D1375608

University of the
West of England

BRISTOL

**FRENCHAY CAMPUS
(BOLLAND) LIBRARY**

Please ensure that this book is returned by the end of
the loan period for which it is issued.

0 4. OCT 2007

1 3. FEB 2008

1 0. APR 2008

Telephone Renewals: 0117 32 82092 (24 hours)
Library Web Address: www.uwe.ac.uk/library

SOVIET AND POST-SOVIET POLITICS AND SOCIETY

ISSN 1614-3515

Recent volumes

Ivan Katchanovski

CLEFT COUNTRIES

Regional Political Divisions and Cultures
in Post-Soviet Ukraine and Moldova

With a foreword by Francis Fukuyama

ibidem-Verlag
Stuttgart

Bibliografische Information Der Deutschen Bibliothek

Die Deutsche Bibliothek verzeichnet diese Publikation in der Deutschen Nationalbibliografie; detaillierte bibliografische Daten sind im Internet über <http://dnb.ddb.de> abrufbar.

Coverpicture: Demonstrators from Western Ukraine during the "Orange Revolution" on Maidan in Kyiv city in the end of 2004. Printed with kind permission from ©Tammy Lynch

∞

Gedruckt auf alterungsbeständigem, säurefreien Papier
Printed on acid-free paper

ISSN: 1614-3515
ISBN: 3-89821-558-X

© *ibidem*-Verlag
Stuttgart 2006
Alle Rechte vorbehalten

Printed in Germany

To my mother, who taught me my first lessons in comparative politics

Contents

List of Tables, Figures and Pictures

Tables

Figures

Pictures

Foreword

The collapse of Communism in Eastern Europe and the former Soviet Union, and the latter's breakup into a series of successor states, is the closest thing we have to a controlled laboratory experiment in political science. The formal political institutions of the communist world were all – in theory, at least – identical to one another: each was ruled by a vanguard party espousing Marxist-Leninist ideology; each had a centralized, hierarchical authoritarian party-state structure; each had a centrally planned economy; and each sought to suppress religion, ethnicity, and nationality as political categories in favor of a universal socialist citizenship. Communist central planning tried to equalize incomes across different regions, and education was stamped out of a single mold. And yet, when the system broke down between 1989 and 1991, a huge variance in transition outcomes emerged. Estonia, Poland, Hungary, and the Czech Republic all made a rapid transition to both stable democracies and market economies, eventually joining both NATO and the European Union. At the other end of the scale, Kyrgyzstan, Turkmenistan, and Uzbekistan all ended up either as outright dictatorships, or else as what Thomas Carothers has labeled "feckless democracies" that are highly corrupt, economically stagnant, and democratic in name only. Somewhere in the middle are countries like Ukraine, Romania, and Bulgaria, which neither made a smooth transition to democracy, nor were consumed by ethnic conflict.

What accounts for this enormous variation in outcome, when the starting conditions were supposedly so similar? A number of theories have fallen victim to the comparative realities of the former communist world. For example, the standard neoclassical growth models would have predicted that those successor states with the largest initial stocks of physical and human capital like Russia or Ukraine should have done the best in making the economic transitions to market economies. Yet these countries grew much less quickly than less industrialized ones like the Baltic States. Geography and the distance of a country from major world centers of trade and industry might explain a great deal, given that countries further away from Western Europe tended to do worse; and yet, why has isolated Mongolia fared better in terms of both political and economic development than most of the Central Asian "stans"? Ethnicity or the prospects for ethnic conflict might be another important explanatory factor; yet the existence of ethnic divisions only begs the further question as to why some ethnically divided countries like the former Yugoslavia, Moldova, Tajikistan, Armenia, and Azerbaijan exploded into civil war or external ethnic conflict, while others like Ukraine did not.

Ivan Katchanovski rigorously tests various competing theories of transition in *Cleft Countries: Regional Political Divisions and Cultures in Post-Soviet Ukraine and Moldova.* Using both quantitative methodology and in-depth historical case studies, he looks at two countries, Ukraine and Moldova, that are divided along ethnic, religious, and regional lines. He finds that political culture more than any other factor explains both the political differences between the divided parts of these countries, and also why these divided countries have had different outcomes in terms of ethnic conflict.

Katchanovski notes that political culture is not the same thing as the "culture factor" used by observers like Samuel Huntington to explain ethnic conflict. Indeed, he finds that traditional markers of culture like religion (i.e., whether one is Orthodox, Catholic, etc.) are not terribly powerful as explanatory variables. Political behavior in the post-Soviet transition period was much more readily explained by habits of mind and action acquired during the nineteenth and twentieth centuries, rather than ancient cultural identities. Experiences of occupation, rule, liberation, and integration all played important roles in shaping national consciousness, and in changing political behavior for better or worse.

Political culture is a variable that has fallen out of favor with many social scientists in recent years, in part because it is hard to define precisely or to measure. And yet, when looking at the nationalist ferment in Ukraine when compared to the passivity in neighboring authoritarian Belarus, it is hard not to see that political culture is incredibly important. *Cleft Countries* thus makes an important contribution both to the growing literature on post-Soviet transitions, as well as to the broader literature on political culture and political development.

Francis Fukuyama
McLean, Virginia
January 4, 2006

Acknowledgements

This book benefited greatly from the advice and suggestions of many people. I am indebted to Seymour Martin Lipset for his guidance and support from the very first steps of this study. I am thankful to Francis Fukuyama, Don Kash, Don Lavoie, and Ilya Prizel for their valuable advice, comments, and suggestions on this manuscript. Robert Crews; Charles King; Peter Reddaway; Philip Roeder; Olga Shvetsova; the participants of the 2001 American Political Science Association Annual Meeting in San Francisco; the 2005 American Political Science Association Annual Meeting in Washington, DC; and the 2000 and 2004 Annual World Conventions of the Association for the Study of the Nationalities in New York provided beneficial input for various parts of this study.

I would like to acknowledge Hans Klingemann from Wissenschaftszentrum, Berlin for providing the World Values Survey datasets; the Harry Frank Guggenheim Foundation, which funded the Laitin/Hough surveys; and David Laitin, the principal investigator who directed the surveys and supplied the datasets. The Kyiv International Institute of Sociology provided regional results of its surveys in Ukraine. I am also thankful to Peter Craumer and Vicki Hesli for supplying the census data on education, the International Foundation for Election Systems for providing data on elections in Moldova, and Samuel Huntington for permitting me to use the term that he coined as the title of the book. This study benefited from conversations and helpful suggestions from many other individuals from Ukraine, Moldova, the United States, and Canada.

I am greatly indebted to the editor of the *ibidem* series *Soviet and Post-Soviet Politics and Society*, Andreas Umland. Brenda Belokrinicev and Nicola Scott were responsible for ensuring that the manuscript is free from English language mistakes. This book uses a standard English transliteration of Cyrillic, except in cases of commonly used names and places.

Last, but not least, I would like to acknowledge my mother, Sophia Katchanovski, for my first real-life lessons in comparative politics. Because of changes in international borders, she experienced the politics of four countries first-hand, as well as the Nazi genocide, the Soviet terror, and ethnic cleansing in Eastern Europe, without ever moving on her own.

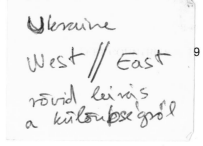

1 Introduction

Since the collapse of Communism and the end of the Cold War, regional divisions, ranging from significant territorial voting differences to intra-state conflicts, have manifested in many countries in different parts of the world. The most notable examples of this include: Kosovo, Bosnia, and Macedonia in the former Yugoslavia; Chechnya and Tatarstan in Russia; Kashmir and Punjab in India; Northern Afghanistan; Quebec and the Western provinces in Canada; Northern Ireland and Wales in the United Kingdom; Southern Sudan; Northern Nigeria; and the Chiapas in Mexico.

Ukraine and Moldova are two post-Communist countries with sharp regional divisions.[1] They became independent states after the failed coup of August 1991 and the break-up of the Soviet Union in December 1991. In all elections and referendums held since 1991, Western regions of Ukraine have supported nationalist, pro-independence and pro-Western parties and politicians, while Eastern regions of Ukraine have backed pro-Communist and pro-Russian parties and politicians. The regional differences are extensive. For example, official results of the repeat second round of the presidential elections in December 2004 showed that Viktor Yushchenko received more than 93 percent of the vote in three Galicia (Halychyna) regions in Western Ukraine and 4–6 percent in two Donbas (Donbass) regions in Eastern Ukraine. Conversely, Viktor Yanukovych, a pro-Russian candidate, received more than 90 percent of the vote in the Donbas regions and less than 5 percent of the vote in the Galicia regions.

Some Ukrainian, Russian, and Western politicians and observers raised possibilities of civil war and territorial disintegration of Ukraine as a result of sharp regional polarization during the 2004 presidential elections and a

---

[1]   See Aarrevaara, 1998; Aberg, 2000; Barrington, 1997; Birch, 2000a, 2000b; Clem and Craumer, 2005; Craumer and Clem, 1999; Hesli, 1995; Hesli, Reisinger, and Miller, 1998; Kaufman, 1996; Khmelko and Wilson, 1998; Kolsto, 2002; Kubicek, 2000; Malanchuk, 2005; Miller, Klobucar, and Reisinger, 2000; Miller, White and Heywood, 1998; Shulman, 1999a; Crowther, 1997a, 1997b; European Centre for Minority Issues, 1997; Kaufman, 1996; King, 2000; Kolsto and Malgin, 1998; O'Loughlin, Kolossov, and Tchepalyga, 1998; Wilson, 2005.

political crisis that followed. (See, for example, Finn, 2004, and Stephen, 2004.) According to Ukrainian and Western media reports and to my personal observations, more than one million people, mostly from Western regions of Ukraine and the city of Kyiv, took to the streets to protest falsification of the results of the second round of the elections and in support of Viktor Yushchenko. The Kuchma administration came very close to using military force against Yushchenko supporters, some of whom favored a violent seizure of power.

Many local authorities, predominantly in the Western part of Ukraine, recognized Viktor Yushchenko as president; however, local authorities in a number of Eastern regions backed Viktor Yanukovych, and threatened to declare an autonomous republic or hold a referendum on the federalization of Ukraine. In the beginning of the 1990s, a similar separatism emerged in the Crimea region when it gained autonomous status within Ukraine.

In the middle of the 1990s, the CIA predicted the break-up of Ukraine along regional lines and a Yugoslavia-style civil war.[2] In 2005, the Fund for Peace identified Ukraine as a country in danger of disintegration; the American organization placed Ukraine in this group along with such countries as Bosnia and Herzegovina, Lebanon, Uzbekistan, and Tanzania. ("Failed States Index," 2005.)

A significant proportion of Ukrainians thought that a break-up of Ukraine was a real possibility. The 2005 survey conducted by the Institute of Sociology of the National Academy of Sciences of Ukraine showed that every fifth respondent (19 percent of Ukrainians) believed that a break-up of Ukraine was the biggest fear among the people of Ukraine. From 11 to 16 percent of the respondents expressed the same opinion in annual surveys conducted in 1999-2004. (Panina, 2005, p. 87.)

A survey, conducted by the Kyiv International Institute of Sociology (KIIS) in 2005, showed that more than a third of all respondents (35 percent), which corresponds to almost half of Ukrainians (42 percent) who had a definite opinion, considered an East-West division in Ukraine as a divide between hostile sides. Journalists from *Dzerkalo tyzhnia*, which commissioned the survey that asked this question, described the regional division as a gulf separat-

---

[2]   See "Better Later than Never, Maybe", 1995.

ing Easterners from Westerners, and concluded that a significant proportion of Ukrainians regarded their compatriots in other regions as enemies. (Mostova and Rakhmanin, 2005.)

However, such assessments are not necessarily reliable. The CIA has a poor track record in its evaluations of political developments in a number of key cases. The American spy agency failed to predict the break-up of the Soviet Union. The CIA gave a wrong assessment with regard to the existence of weapons of mass destruction in Iraq. The Fund for Peace based its identification of Ukraine as a state in danger of disintegration on computer analysis of news reports. Media coverage affected Ukrainians' perceptions about the possibility of Ukraine's break-up. Similarly, sensationalist and anecdotal stories in Western and Ukrainian media created irrational fears about the consequences of the Chornobyl disaster, fears that were grossly inflated compared with the conclusions of the scientists who studied these issues.

Moldova, a country much less studied than Ukraine, its bigger post-Soviet neighbor, offers a perfect case for comparison. Ukraine and Moldova differ in terms of their size, but their levels of economic development are similar. Ukraine is the second largest country in Europe after Russia in terms of its territory (603.7 thousand sq. km, or 233.1 thousand sq. miles) and fifth largest in terms of its population (49 million in 2002.) The territory and population of Ukraine are comparable to France's. Moldova is similar in terms of its size (33.7 thousand sq. km, or 13.1 thousand sq. miles) to Belgium. In terms of its population, Moldova (4.5 million in 1999) is comparable to Croatia or Norway. The Gross National Product (GNP) per capita at purchasing power parity exchange rate in 1995 was $2,400 in Ukraine and $2,070 in Moldova (European Bank for Reconstruction and Development, 1997.) Ukraine is a more urbanized and industrialized country than Moldova, which is more rural and agricultural.

As in Ukraine, nationalist pro-Moldovan and pro-Romanian parties and politicians have received their strongest support in the Western (right-bank) part of Moldova. The Transdniestria region, in the East of the country, tried to preserve many elements of the Soviet political system and to secede from Moldova. This political conflict turned violent when the Transdniestrian secessionists, supported by the presence of Russian troops, declared their region independent from Moldova. Another dispute emerged between the

Gagauz-populated districts in the South and the Central government of Moldova. However, this conflict was solved peacefully, and the Gagauz region gained substantial autonomy.

Political scientists – who study why people in different regions have different political attitudes, vote for different parties and politicians, want to secede from their neighbors, and engage in violent clashes – have developed various theories to explain regional cleavages and conflicts. They have identified economic, ethnic, cultural, religious, and political leadership issues as factors of regional division. Economic theories focus on the self-interest of politicians and disparities in levels and structures of economic development. Theories of ethnicity and religion emphasize the function of ethnic and religious differences, language, and nationalism. Theories of leadership stress the role that political leaders and elites play in regional divisions, claiming that the power struggle among domestic leaders and involvement of foreign leaders are the elite-level causes of regional conflicts. Political culture theories emphasize the value differences that have evolved from religious, historical, and other similar divisions.

Previous studies have identified ethnic, economic, religious, and cultural factors that affect regional cleavages and conflicts in post-Communist Ukraine and Moldova. In this study, *the first question* is – how significant is the role of culture when compared with other factors in the regional political divisions in these countries? This book tests the hypothesis that regional political culture, which has emerged as a result of different historical experiences, accounts for a significant part of the variation in support for nationalist/pro-Western and Communist/pro-Russian parties and politicians across regions of Ukraine and Moldova.

The second question is – which factor or factors turn regional political cleavages into violent conflicts? This study uses a comparison of two neighboring post-Soviet countries – post-Communist Ukraine and Moldova, which have many similarities in terms of their historical development, political systems, economies, and other factors – to determine which factors transform regional political cleavages into violent conflict.

This book examines the role of political culture in relation to economic, ethnic, and leadership factors in regional political divisions in Ukraine and Moldova from 1991 to 2005. It argues that culture – which has emerged as a result of distinct historical institutions, policies, and experiences – plays a major role in regional political divisions.

Ukraine and Moldova both consist of regions that have belonged to different states for significant historical periods. For a great span of time, the territory and population of Ukraine were divided among the Russian Empire, the Ottoman Empire, and the Austro-Hungarian Monarchy. After World War I, Eastern Ukraine and the Transdniestrian region of Moldova belonged to the Soviet Union, while Western Ukrainian regions became parts of Poland, Romania, and Czechoslovakia. Moldova's Western province, called Bessarabia, belonged to Romania between World War I and World War II.

The pre-World War II division is used in this study to distinguish between Western Ukraine and Eastern Ukraine and between Western Moldova (Bessarabia) and Eastern Moldova (Transdniestria). This definition of Western and Eastern regions underlines different historical legacies. Western Ukraine refers to part of Ukraine that was not only located in the geographical West but that also had a distinct history of its own before World War II; Eastern Ukraine refers to all other regions that are located to the east of Western Ukraine. Such definitions were common before World War II, and they remain widespread in present-day Ukraine. The use of this dichotomy is as justified as the use of the historically-based Western Germany vs. East Germany dichotomy, and of the South vs. the North dichotomies in Italy and in the United States, in studies of regional cleavages in those countries.

The Soviet Union incorporated Western regions of Ukraine and Moldova as a result of World War II. For several decades, these regions experienced Soviet policies aimed at eliminating the economic, ethnic, and religious differences between them and their Eastern counterparts. For this reason, from a comparative perspective, post-Communist Ukraine and Moldova, like modern Italy and Germany, represent a quasi-experiment. (See Almond, 1983, Putnam, 1993, Rohrschneider, 1996.)

Political systems, institutions, and policies in Ukrainian and Moldovan regions of the Russian Empire, the Ottoman Empire, and the Austro-Hungarian Monarchy differed significantly. Large differences characterized political and economic systems, institutions, and policies of Poland, Romania, Czechoslovakia, and the Soviet Union during the interwar period. Nazi and

Romanian policies in Ukrainian and Moldovan regions throughout World War II reinforced these variations.

For example, political institutions and polices in Ukrainian regions in the Austrian-Hungarian Monarchy created more favorable conditions for the development of Ukrainian nationalism and national identity than was the case in the Russian Empire. These conditions included a more democratic political system, along with educational and religious policies that were more supportive of the formation of Ukrainian national identity. The existence and activity of the Ukrainian Greek Catholic Church helped to promote Ukrainian national identity in Galicia, a region that was part of the Austrian-Hungarian Monarchy. During World War II, the Nazi policy towards Ukrainians was less severe in Galicia than in other regions of Ukraine.

Historical conditions were also more favorable for the development of national identity in Western Moldova, the historical region of Bessarabia, than in the Transdniestria region. The differences in political systems and policies were most significant during the inter-war period, when Western Moldova was unified with Romania and the Autonomous Moldovan Republic, which included all of Transdniestria, was part of Soviet Ukraine.

The focus on the West-East divisions in Ukraine and Moldova involves a certain simplification of political regionalisms in these post-Communist countries. This simplification, which relies on historical differences, in no way denies existence of other types of regional cleavages, as for example between capital cities and neighboring regions in Ukraine and Moldova, or between Central regions and Eastern regions in Ukraine.

This book links the political distinctiveness of Gagauzia in Moldova and Crimea in Ukraine to the differences in their historical legacies. The critical juncture in the evolution of Gagauz political culture was the nineteenth-century mass migration of the Gagauz people from Bulgaria to the Southern part of Moldova, with the aid of the Russian government, to avoid persecution by the Ottoman Empire.

In the case of Crimea, the historical experience of Ukrainians and Russians differed significantly from that of Crimean Tatars. For several centuries when Crimea was a vassal state of the Ottoman Empire, the Crimean khanate carried out frequent raids in Ukraine and Southern Russia, during which a great number of Ukrainians and Russians were captured and sold as slaves. The origin of Ukraine's name, which in Ukrainian means "the border-land" or "on the edge," is traced to this period. Ukraine was a frontier area of the Polish-Lithuanian Commonwealth and the Russian Empire, which bordered the Ottoman Empire.

While the Russian conquest of Crimea ended slavery, it also had a significant affect on the historical experience of Crimean Tatars. To avoid discrimination and persecution by the Russian government, many Crimean Tatars migrated to the Ottoman Empire. Another important factor in the evolution of the political culture of the Crimean Tatars was their exile, mandated by Stalin, to Central Asia; this collective punishment was doled out because a fraction of Crimean Tatars collaborated with the Nazis during World War II.

This book uses the term *cleft countries* to refer to the considerable and persistent regional political cleavages in Ukraine and Moldova. Huntington (1996) also uses this term, though he uses it specifically in reference to countries divided along civilization lines that are defined by Western Christianity, Orthodox Christianity, Islam, and other religions. He considers Ukraine as being divided between Catholic West and Orthodox East. However, this book will show that religion is not the primary factor responsible for the regional cleavages in Ukraine.

This study focuses on one dimension of political culture in regions of Ukraine and Moldova: pro-Communist/pro-Russian orientation versus pro-nationalist/pro-Western orientation. Other dimensions of political culture, such as democratic values, political tolerance, support for market reforms and privatization, and social capital will be discussed as they relate to the main focus of this book.[3]

It is important to emphasize that a vote for the Communist and nationalist parties does not necessarily imply complete support of their programs, or support for their most radical elements. Pro-Communist/pro-Russian political orientation refers to the support of political parties and candidates who are, to a significant extent, ideological successors of the Communist Party of the Soviet Union or those who favor closer ties with Russia. Similarly, the term pro-nationalist/pro-Western refers to a broad part of the

---

[3]   For the same approach extended to the analysis of social capital and privatization in regions of Ukraine and Moldova, see Katchanovski, 2001.

political spectrum. It encompasses Ukrainian and Moldovan nationalisms in either a civic form, which embraces ethnic minorities, or an exclusive ethnic form. This spectrum also includes advocacy for the independence of Ukraine and Moldova and a speedy integration of these countries into Western organizations, such as the North Atlantic Treaty Organization (NATO) and the European Union (EU), as well as, in the case of Moldova, its unification with Romania.

This study argues that political culture is not stagnant, but evolves, albeit slowly, under the influence of institutions and policies. For example, differences in historical experience, not only between Western Ukraine and Eastern Ukraine but also within these regions, have contributed to differences in electoral behavior and political attitudes. This approach helps us to understand the political differences between Galicia and Volhynia, both of which are regions of Western Ukraine. While both these historical regions were part of Poland between World War I and World War II, Galicia was under Austrian rule and Volhynia was under Russian rule for more than a century before World War I. Such differences are often overlooked in studies of Ukrainian and Moldovan regionalism.

An analysis of the cultural legacy of historical institutions and policies is useful in understanding regional cleavages and conflicts not only in Ukraine and Moldova, but also in other regionally divided countries. For example, regional conflicts in the former Yugoslavia closely parallel historical divisions between the Austro-Hungarian Monarchy and the Ottoman Empire (Slovenia and Croatia vs. Serbia and Montenegro), while other conflicts parallel different historical experiences of Orthodox Christians and Muslims during the Ottoman rule (Kosovo, Bosnia, and Macedonia).

Region is the main unit of analysis in this study. This book compares political behavior and attitudes in different historical regions of Ukraine and Moldova: regions that experienced long periods of Russian and then Soviet rule; regions that were under Austro-Hungarian and then Polish, Romanian, and Czechoslovak rule until World War II; and regions with a legacy of the Ottoman rule. This study analyzes the regional results of all national elections and referendums held in Ukraine and Moldova between 1991-2005, as well as regional dimensions of a variety of survey data.

This book argues that, in contrast to the Transdniestria region of Moldova, the behavior of regional, national, and foreign leaders contributed to the absence of violent regional conflicts in Ukraine. For reasons of ideology and self-interest, political leaders in Transdniestria, with the support of the 14th Russian army, chose a separatist option, which turned into a violent conflict. The de facto independence of the Transdniestrian Republic satisfied both rent-seeking interests and the pro-Russian orientation of its leadership. Similar factors motivated political leaders in Ukraine to choose a different option. The main ideological goal of nationalist leaders in Western Ukraine was reached when Ukraine became an independent state. A significant number of these leaders were accommodated by access to positions of power. Many of the former Communist and pro-Russian leaders, such as Leonid Kravchuk and Leonid Kuchma, radically changed their political orientation to maintain power. The actions of certain key national, regional, and foreign leaders prevented the major political crisis in Ukraine at the end of 2004 from escalating into violent conflict.

This study deals with regions of Ukraine and Moldova, but it also provides insight on the significant disparities in the political development of post-Communist countries in Eastern Central Europe and the former Soviet Union; the geographic patterns of differentiation among these countries parallel those of Ukrainian and Moldovan regions. The most successful political reforms have taken place in the countries located in the Western part of the former Communist domain, such as Poland, Slovenia, the Czech Republic, Hungary, and the Baltic States. These countries have achieved more progress in their democratization and integration into the European Union and NATO than countries located further to the East. Democratization and political reforms have been much more limited in Central Asian states, Armenia, Azerbaijan, Belarus, Georgia, Serbia, Macedonia, and Russia. Most of the countries in the first group, like many regions in Western Ukraine, share the legacy of Austro-Hungarian rule before World War I, while the countries in the second group, like Eastern Ukraine, experienced Russian and Ottoman rule.[4] (See Katchanovski, 2000; Katchanovski and La Porte, 2005.)

---

[4]   Some scholars argue that it is not political culture but other factors, such as geographic proximity to Western Europe or initial post-Communist elections, that are

This book employs both comparative and statistical methods. A comparative approach is used in the analysis of regional voting patterns in post-Communist elections and referendums. An analysis of the evolution of regional political culture, religious and ethnic cleavages, and the role of political leadership relies on comparative historical methods. Statistical methods are used to analyze regional voting data and data from the World Values Surveys in Ukraine and Moldova and the Laitin/Hough survey in Moldova.[5]

This study utilizes historical sources, not only from the West, but also from Ukraine and Moldova. Such an approach corrects the ideological interpretations prevalent under Soviet rule and, to some extent, in the post-Communist period, as well as biases in the Western scholarship of these countries. The Soviet state and regimes in other Communist countries promoted an ideological view of history; they relied on party propaganda, and banned research into and public discussion of many crucial historic events, such as mass political terror and famines in Soviet Ukraine and Soviet Moldova in the 1930s and 1940s. Cold War politics and other related factors affected research on Ukraine and Moldova in the West. For example, many Western studies that discuss World War II in Ukraine fail to take into account regional differences, and thus often denote Eastern Ukrainians as Russians or Soviets. Davies (1996, p. 54) states the following in his study of European history:

> Their [Ukrainian] population is similar in size to that of England or France, and contains important minorities; but the Ukrainians find very little place in the history books. For many years, they were presented to the outside world as 'Russians' or 'Soviets' whenever they were to be praised, and as 'Ukrainians' only when they did evil.

Similarly, most Western studies of the Ottoman Empire overlook Ukrainian and Russian slavery in the Crimean khanate, as well as the forced migration of tens of thousands of the Gagauz, Bulgarians, and other Orthodox

---

chiefly responsible for the cross-national variation among post-Communist countries. (See Fish, 1998; Kopstein and Reilly, 2000.) These factors are much less important at the regional level in Ukraine and Moldova.

[5]   The Laitin/Hough survey was also conducted in Ukraine, but it included only regions of Eastern Ukraine.

Christians from the Ottoman Empire to Southern Moldova and Ukraine under Russian rule. (See, for example, Lieven, 2001; and Quataert, 2000.)

Historians have studied Ukrainian and Moldovan regions as part of the histories of the Russian Empire, the Austro-Hungarian Monarchy, the Ottoman Empire, Poland, Romania, and the Soviet Union. For this reason, they still debate whether Ukraine has its own history. (See Hagen, 1995; Plokhy, 1995.) Very few studies have examined the historical development of all regions of Ukraine and Moldova (see King, 2000; Magocsi, 1996; Subtelny, 1988; Szporluk, 1979).

This book is the first comprehensive study to analyze regional political divisions in Ukraine and Moldova from a comparative perspective. Research into the politics of the former Soviet Union has often been confined to Russia. Since Ukraine and Moldova became independent states after the collapse of Communism and the break-up of the Soviet Union in 1991, studies of their political development have grown significantly.

However, most of these studies examine one country at a time. They are often unable to define the role of the various factors causing regional divisions because economic, ethnic, language, religious, and cultural differences coexist. For example, Transdniestria, which seceded de facto from Moldova, is a more economically developed region with a large proportion of Russian speakers, most of whom are ethnic Russians and Ukrainians. In addition, Transdniestria, in contrast to other regions of Moldova, had not been part of Romania for a long period of time. Moldovans descend from the Dacian people in the Roman Empire and Vlachs, while Ukrainians and Russians are Slavs. The Moldovan language is a dialect of Romanian, and is similar to other Latin languages such as Italian and French; even though Ukrainian and Russian are separate languages, Ukrainian, like some other Slavic languages, can be largely understood by a Russian speaker and vice versa.

The Gagauz, concentrated in the South of Moldova, are Turkic-speaking people, but they are Orthodox Christians like the majority of the Moldovan population. Other regionally concentrated Turkic ethnic groups are predominantly Muslim. Since the Gagauz are unique in this aspect, the study of their political behavior and attitudes is especially interesting when juxtaposed with religious experience.

Regional divisions in Ukraine and Moldova also affect their neighbors: Russia, and the current and future members of the European Union and NATO. As noted, regional divisions in Ukraine and Moldova coincide with pro-Western and pro-Russian orientations. Historic, geographic, ethnic, political, and economic links between Ukrainian and Moldovan regions on the one hand and Russia, Poland, Romania, Hungary, Turkey, Austria, Bulgaria, Slovakia, and the Czech Republic on the other underline broader repercussions of regional cleavages and conflicts in Ukraine and Moldova; the presence of large ethnic Russian minorities in Ukraine and Moldova illustrates this point.

Regional conflicts in Ukraine and Moldova can affect not only the political security but also the energy security and economic stability of many other countries. In late 2005 and early January 2006, a conflict over the price of natural gas, between Russia on the one hand and Ukraine and Moldova on the other hand, demonstrated the importance of the geographic and economic links that Ukraine and Moldova have to Russia and many other European countries. Russia's decision to end subsidized gas pricing to Ukraine and Moldova, after the governments in these two post-Soviet countries rejected political and economic integration with Russia, culminated in the suspension of deliveries of natural gas to Ukraine and Moldova on January 1, 2006 by Gazprom, the Russian state gas monopoly. Russia also suspended deliveries of Turkmen natural gas to Ukraine after it outbidded Ukraine as a principal buyer of gas from Turkmenistan. However, Russia's principal route for the delivery of gas to many Western European, Central European, and Southern European countries crosses Ukraine; Ukrainian government officials authorized the siphoning of transit gas, which they claimed was their Turkmen gas, and the supply of some gas to Moldova. As result of the conflict, the volume of Russian natural gas delivered to many countries, including Germany, France, Italy, Poland, Romania, Austria, Slovakia, Serbia, Croatia, and Hungary, declined significantly for several days until Ukraine and Russia could reach a compromise.

The next chapter of this book presents a theoretical framework for historical experience, political culture, and region. It compares regional divisions in Ukraine and Moldova with significant regional divisions in other post-Communist countries, as well as advanced Western countries and developing countries. The third chapter examines both the character and the extent of regional political divisions in post-Communist Ukraine and Moldova. The fourth chapter analyzes how distinct historical experiences have led to the emergence of regional political cultures in both countries; it also explores religious cleavages as they relate to historical experience. The fifth chapter compares the role of culture to the role of ethnic, economic, and political leadership factors in regional political cleavages and conflicts in Ukraine and Moldova. The concluding chapter summarizes the main results of this study and its implications for Ukraine and Moldova, as well as other cleft countries.

2   Cleft countries: A theoretical and comparative framework

Regional divisions exist to various degrees in practically every country in the world. One can almost always find an area, be it a metropolis, capital, administrative, or historical region, that differs politically from other areas. Regional political divisions increased in scope and significance with the end of the Cold War and the collapse of Communism,[6] while global political cleavages and conflicts, which had dominated Cold War politics, subsided (Fukuyama, 1992). The most notable exception is the rise of Islamic fundamentalism, which advances global aims. Although religious-based divisions are often regarded as a global clash of civilizations, such conflicts and cleavages often manifest themselves at the regional level.

This chapter presents an overview of regional political divisions within a theoretical and comparative framework. The chapter focuses only on those divisions that play an important role in national or international politics, specifically those that have produced significant intra-state conflicts or regional cleavages among electorate, secessionist, or autonomist movements.

2.1   Theoretical framework

While functional cleavages that include divisions between ideological movements, religious and ethnic groups, and socio-economic classes cut across different regions, territorial cleavages encompass divisions between center and periphery as well as cleavages between territorially concentrated linguistic, ethnic, and cultural minorities and majorities (Lipset and Rokkan, 1967). Regional conflicts, insofar as they reflect mass political attitudes, represent the most extreme manifestation of territorial cleavages.

---

[6]   See Barber, 1995; Brown, 1996; Gurr, 1994; Gurr, Marshall, and Pitsch, 1999; Jalali and Lipset, 1992-93; and Minahan, 1996.

Most studies of political regionalism, including those dealing with Ukraine and Moldova, focus on ethnic, linguistic, economic, or political leadership factors of regional divisions.[7] Ethnic and linguistic theories attribute regional conflict to differences and rivalries between ethnic or linguistic minorities and majorities. In the case of Ukraine and Moldova, this view emphasizes the large number of ethnic Russians and Russian speakers present in the Eastern part of Ukraine and the Transdniestria region of Moldova. (See Arel, 1995; Gurr et. al., 1999; Laitin, 1998).

According to Ukraine's 2001 national census, ethnic Russians made up about one fifth of the country's population, most of them in Eastern Ukraine. Russians form the majority of the population in Crimea and represent about one fourth of the Transdniestrian population. However, most Russians in Moldova live outside of the Transdniestrian region. Before the breakup of the Soviet Union, ethnic Ukrainians made up about 30 percent and ethnic Moldovans about 40 percent of the Transdniestrian population.

Some scholars attribute the regional political divisions in Ukraine to language differences between Russian speakers and Ukrainian speakers, and in Moldova to differences between Russian speakers and Romanian speakers (see Arel, 1995). The number of Russian speakers in the Eastern regions of Ukraine and Moldova is much higher than the number of ethnic Russians, because many Ukrainians and Moldovans in these regions have adopted the Russian language.

Language became one of the central political issues in postcommunist Ukraine and Moldova. Ukrainian nationalists advanced Ukrainian as the official state language. Communists and their allies wanted to preserve the dominant position of Russian in Eastern Ukraine by giving it status as an official language. Moldovan nationalists favored the declaration of Romanian as the state language. Many Russian speakers in Moldova, especially in the Transdniestrian and Gagauz regions, opposed such proposals.

Ukrainian and Russian belong to the East Slavic group of languages and are both written in the Cyrillic alphabet. Moldovan is considered a re-

---

[7]   See Bookman, 1991, 1993; Brown, 1996; Evangelista, 1996; Fearon and Laitin, 2003; Gagnon, 1994; Gellner, 1997; Gurr, 1997; Hale, 1998; Hardin, 1995; Hechter, 1999; Horowitz, 1985; Kohn, 1955; Laitin, 1995,1998; Lake and Rothchild, 1998; Saideman, 1998; Smith, 1998; and van den Berghe, 1981, 1986.

gional variation or dialect of Romanian language. The Soviet government treated Moldovan as a separate language from Romanian and imposed Cyrillic as the Moldovan alphabet. The parliament of post-Communist Moldova restored the Latin alphabet and declared Moldovan the official language of Moldova. Gagauz, like Turkish, Azeri, and Turkmen, belongs to a southwest group of Turkic languages (King, 2000, p. 213).

Another group of theories attributes regional political divisions to economic differences and rivalries. Theories of relative deprivation, uneven economic development, economic dependency, and internal colonialism emphasize the role that differences in levels of regional economic development, taxation, and spending play in the emergence of regional cleavages and conflicts. In the case of Ukraine and Moldova, this view traces regional political divisions to higher levels of urbanization, industrialization, and income in regions of Eastern Ukraine and Transdniestria as compared to Western Ukraine and Bessarabia. (Birch, 2000b; Bookman, 1991; Craumer and Clem, 1999; Hechter, 1999; Herrera, 2005; Hesli, 1995; Motyl and Krawchenko, 1997).

The third group of theories focuses on the role that leadership plays in regional political divisions. This group attributes regional cleavages and conflicts to the actions and interests of domestic and foreign leaders, or to competition among elites. For example, Transdniestrian conflict in Moldova is linked to the actions and interests of the leadership of Russia, which used its troops in the region to support Transdniestrian secessionists, or to the belligerent leadership of the Transdniestrian separatists. (See Brown, 1996, p. 582; Evangelista, 1996, pp. 121-123; Kaufman 1996).

The fourth group of theories of regional cleavages and conflicts underlines the role of political culture. This group emphasizes differences in political values, and historical and religious legacies. As noted, Ukraine and Moldova include regions with different histories. In addition, several Western Ukrainian regions are mostly Greek Catholic, in contrast to the predominantly Orthodox regions of Eastern Ukraine. (See Birch, 2000a, 2000b; Huntington, 1996, pp. 138, 165; King 2000; Roper and Fesnic, 2003).

Previous studies of regional political divisions in Ukraine and Moldova, with few exceptions, analyzed a single country or region and the results of only one election and survey, and these studies differ in their interpretations of regional differences. They employ different classifications of regions in Ukraine. Many scholars divide Ukraine into four geographical regions: West, Center, South, and East; other scholars divide Ukraine into Western and Eastern parts along the Dnieper River. Such classifications are based to a significant extent on geographical location, and they are affected by subjective judgments. (See Barrington and Herron, 2004). Findings of statistically significant regional differences in levels of support for certain political parties and politicians in certain elections or surveys cannot be generalized with sufficient confidence as measures of regional political cultures, because electoral attitudes are much more fluid than values.

The number of Ukrainian and Moldovan studies of the regional divisions in these countries has been growing. However, these studies tend to be descriptive. (See, for example, *Politychna kul'tura*, 2004). They often contain value judgments or biased opinions concerning a particular political orientation or a particular region. (See, for instance, Riabchuk, 2001, 2003). For example, a popular study by a writer born in the Volyn region in Western Ukraine contrasted political orientations that dominated present-day regions of 'Polish Ukraine' or 'Ukrainian Ukraine' and regions of 'Russian Ukraine' or 'Sovietized Ukraine.' Its author equated studies of Ukrainian regionalism by "seemingly respected" foreign analysts with Soviet Communist Party propaganda, because these experts spread "myths" about nationalist West and pro-Russian East and did not refer to pro-Russian orientation in Ukraine as Russian nationalism. The article described features of Russian Ukraine as "ugly." This study stated, contrary to available statistical data, that Donbas in Eastern Ukraine had the highest rates of crime, drug addiction, alcoholism, abortions, divorces and sexually transmitted diseases in Ukraine, and, without providing any evidence, it linked these rates to the Russian and Soviet legacy of the region.[8] (Riabchuk, 2001).

Many publications by scholars and other intellectuals from Eastern Ukraine present a similar caricature of Western Ukraine. For example, a study by an internationally renowned Canadian scholar whose Russian an-

---

[8]   The crime rate and the divorce rate were generally higher in Eastern regions than in Western regions of Ukraine, but these rates were not the highest in Donbas. For example, the Dnipropetrovsk region had the highest crime rate in 1996. The divorce rate was highest in Kyiv city. (See Katchanovski, 2001; Statystychnyi, 1997). The Odesa region had the highest AIDS infection rate in Ukraine. (See Varnalii, 2005.)

cestors lived in Eastern Ukraine associated independent Ukraine and nationalist/pro-independence supporters, who primarily were Western Ukrainian, with "images of peasant embroidered shirts, the nasal whine of ethnic instruments, phoney Cossacks in cloaks and boots, nasty anti-Semites" (Ignatieff, 1993, p. 79). Similar problems affected Transdniestrian and Moldovan studies of regionalism in Moldova.

This book analyzes all factors of regional political divisions, but its main focus is on culture, in particular the different historical legacies in regions of Ukraine and Moldova. Political culture refers to values and norms that are shared by individuals and are persistent over a long period of time, in contrast to attitudes, which are much more volatile (see Almond and Verba, 1965; Lipset, 1996). Historical legacies, along with religious traditions, national identity, family structure, and moral values, represent different elements of culture (Fukuyama, 1995a).

It is important to note that culture refers to a distribution of values among various groups of individuals. Not every individual in a particular group shares the dominant culture of that group. The failure to make this important distinction manifests itself in stereotypes and prejudices, wherein every individual from a certain group is assumed to be representative of the values and norms ascribed to the group as a whole.

The concept of culture is often viewed as an alternative to theories of rational choice. Rational choice theorists treat individuals or groups as rational and self-interested utility maximizers, and these scholars often simply reject the relevance of political culture because of its alleged incompatibility with the rational choice framework. However, one can view culture and instrumental rationality as different ideal types of political action or behavior. Weber (1922/1978, pp. 24-25) distinguished four ideal types of action: instrumentally rational, value-rational, effectual, and traditional. Following neoclassical economists, rational choice scholars focus on the instrumentally rational type of action and tend to ignore the other types of actions, which are difficult to incorporate into mathematical models (Almond, 1990). However, non-instrumentally rational types of actions can also be grounded in methodological individualism and then studied (See Boudon, 1998, 1996; Schutz, 1971). The traditional type of action, which according to Weber's (1922/1978,

p. 25) definition, is "determined by ingrained habituation," corresponds to the concept of culture.

Historical legacy represents a major source of political culture (See Diamond, 1993; Elazar, 1966, p. 84). Shared historical experiences tend to bring the values and norms of individuals close to one another, while different histories have the opposite effect. Socialization in family, school, and a circle of friends serves as a mechanism that transmits these values and norms from one generation to the next. As result, different historical legacies shape the political cultures of regional ethnic, linguistic, and racial groups and social classes.[9]

The study of the influence of historical legacies in regional politics has a long tradition. Siegfried (1930, 1949), who led the French social geography school, showed the importance of historical legacies in French politics. Most recently, Putnam (1993) underlined the influence of historical factors in his study of Italian regional governments.

In many advanced Western countries, voter alignment and party systems reflect historical cleavage structures (Lipset and Rokkan, 1967). Divergence in the levels of corruption, economic liberalization, and economic growth in post-Communist countries is attributed to a great extent to different historical legacies and religious traditions (Katchanovski, 2000). The legacies of British colonial institutions in North America and Spanish and Portuguese colonial institutions in Latin America explain the different forms of governments and governance in these regions in post-colonial times. The legacy of British rule in the United States and Canada was more favorable for the emergence and evolution of a decentralized government than was the legacy of Spanish and Portuguese rule in Latin America (North, 1990). Different historical legacies in the United States and Canada have had a major effect on the divergence of political values and union membership rates in these neighboring countries. (Lipset, 1990; Lipset, Meltz, Gomez, and Katchanovski, 2004).

---

[9]   Culture can influence both ethnic identity and economic development. For example, Gellner (1997) argues that a nation is based on shared culture, and that language is the central element of this shared culture.

Critical junctures in history, such as the unification, conquest or break-up of a country or its defeat or victory in war, provide a major impetus for the formation of political culture. Using an analogy proposed by Max Weber (1949, pp. 181-183), the critical juncture represents a point in the evolution of political culture when the dice become "loaded." In the course of subsequent historical development, these loaded dice then cause the culture to evolve in a particular direction.

Weber's analogy implies that not all historical legacies are equally important. A period when national identity begins to develop and spread is more crucial in the evolution of a national political culture than the preceding historical periods. For example, the emergence of mass national identity in the Russian Empire and the Soviet Union varied significantly in time among different ethnic groups and regions: with the Ukrainians, Moldovans, Belarusians, and Russians, it developed later than with the Estonians, Latvians, and Lithuanians but earlier than with the people of Central Asia. Prior to this, local, religious, and status-based identities were dominant, and illiterate peasants constituted the majority of the population. For example, according to 1897 census data, literacy rates were 23 to 33 percent in the Ukrainian provinces of the Russian Empire, 6 percent among ethnic Moldovans, 7 percent among the Gagauz, 5 percent in Central Asia, and 14 percent in Transcaucasus, compared to 91 percent in the Baltic provinces (see Kaiser, 1994, p. 69; King, 2000, pp. 23, 211). By 1939, the level of literacy had increased to 88 percent in Ukraine and 46 percent in Moldova (Kaiser, 1994, p. 139). Historical experiences during the periods when mass literacy was achieved had a much more profound impact on the formation of national identity than did historical experiences in either earlier or later periods.

This book argues that the division of Ukraine between the Russian Empire and the Austro-Hungarian Monarchy, at the end of the eighteenth century, and the division of Ukraine and Moldova between the Soviet Union, Poland, Romania, and Czechoslovakia, at the beginning of the twentieth century, were critical junctures in the emergence of distinct regional political cultures. These divisions coincided with the crucial period in the development of national identity. Differences in political systems, institutions, and policies in these countries led to the emergence of different political cultures in Ukrainian and Moldovan regions. Historical conditions in the Austro-Hungarian Monarchy, interwar Poland, Romania, and Czechoslovakia were generally more favorable for the spread of nationalism and the development of a national identity than were the conditions in the Ukrainian and Moldovan regions of the Russian Empire and the Soviet Union.

Similarly, the distinct historical experience of Crimean Tatars and the Gagauz shaped their political behavior and attitudes during the post-Communist period. In particular, institutions and policies towards Crimean Tatars differed significantly among the Ottoman Empire, the Russian Empire, and the Soviet Union. The link between their historical legacy and Islam in the Ottoman Empire, and their experience during their mass exile during the Soviet period, were crucial factors in the formation of a distinct national identity among Crimean Tatars. The historical experience of the Gagauz provides a key to understanding their seemingly anomalous political behavior and attitudes in post-Communist Moldova. In contrast to most other Turkic-speaking groups, the Gagauz demonstrated a pro-Russian and pro-Communist orientation. This book explains this anomaly as a cultural legacy of the institutions and policies of the Ottoman Empire, the Russian Empire, and the Soviet Union. Because they were Orthodox Christians, under the Ottoman Empire which discriminated against and persecuted Orthodox Christians. the Gagauz were forced to flee to Moldova and Southern Ukraine with assistance from the government of the Russian Empire.

Some scholars attribute regional conflicts to "ancient hatred."[10] This view traces the emergence of political cleavages to historical conflicts in an-

---

[10] Historians and area scholars have identified numerous conflicts and divisions dating back to the ancient history of Ukraine and Moldova. Their territories have been conquered, fought over, and divided between different states many times during the course of the past two thousand years. In the case of Moldova, these divisions go back to the Roman Empire and its aftermath. Dacian tribes, who are considered to be Moldovan ancestors, came under the control of the Roman Empire, and then numerous nomadic tribes and ancient Slavs invaded their territory. (See King, 2001). The territory of Ukraine was the ancient homeland of Slavic tribes, who then migrated and colonized the Balkans, Central Europe, and European Russia during the first millennium. Ukrainians, Russians, Belarusians, Czechs, Slovaks, Poles, Serbs, Slovenes, Macedonians, Bulgarians, and Slavic Muslims in Bosnia all trace their origin and languages to this historic split. In turn, ancient Greeks, Goths, Vikings, Khazars, and many nomadic tribes settled or raided various areas of territory that would later become Ukraine. The emergence of Ukrainians, Russians, and Belarusians is attributed to the break-up of the Kyiv Rus as a result of internal feuds and its division between

cient times and the mythologization of these conflicts in modern times. For example, Huntington (1996) argues that the clash of civilizations is the main characteristic of post-Cold War politics. He defines "civilizations" as religions, such as Western Christianity, Orthodox Christianity, Islam, Buddhism, and Confucianism, and attributes regional conflicts in the former Yugoslavia, the former Soviet Union, and in many developing countries to the clash of civilizations.

Huntington (1996, pp. 138, 165) views Ukraine as a cleft country that is divided along civilization lines between the Greek Catholic West and the Orthodox East. However, more than half of the population in Western Ukraine is not Catholic, but Orthodox Christian. All the major ethnic groups (Moldovans, Ukrainians, Russians, and the Gagauz) in Moldovan regions are predominantly Orthodox Christian. (See Table A.1 in the Appendix.)

This study argues that the role of ancient conflicts and legacies in the emergence of regional political cultures has been minimal in both Ukraine and Moldova. Mass illiteracy, the absence or weakness of religious identity, and cultural decline during long periods of foreign rule meant that the historical legacies from ancient times were not transmitted culturally from one generation to the next. For example, an "ancient hatred" would make it difficult to explain the pro-Russian values of the Gagauz and the absence of conflict between Ukrainians and the Gagauz. Nomadic ancestors of the Gagauz were often engaged in violent conflicts with the ancestors of modern Ukrainians and Russians in Kyiv Rus about one thousand years ago.

However, modern mythologization of ancient history and its use by political leaders as a means of ideological legitimization and mobilization can be a powerful factor in generating political conflicts. For example, Nazi leaders based their policy in Eastern Europe on the racial mythologization of ancient history. The Nazis viewed World War II and the occupation and colonization of Slavic lands in Eastern Europe as a continuation of the drive to the East by ancient Germanic tribes.

Adolph Hitler and other leading Nazi policy-makers considered the absolute majorities of Ukrainians, Russians, and Belarusians to be racially in-

---

Mongolo-Tatars, Poles, and Lithuanians in the first half of the last millennium. (See Barraclough, 1998; Davies, 1996; Subtelny, 1988).

ferior. Because of German influence in Galicia, including the legacy of Austrian rule, some Nazi leaders regarded Ukrainians in Galicia as members of a Slavic group that was distinct from Ukrainians and that spoke its own Galician language. At the same time, Nazi leaders often described Ukrainians in Eastern Ukraine as Russians. (See Kosyk, 1993). The Nazis' views on race, based on their ideological interpretations of anthropology and history, manifested itself in significant variations in their policy, and thereby produced different historical experiences for Ukrainians in Galicia and Eastern Ukraine during World War II.

The cultural differentiation between regions of Ukraine and Moldova resembled the difference between the United States and Canada, both of which were at one time part of British North America. The historical development of the United States and Canada took different paths when the United States won the revolutionary war for independence and Canada remained a British colony. In contrast to Canada and European countries, the United States developed as a religiously sectarian country. Political values in the United States are more individualist and laissez-faire than those in Canada. Conversely, political values in Canada are more collectivist and statist than in the United States. (Lipset, 1990, 1996; Lipset, Meltz, Gomez, and Katchanovski, 2004; Weber, 1946, pp. 302-322).

From a historical perspective, political culture can be viewed as analogous to a geological structure, which includes layers or deposits accumulated over long time. (See Diamond, 1993, pp. 412-413; Elazar, 1966, pp. 94-96). In the cases of Ukraine and Moldova, this implies that political culture in different historical regions would vary, and that it would include different historical legacies. For example, the political culture of national identity in the Ukrainian regions of Galicia reflects the legacy of Austrian rule before World War I, Polish rule during the interwar period, German rule during World War II, and the Soviet rule between 1939 and 1941 and after World War II. The political culture of the neighboring historical region of Volhynia reflects similar legacies, with the exception of Austrian rule, because this region was part of the Russian Empire before World War I. National identity values in the Bessarabia region of Moldova incorporate the historical legacies of Russian rule before World War I, Romanian rule during the interwar and World War II years, and the Soviet rule in 1940-1941 and after World War II.

In contrast, the political culture of national identity in the regions of Eastern Ukraine and in the Transdniestria region of Moldova reflects legacies of Russian rule before World War I and then Soviet rule, which was only interrupted by Nazi and Romanian rule during World War II. Soviet rule lasted much longer in Eastern Ukraine and the Transdniestria region of Moldova than in Western Ukraine and Western Moldova, and this affected the formation of their respective political cultures.

Political culture evolves slowly, and it takes a long time to change values. Historical experiences during wars and other short-term upheavals are less likely to radically reshape political culture; however their effects on values are much more intense. For example, World War II left a noticeable historical imprint on values in many countries because of its intensity and because of the totalitarian character of Nazi occupational policy.

Political culture theory entails that political values are not abandoned as soon as the costs of holding them outweigh the benefits, as implied by the path dependency theory. For example, it was contrary to rational self-interest for many Western Ukrainians and Western Moldovans to maintain their nationalist values after their regions had been incorporated into the Soviet Union, because the Soviet policy of mass terror during Stalin's rule was a powerful incentive for them to reverse their original values. Anyone suspected of being a Ukrainian nationalist faced execution, arrest, exile to Siberia, and other harsh punishment. This means that the path dependence mechanism would be broken and that political preferences in different historical regions would converge, unless it is assumed that West Ukrainians preferred a situation in which it was higly probable that they would be arrested, exiled, or executed.

Like historical legacy, religious tradition influences the evolution of culture. (See Huntington, 1996; Weber,1904-1905/1958). Because religious identities can be culturally transmitted even to an illiterate population, they often precede the formation of national identities. For example, historical experience in the Ottoman Empire differed significantly, depending on the religious affiliation of people. The Ottoman political system, a Muslim theocracy, included nominally autonomous units that were based on religious affiliation: Muslim, Orthodox Christian, Armenian Christian, and Jewish. The government treated non-Muslims as members of lower social groups. Thus, Christians had to pay higher taxes, wear different clothing, and face religious and legal discrimination; they could not carry arms and a significant number of them were forced into slavery or massacred in the frequent wars and uprisings. (See Crampton, 1997; Rummel, 1994; Todorova, 1996).

Modern Western historians tend to portray the Ottoman Empire as more tolerant towards its religious minorities than were many other European monarchies. However, the perception of this period in Armenia, Bulgaria, Greece, Macedonia, Moldova, Serbia, Romania, Russia, and Ukraine is the complete opposite. In historical research, popular culture, and folk ballads, the period of Ottoman rule and the rule of the Crimean khanate, its vassal state, is viewed as the "dark ages," "enslavement," or a "yoke" (See Quataert, 2000, pp. 193-194; Subtelny, 1981;Todorova, 1996). Even though Christians in the Ottoman Empire were formally granted a high degree of autonomy, leading positions in the Church and government in Orthodox Christian areas were largely occupied by Greeks. For example, Moldovans played little role in the Greek-dominated governance of Moldova when their country was a vassal state of the Ottoman Empire. (See King, 2000).

Such historical experiences cannot be attributed solely to modern-day nationalist myth-making, because these perceptions, as exemplified by folk ballads, appeared in the Orthodox countries of the former Ottoman Empire before the advent of nationalism. Even though in modern times the role of religion declined significantly in these countries, the legacy of the distinct historical experience during the Ottoman rule contributed to the evolution of national and regional political cultures, which, to a considerable extent, parallel the divisions between Christians and Muslims in the Ottoman Empire.

2.2   Historical legacies and regional divisions in a comparative framework

Variation in regional political behavior and attitudes in many countries is linked to the political culture that is associated with historical legacy. The wave of democratization in post-Communist countries and many developing countries after the collapse of Communism and the end of the Cold War brought to the surface regional divisions that had been hidden or suppressed

by totalitarian and authoritarian regimes. Communist governments in the Soviet Union, Yugoslavia, and Czechoslovakia, suppressed all forms of
regionalism or nationalism, which were not sanctioned by the ruling parties.
However, these countries disintegrated in the early 1990s.[11]

Yugoslavia broke apart in 1991, and the republics that first seceded
had very different historical legacies. Slovenia and Croatia in the former
Yugoslavia were parts of the Austro-Hungarian Monarchy until World War I,
while most of Serbia, Montenegro, and Macedonia were under the rule of the
Ottoman Empire until the end of the nineteenth century or the beginning of
the twentieth century. Bosnia-Herzegovina was also part of the Ottoman Empire for several centuries, but it later came under the brief control of the
Habsburg Monarchy. The historical experiences of Croatians, Serbs, Bosnian
Muslims, and Slovenes during World War II also differed significantly.

Many of the countries that emerged from the break-up of Yugoslavia
have shown the profound divisions in regions populated by ethnic and religious minorities. Violent conflicts swept across Kosovo region in Serbia; Muslim, Croatian, and Serbian regions in Bosnia; Eastern Slavonia and Krajina in
Croatia; and the Albanian regions of Macedonia. Divisions also became ap-
parent between North and South Albania, and between Montenegro and Serbia in the former Yugoslavia.

These divisions parallel, to a significant extent, the different historical
experiences under the Ottoman rule. The historical experience in the Ottoman Empire varied significantly depending on religion. Bosnian Muslims
emerged as a distinct group when a portion of the Serb and Croat populations
of this region adopted Islam during the Ottoman rule, while another part preserved their Christian faith. Similarly, most Albanians converted from Christianity to Islam during the Ottoman rule. At the same time, many Serbs were
forced to migrate from Kosovo to the Krajina and Slavonia regions of Croatia
after the Habsburg-Ottoman war, which took place from 1683 to 1699. (See
Rusinow, 1996).

Because of the different historical legacies, Orthodox Serbs continue
to perceive these conversions as "betrayals" and to associate Bosnian Muslims and Kosovo Albanians with Turks. The Battle of Kosovo (1389) gained

---

[11]   See Bookman, 1994; Leff, 1999; and Musil, 1995.

mythic status among Serbs because it signified the beginning of the Ottoman domination, which lasted until the nineteenth century. Similar historical distinctions characterized Orthodox Macedonians and Albanians, who lived in Western Macedonia. The differences in historical legacies between Montenegrins and Serbs and between Northern and Southern Albanians can also be traced to Ottoman times. The Ottoman rule was nominal in Montenegro and Northern Albania because of the mountainous location of these regions. (See Zickel and Iwaskiw, 1994).

The historical experience of Croatians, Serbs, Bosnians, and Albanians differed during World War II. For example, Nazis regarded Croatians as descendants of ancient Germanic tribes, and treated them as racially superior to Serbs. During the war, the policy of a Croatian state, created by the Nazis, resulted in mass extermination of the Serbian minority.

The historical events associated with critical junctures were often mythologized and used by nationalist politicians to promote their goals and mobilize public support in regional conflicts. For example, Serbian nationalists referred to the Battle of Kosovo in their attempt to justify policies of discrimination and ethnic cleansing against Kosovo Albanians, even though Albanian troops fought alongside Serbian troops against the Turkish invaders in the battle. Similarly, the number of Serbs who fell victim to policies of mass extermination, expulsion, and conversion carried out by the Nazi-backed Croatian *Ustashi* government during World War II was exaggerated by Serbian nationalists and used to justify wars and ethnic cleansing in Croatia and Bosnia. At the same time, the Croatian government, led by Franjo Tudjman, minimized the number of Serbian victims and restored some of the symbols of the *Ustashi* regime. (See, for example, Judah, 1997).

In the Baltic States, distinct historical legacies contributed to the evolution of political cultures that were different from those of the other republics of the former Soviet Union. Estonia, Latvia, and Lithuania were independent states before their incorporation into the Soviet Union as a result of the Soviet-Nazi pact and World War II. In addition, the Baltic States had distinct religious identities before they came under Russian control in the eighteenth century. In contrast to the predominantly Orthodox Russians, ethnic Estonians were predominantly Protestant, ethnic Lithuanians were Catholic, and ethnic Latvians were Protestant and Catholic in about equal proportions.

The distinct historical legacy in the Baltic States was reinforced during World War II. The Nazi occupation policy towards Estonians and Latvians differed significantly from their policy towards Belarusians, Russians, Ukrainians, and Poles, which in turn differed from their policy towards Jews. While Nazis regarded Estonians and Latvians as largely suitable for Germanization, they viewed the absolute majority of Slavic people as racially inferior and suitable only for extermination, enslavement, and ethnic cleansing. Nazis pursued a policy of complete elimination against European Jews and Gypsies, whom they regarded as racially alien groups. (See Madajczyk, 1962; Rummel, 1992).

Like the Volhynia region of Western Ukraine, Western regions of Belarus became a part of Poland in the period between the two world wars, while Eastern regions were part of the Soviet Union. However, in contrast to Ukraine and Moldova, by the mid-1990s Belarus had become an authoritarian state. Elections in Belarus were no longer free after President Lukashenko disbanded parliament and concentrated power into his hands. (See Mihalisko, 1997; Zaprudnik and Urban, 1997). Nevertheless, poll data suggests that the Western regions of Belarus differ politically from Eastern Belarus. For example, the 1996 World Values Survey shows that a significantly higher proportion of respondents in Western Belarus (20 percent) than in Eastern Belarus (6 percent) supported the Popular Front, the main nationalist organization. The Popular Front opposed union with Russia, which was pursued by Alexander Lukashenko.

Czechoslovakia, another post-Communist country, broke apart in 1992, and the Czech Republic and Slovakia became separate states. Although the Czechs and the Slovaks are both Western Slavic nations and have similar languages, they have different historical legacies. Even though the Czechs and the Slovaks formally belonged to the Austro-Hungarian Monarchy from the seventeenth century until the beginning of the twentieth century, they were in two parts of the empire that became quite autonomous during the nineteenth century. Hungarian rule affected the historical experience of the Slovaks, while the historical experience of the Czechs was linked to Austrian rule. The influence of Catholicism was stronger in Slovakia than in Czech lands. (Kirschbaum, 1995, p. 38; Kucera and Pavlik, 1995, pp. 32-33; Ulc, 1996, p. 332).

There were regional conflicts in the former Soviet republics, including in Chechnya in Russia, Nagorno Karabakh in Azerbaijan, Abkhazia and South Ossetia in Georgia, and several regions of Tajikistan (see Bremmer and Taras, 1997; Lieven, 1998). A violent conflict took place between Ossetians and Ingushes in a southern region of Russia (Omrod, 1997). Russia has also experienced significant regional political divisions that took a non-violent form. For example, Tatarstan gained significant autonomy in the Russian Federation. Non-violent divisions between Northern regions populated by Russians and Southern regions populated by Kazakhs have emerged in Kazakhstan. (O'Loughlin, Shin, and Talbot, 1996; Treisman, 1997). Significant regional divisions became evident in Kyrgyzstan during the "Tulip Revolution" in 2005. The opposition, which overthrew the government of President Askar Akaev, was much more popular in the South than in the North.

Many of these regional conflicts in the former Soviet Union are associated with distinct historical legacies, and these are often linked to religion. For example, Chechens, Abkhazians, and Ingushes adopted Islam under the influence of the Ottoman Empire in the seventeenth century, while Don Cossacks, Georgians, and Ossetians preserved their Christian religion. As noted, this meant differential treatment during direct or indirect Ottoman rule, for instance in determining the likelihood of enslavement or massacre. Similarly, in Nagorno Karabakh, the experience of predominantly Shiite and Turkic-speaking Azeris differed from the experience of Christian Armenians from the period when the region was part of the Persian Empire until the beginning of the nineteenth century. (Hunter, 1997).

The Russian conquest of the Caucasus and Transcaucasus in the nineteenth century reversed the situation. Many Muslim people in the region, including a large proportion of the population of Abkhazia, were forced to migrate to the Ottoman Empire because of the violence that accompanied the Russian conquest and the discriminatory treatment of Muslims by the Russian government. Under Soviet rule, Chechens and Ingushes were expelled by Stalin to Central Asia as a collective punishment for collaboration with Nazis by some of them. Abkhazians avoided this fate, but in the 1930s, Stalin, who was an ethnic Georgian, lowered the administrative status of their region in Georgia. (See Lieven, 1998; Lieven, 2001, p. 153; Minahan, 1996, pp. 1-3).

Distinct historical legacies reinforce the cleavages between ethnic Russians and Tatars in Tatarstan, and between Russians and Kazakhs in Northern Kazakhstan. Russians viewed the Mongol and Tatar conquest of the Middle Ages as the "yoke" that was accompanied by cultural and physical destruction. The Russian Tsars in the sixteenth to nineteenth centuries incorporated these regions, which had belonged to successor states of the Mongol Empire. The Russian and Soviet rules had a significant effect on the development of national identity among Tatars and Kazakhs because, prior to the Russian conquest, most of them had been nomads and Islam was relatively weak in their regions. (See Frank and Wixman, 1997; and Olcott, 1997).

The regional political cleavages in Poland and Romania also have historical components. The partition of Poland among the Austro-Hungarian Monarchy, the Russian Empire, and the German Empire from the end of the eighteenth century until World War I is associated with significant variations in the voting behavior of post-Communist Poland (Gorzelak, 1998; Zarycki and Nowak, 2000). A more liberal and democratic system in the formerly Austrian region of Galicia, the Western part of which is in Poland and the Eastern part in Ukraine, fostered a stronger Polish national identity in this region than in the regions that belonged to Prussia and the Russian Empire. A survey of local governments conducted in the mid-1990s found that their location in different historical regions strongly affected the performance of local governments in Poland. Local governments in Northwest Poland, an area that belonged to Germany until World War II, exhibited the best performance, as measured by such indicators as foreign capital investments, contacts with municipalities abroad, registration of new companies, and the existence of a local newspaper. They were followed by regions that were parts of the German Empire until World War I. The formerly Austrian region of Galicia was next. The region that belonged to the Russian Empire until World War I demonstrated the weakest performance. (Gorzelak, 1998, pp. 124-126).

The Transylvania region, which contains a large Hungarian minority, was under Austro-Hungarian rule until World War I, in contrast to the rest of Romania (Minahan, 1996, pp. 579-581). This region played an important role in the anti-Communist movement and it voted differently from the rest of Romania in elections held after the collapse of Communism (Roper and Fesnic, 2003).

It is noteworthy that differences between Romania and Moldova are mostly historical, since the languages and ethnic origins of people in both countries are similar. In contrast to Romania, which became independent after the end of Ottoman rule in the nineteenth century, Moldova was under Russian rule until World War I. Moldova became a part of the Soviet Union after a unification with Romania during the interwar period. These historical differences contributed to the emergence of a distinct Moldovan identity. For example, most ethnic Moldovans do not support the unification of their country with Romania.

Historical legacy is helpful in understanding the divisions not only *within*, but also *among* post-Communist countries. There is significant geographic variation in the democratization and economic reform policy in the formerly Communist countries of Eastern Central Europe and the post-Soviet Republics. The most successful democratic and economic reforms have taken place in Poland, Slovenia, the Czech Republic, Slovakia, Hungary, and the Baltic States. These countries receive the highest scores on overall measures of democratization and economic liberalization. Reforms have been much more limited or have faced setbacks in Central Asian Republics, Transcaucasian States, Belarus, Moldova, Ukraine, Serbia, Macedonia, and Russia. It is noteworthy that most countries in the first group shared a legacy of Austro-Hungarian rule and religious traditions of Western Christianity, while the second group of countries experienced Russian and Ottoman rule as well as Orthodox Christianity and Islam. (See Katchanovski, 2000; Katchanovski and La Porte, 2005).

Significant regional political cleavages exist in many developed Western countries. In the United States, the South preserves its political distinctiveness, even though regional political divisions have diminished since the American Civil War between the North and the South (Burnham, 1974; Lipset 1981/1959, pp. 322-325, 372-384). For most of the twentieth century, the Democratic Party dominated Southern politics, especially at the state and local levels (Lamis, 1999). However, by the end of the 1990s, the Republican Party had won the majority of Congressional seats and Governorships in the Southern states (Bullock and Rozell, 1998; Lamis, 1999). This shift in US regional voting patterns represented a major electoral realignment (Glazer, 1996; Speel, 1998). However, political values in the South have not changed as rapidly as has party support. Survey data shows that Southerners remain more conservative on political and social issues than do Northerners (See Miller and Shanks, 1996; Moreland, Baker, and Steed, 1982; Reed, 1972/1986; Steed, Moreland and Baker, 1990; Weakliem and Biggert, 1999).

These regional cleavages in the United States are linked to differences in political culture (see, Elazar, 1996; Erikson, McIver and Wright, 1987; Johnson, 1976; Reed, 1972/1986). Elazar (1966) identifies traditionalistic, moralistic, and individualistic regional political cultures in the United States and argues that the traditionalistic culture is predominant in the South. In contrast, the moralistic culture dominates in most of New England, the Northwest, and the Far West, while the individualistic culture dominates such states as New York, New Jersey, Pennsylvania, Massachusetts, Ohio, and Illinois.

Distinct immigration patterns and historical experiences led to the emergence and evolution of regional subcultures in the United States (Elazar, 1966; Johnston, 1976). Different ethnic and religious groups settled in different regions. For example, Elazar (1966, pp. 96-102) links the moralistic culture to the Puritan immigrants and Mormons. Reed (1972/1986, pp. 84-87) attributes the endurance of the regional culture in the South to socialization in the family, church, and even local media and schools, which are staffed and run mostly by Southerners. He links the emergence and evolution of this regional culture to the historical legacies in the South. Reed (1972/1986, pp. 88-90) argues that the perception of an outside threat, such as the abolitionist and civil rights movements, helped to create a distinct Southern identity.

Regional divisions play a significant role in Canadian politics (Schwartz, 1995). Quebec is the most politically distinct region in Canada. There is a considerable level of support among French-speaking residents of Quebec for the secession of the province from Canada. Almost half of the voters in Quebec support sovereignty (Nevitte, Blais, Gidengil, and Nadeau, 2000, pp. 118-119). The New Democratic Party (NDP), Canada's national social-democratic party, is traditionally strong in Western regions, most notably in Saskatchewan, Manitoba, and British Columbia (Johnson, Blais, Brady, and Crete, 1992, pp. 60-63; Lipset, 1968/1950). In the 1997 elections, the NDP significantly increased its vote in the Atlantic regions of Canada (Nevitte, et. al, 2000, pp. 12-14, 108-110). The proportion of the votes received by the Reform Party in the 1993 and 1997 elections was considerably higher in the

Western regions, especially Alberta, than in the Eastern regions (Nevitte, et. al., 2000, pp. 12-15).

As in the United States, immigration patterns contributed to the emergence and evolution of regional subcultures in Canada. For example, unlike the rest of Canada, Quebec was settled primarily by French Catholic immigrants. Several studies have linked regional differences in political behavior and attitudes in Canada to regional political culture. (See, for example, Vengroff and Morton, 2000). Strong regional differences in Canadian party support remain even after other variables, such as income, religion, gender, and age, are taken into account (Nevitte, et. al., 2000, p. 15).

Historical legacy, including post-war divisions, affected the formation and evolution of regional political subcultures in Germany (Rohrschneider, 1996). Elections and opinion polls have revealed significant political differences between regions of the former East Germany and West Germany after their unification in 1990 (see, for example, Rohrschneider, 1996). The Communists and radical right parties and groups, including neo-Nazis, have received much stronger support in the East than in the West. The Christian Democratic Union has enjoyed a disproportionate level of support in Bavaria, a region that differed in its historical development from other regions of Germany (Linz, 1967; Minahan, 1996, pp. 71-74; Sallnow and John, 1982, pp. 18-25; Urwin, 1982b).

Large regional political divisions have manifested themselves in Italy. For example, the Communists received much higher electoral support in the Central and Northern regions than in the South (Dogan, 1967; Sallnow and John, 1982, pp. 80-94). The Northern League, a coalition of regionally based movements, emerged as an influential political force in the North of Italy in the 1990s (Woods, 1995). Putnam's (1993) study showed a significant division in Italy between the North and the South in the area of governance. Political differences between Italy's Northern and Southern regions are traced to different historical legacies dating back to early medieval times.

Movements for secession in Northern Ireland in the United Kingdom, in the Basque region in Spain, and in Corsica in France have become violent (Heiberg, 1982; Laitin, 1995; Newman, 1996; Urwin, 1982a). In contrast, nationalist parties have relied on electoral politics to achieve their goals in Scotland and Wales in Great Britain and Catalonia in Spain (Berrington, 1985; Newman, 1996).[12]

Historical legacies linked to religion have contributed to the cleavages and conflict between Catholics and Protestants in Northern Ireland. Within England proper, the Conservatives traditionally have received a high level of support in the South (Sallnow and John, 1982, pp. 52-60; Urwin, 1982a). London, which is now a stronghold of the Labor Party, has been a major exception to this pattern (Rose, 1974a, pp. 513-515). Different patterns of historical development in the Basque and Catalan regions of Spain shaped distinct political identities in these regions. (See Diez, 1995; Minahan, 1996, pp. 111-114, 168-170).

In Belgium, political divisions between the Flemish and Wallon regions led to both the establishment of a federal system and the existence of regionally based parties by the early 1990s (Newman, 1996). Historical legacy associated with linguistic differences contributed to the emergence of these political divisions. French-speaking Walloons are concentrated in the South, while the Flemish, who speak a language related to Dutch, live mostly in the North (Minahan, 1996).

Regionalist movements have emerged in the Basque country and Alsace in France, but their influence is limited (Loughlin, 1985). Leftist parties, including the Socialists and the Communists, had a strong influence in the South of France for a significant part of the post-war period (Sallnow and John, 1982, pp. 61-71). However, in the 1990s, the National Front, a nationalist and anti-immigrant movement, received its strongest support in the South.

Party electoral support has varied significantly among regions in Norway. Leftist parties and the Conservative Party have received disproportionate shares of the votes in the East and North of Norway. Support for the Socialist and Communist parties has also been much stronger in the East and North than in the West, which has been a traditional stronghold of the Protestant fundamentalist Christian People's Party (See Aarebrot, 1982; Rokkan, 1967; Sallnow and John, 1982, pp. 129-133; Valen and Rokkan, 1974).

Regional political divisions in other advanced Western countries, such as Switzerland, Finland, Ireland, Portugal, Greece, Austria, Denmark,

---

[12]   The Labor Party has often received a disproportionate share of votes in Scotland.

and Sweden, have manifested primarily in varying levels of support for political parties (see Rose, 1974b; Sallnow and John, 1982). In Switzerland, the vote for many parties, including the Social Democratic Party and the Radical Democratic Party, had a high degree of regional concentration (Sallnow and John, 1982, pp. 26-30; Urwin, 1983, p. 230). In Finland, the Communists enjoyed stronger electoral support in the North after World War II, but by the 1990s their influence on the national level had declined. The Swedish People's Party, which represents the Swedish minority in Finland, received most of its votes in the Southwest (See Alapuro, 1982; Allardt and Pesonen, 1967).

Significant regional divisions, which often coincide with territorially based ethnic or religious groups, exist in many Asian countries. For example, there are several politically distinctive regions in Communist China. Hong Kong and Macao reunited with China at the end of the 1990s. However, they preserved their own political systems and cultures, which had emerged as result of British and Portuguese colonial rule (Chang and Chuang, 1998). In South Korea, regional political divisions have manifest in significant differences in levels of support for parties and presidential candidates in the Youngnam and Honam regions (Steinberg, 1995).

Violent regional conflicts have taken place in Afghanistan, India, Sri Lanka, Indonesia, Myanmar, Yemen, Turkey, Iran, Iraq, and Lebanon. For example, a violent conflict continues in Kashmir in India. This region has been in dispute by India and Pakistan since the former British India was split into two countries in 1947. A million people died in the violence that erupted during the split. The dispute over Kashmir escalated several times into wars between India and Pakistan, and the territory of Kashmir was de facto divided between these two countries. The regional conflict over Kashmir took on a global dimension when India and Pakistan tested nuclear bombs in 1998. In addition, India and Pakistan have had other regional political divisions within their territories. Separatist movements have been active in the Indian regions of Punjab, Assam, and Nagaland. (See Das Gupta, 1995). Regionally based political movements have emerged in Baluchistan, Sindh, and the Northwest Frontier Province in Pakistan (*Minorities*, 2000).

Secessionist armed movements have been active in the Northern and Eastern regions of Sri Lanka, the Southern islands of the Philippines, the Aceh province in Indonesia, and in many regions of Burma (Myanmar). A pro-independence movement waged an armed struggle in East Timor after the former Portuguese colony was taken over by Indonesia in 1975. East Timor became independent after the majority of its residents voted in favor of independence in the 1999 referendum. War broke out in Yemen in 1994 between the South and the North, which had previously waged wars on each other when they were separate countries. North Yemen and South Yemen became one country in 1990. Armed insurgency in the Kurdish regions in the 1990s spanned Turkey, Iraq, and Iran. The insurgency that followed the American invasion of Iraq in 2003 is concentrated in the central provinces, an area known as the Sunni triangle.

Most of these regions are populated by ethnic or religious minorities, many of whom have distinct historical legacies. For example, the Sunni triangle in Iraq, as its name suggests, is dominated by Sunni Muslims who enjoyed preferential treatment during British colonial rule and after Iraq became an independent country. In contrast, Iraqi Shiites in Southern regions and Sunni Kurds in the North of Iraq faced discrimination and persecution for a long period of time. Pashtun tribes in the Northwest of Pakistan and in Southern Afghanistan, Kachins in North Myanmar, and tribes in Eastern India and Eastern Bangladesh live predominantly in mountainous areas, the topography of which made colonial and central government rule less effective than in other regions in these countries. Kurds and the people of Tibet also live in mountainous areas. Southern Yemen has a legacy of British colonial rule, in contrast to Northern Yemen. East Timor was a Portuguese colony, while West Timor was a Dutch colony and part of independent Indonesia. Dutch control over the Aceh province was established much later than in other parts of Indonesia. (See Minahan, 1996).[13]

The spread of both religion and colonization presents critical junctures in the emergence of distinct political cultures in many other regions of Asian countries. Muslim populations in the Xinjiang province in China, the Southern islands of the Philippines, Kashmir in India, Western Myanmar, Southern Thailand, and Northern Cyprus reflect distinct historical and religious legacies compared to the majority of the non-Muslim population in other

---

[13]   Minahan (1996) provides references to detailed historical studies in these and many other cases.

regions of these countries. As noted, the historical experience of Christians and Muslims in the Ottoman Empire, to which Cyprus belonged for several centuries, differed significantly. Similarly, the Sikh population of Punjab in India, Hindu Tamils in the North and East of Sri Lanka, Maronite Christians in Mount Lebanon, and Buddhist Tibetans have distinct historical legacies, linked to their religions. These differences existed prior to colonial rule and continued through colonial rule and after independence. (See Barraclough, 1998; Minahan, 1996).

Regional conflicts and cleavages have affected many African countries in the end of the twentieth century. Regional wars swept across Angola, Chad, the Democratic Republic of Congo (Zaire), Ethiopia, Sierra Leone, Somalia, Sudan, and Uganda. Significant regional divisions have persisted in Nigeria, Kenya, Senegal, South Africa, Zimbabwe, and other African countries (see Coulon, 1995; Diamond, 1995; Friedman, 1995; Minorities, 2000).

These divisions often occur in regions populated by ethnic, tribal, or religious groups that have distinct historical legacies. For example, Zanzibar in Tanzania, the Oromo region, Ogaden, and the former Eritrea province in Ethiopia, Northern regions of Sudan, Chad, Nigeria, Uganda, Cameroon, Ghana, Niger, and Mali are predominantly Muslim, in contrast to predominantly Christian and animist populations in other regions of these countries. Distinct historical legacies emerged as result of these religious differences. For example, during the nineteenth century, many parts of Western and Eastern Africa experienced religious wars, waged primarily by Muslim states. A considerable number of non-Muslims were subjected to slavery because Islam prohibited the enslavement of fellow Muslims. (See Barraclough, 1998, pp. 238-239; Miles, 1994; Minahan, 1996).

The partition of Africa by European countries established artificial borders. As a result, many colonial and post-colonial countries included groups with different historical legacies. Colonial and post-independence history also contributed to the evolution of regional cultural differences. For example, the British ruled North Somalia, while Southern Somalia was an Italian colony. During British rule and during independence in Nigeria, Belgian rule in Zaire and Rwanda, and French rule in Niger and Mali, some religious and ethnic groups occupied preferable political or economic positions. Similarly,

Muslims from Northern regions dominated military governments in Nigeria after it gained independence. (See Miles, 1994; Minahan, 1996).

Significant regional political divisions have been present in many Latin American countries. Regionally based insurgency movements have emerged in Mexico, Peru, and Colombia (see Mares, 1997). Armed insurgency flared in the State of Chiapas in Mexico. *Sendero Luminoso* (the Shining Path), a radical leftist organization, waged a guerrilla war against the central government of Peru. *Sendero Luminoso*, whose military strength was significantly diminished by the end of the 1990s, has been based in the highland regions of Peru (Cotler, 1995). Left-wing rebel movements in a number of regions have waged war against the central government in Colombia.

Political cleavages between the South and the North have existed in Mexico and Brazil. For example, in Mexico, the Northern States score higher on the democratization index than do the Southern States. The democratization index is derived from expert evaluations of political competition, electoral integrity, human rights, and media openness. (Lawson, 1998, p. 24). After democracy was restored in Brazil in the 1980s, election results indicated a stronger support for the leftist parties in the Southeastern part of the country (see Mainwaring, 1995). Similarly, voting preferences in metropolitan capital areas in Uruguay and Argentina differed from voting preferences in the provinces (Gonzalez, 1995, McGuire, 1995).

Organizations intended to represent Native Indians on various political and economic issues have emerged in Mexico, Peru, Ecuador, Bolivia, Nicaragua, Guatemala, Honduras, Colombia, and other Latin American countries (see *Minorities at Risk*, 2000). Indigenous people in Latin American countries live mostly in the highland and Amazon regions. For, example, the 2000 presidential elections revealed distinct political preferences of Native Indians in Peru (Faiola, 2000). In Ecuador, the level of support for presidential candidates in the 1988 and 1992 elections differed significantly among the coastal regions, the sierra, and the Amazon (Conaghan, 1995, p. 439). An indigenous organization stormed parliament and succeeded in ousting the president of Ecuador in January of 2000 (Buckley, 2000). In Nicaragua, a movement for autonomy emerged in the Atlantic region, which has a large Native Indian population.

The critical junctures in the emergence of distinct political values in Latin American countries can be traced to colonial rule, post-independence rule, and immigration patterns. As noted, many of these divisions occurred in areas that are populated by indigenous people and are difficult for central governments to control because of their remoteness or inaccessibility. The historical experience of Native Americans during the Spanish and Portuguese colonial rule and in the post-independence period differed significantly from that of European descendants who held dominant political and economic positions. This applies, for example, to the Mayas in Chiapas. In the Atlantic region of Nicaragua, a distinct culture evolved as a result of the British and American influence in contrast to other regions of Nicaragua, which were influenced by Spanish rule. Immigration, dominated by settlers from European countries, contributed to the emergence of distinct regional culture in the South of Brazil. (See Minahan, 1996).

A number of factors complicate the analysis of regional political divisions. Regional economic, ethnic, and cultural differences often coexist, which makes it difficult to separate their relative importance. For example, Kosovo is a much less economically developed region than other regions in Serbia. Kosovo is primarily populated by Albanians, whose ethnicity and language differ from the ethnicity and language of Serbs. Most Kosovo Albanians are Muslims, while most Serbs are Orthodox Christians. In addition, Serbs and Kosovo Albanians have different historical experiences, for example, during the Ottoman Empire and after the independence of Serbia in the second half of the nineteenth century. Kosovo became a part of Serbia in 1912 as a result of one of the Balkan wars.

Compared to many other countries, Ukraine and Moldova are better suited for an analysis of regional political divisions. A large number of regions and the availability of data make it possible to conduct a multivariate statistical analysis of the regional political divisions in Ukraine and Moldova. There are 27 administrative-territorial regions in Ukraine and three major regions in Moldova.[14]

---

[14]   Statistical studies that use regions as the main units of analysis to make inferences about behaviors of individuals face an ecological inference problem (King, 1997). The ecological inference problem is not a major problem for this specific study, which analyzes regional political behavior. However, the use of survey data, such as the

Data problems are much less serious in Ukraine and Moldova than in many other regionally divided countries. Relatively democratic and free elections held in Ukraine and Moldova since 1990 provide data on regional political behavior.[15] Surveys, such as the 1996 World Values Survey and the 1998 Laitin/Hough survey, provide comparable data on regional political attitudes in Ukraine and Moldova.[16] The data on regional economic development and the ethnic composition of the population are obtained from Ukrainian, Moldovan, Transdniestrian, and Soviet government publications and from international organizations such as the United Nations.

This study also uses findings of field research conducted in different regions of Ukraine during various time periods from 1990 to 2005, in particular during the 2004 presidential elections. In addition to regional results for elections, referendums, and surveys, this book employs numerous local and Western media reports about the behavior and ideological orientations of leaders in Ukraine and Moldova and the role of foreign leaders in the regional divisions in these countries. Critical analyses of these reports, which cannot be always cited for reasons of space, help us to reduce their shortcomings.

Western media sources are generally more informative and balanced than Ukrainian and Moldovan news reports, which are often slanted in favor of government and political forces as well as by personal value judgments on the part of journalists. However, Ukrainian and Moldovan mass media sources provide detailed accounts and original materials; these are often absent from the reports of Western journalists, who with few exceptions, have no permanent presence in Ukraine and Moldova and lack knowledge of local languages. For example, some journalists and experts in leading American and British newspapers described Western and Central Ukrainian regions that voted for Viktor Yushchenko and in one case Yushchenko himself as

---

World Values Survey and the Laitin/Hough survey, will help to check whether differences in political behavior are also found on the individual level in Ukraine and Moldova. Survey data makes it possible to control additional factors, such as age and gender.

[15] The turnout rate in post-Communist elections and referendums in Ukraine and Moldova was typically between 55 and 85 percent.

[16] Survey data provides a way to quantify regional political cleavages (see Dalton, 1996). However, such surveys often rely on administrative or geographic classification of regions, which differ from the regional cleavages. This study uses a different typology of regions: a typology based on historical divisions.

Catholic, even though most of these regions and the winner of the 2004 presidential elections were Orthodox. (See Bremmer, 2005; Fireman, 2004; Sestanovich, 2004; Stephen, 2004).

Misconceptions also have affected some academic studies of Ukraine and Moldova because of the inherent difficulty of researching political and historical developments in different regions that have belonged to different countries and used different languages. For example, a recent historical book – which received an award from the American Historical Association for outstanding twentieth-century European international history writing, and from the Association for Women in Slavic Studies for the best book in Slavic/East European/Eurasian studies – referred to a region that is now part of central Ukraine as "no place" and as Polish-Russian borderland and Soviet heartland. That study used the Polish term *Kresy*, which generally refered to the former Polish Eastern borderlands and included regions of modern-day Western Ukraine, Central Ukraine, Belarus, and Lithuania, to describe parts of Zhytomyr, Kyiv, Vinnytsia, and Khmelnytsky regions of modern Ukraine during Soviet rule. It maintained that this borderland region was still contested by both Ukrainian and Polish scholars because the issue of whether the local population is mostly Polish or Ukrainian remained unresolved even after Ukraine became independent. (Brown, 2000, p. 43; 2004). This was equivalent to referring to Alaska in the 1920s to 1950s by its historical Russian appellation meaning "Russian America" and describing it as a still-contested Russian-American borderland.

The book argued that Polish political, cultural, and economic domination, in particular in realms of language and religion, continued in the formerly Polish part of central Ukraine during Russian rule and even, in some cases, during the initial period of Soviet rule, and that the Polish legacy affected the evolution of national identity and other aspects of political culture in regions of Central Ukraine. However, Russian, Soviet, and Ukrainian census data show that, except for urban areas and some rural districts, this region was overwhelmingly populated by Orthodox Ukrainian-speaking Ukrainians. Polish speakers, mostly concentrated in large cities and two rural districts, constituted only 6 percent of the region's population at the end of the nineteenth century. That historical study dismissed statistical data in favor of largely anecdotal evidence; it extrapolated the historically undeveloped Ukrainian national identity of part of an ethnically mixed, forested, rural, and poor region, known as *Polissia*, into Western Ukrainian regions such as Galicia and Volyn that had once belonged to Poland. (See Brown, 2000, 2004).

The relative stability of the Ukrainian and Moldovan populations makes it easier to analyze their regional historical legacies. Ethnic Ukrainians and Moldovans did not experience the large regional migrations due to economic or political factors that many other countries did. During Soviet rule, a system of compulsory registration of the population (*propyska*) restricted mass migration from one region to another by imposing strict limitations on jobs and housing.

As noted, from a comparative perspective, Ukraine and Moldova represent a quasi-experiment. Like Italy, Germany, and Yemen, Ukraine and Moldova consist of regions that have belonged to different countries during significant historical periods. By the end of the eighteenth century, the Russian Empire included the Eastern parts of Ukraine and Moldova, while the Austro-Hungarian Monarchy ruled several Western regions of Ukraine. Before that, the Ottoman Empire had controlled Crimea and Moldova. As a result of World War I and the Civil War, the present territories of Ukraine and Moldova were divided among various Central and East European countries until World War II. Eastern Ukraine and the Transdniestrian region of Moldova belonged to the Soviet Union. In contrast, Western Ukrainian regions were incorporated into Poland, Romania, and Czechoslovakia after the break-up of the Austro-Hungarian Monarchy. Moldova's Western region belonged to Romania before World War II.

Therefore, Ukrainian and Moldovan regions experienced different political systems, institutions, and policies over a long period of time. After their incorporation into the Soviet Union, the Soviet economic and political system, which existed already in Eastern Ukraine and the Transdniestrian region of Moldova, was established in Western Ukraine and Western Moldova. Soviet policy aimed at a Communist-style modernization and the elimination of regional economic, cultural, and ethnic differences.

The study of regional political divisions in Ukraine and Moldova allows us to distinguish the effect of historical legacies compared with the effects of factors of religion, level of economic development, ethnicity, and political leadership. These factors do not completely overlap with one another.

Both historical parts of Ukraine and Moldova include regions with different ethnic composition and levels of economic development. Similarly, historical legacies do not completely coincide with religious traditions in these two countries.

This fact, the large number of regions, and the availability of both survey and aggregate data make it possible to use multivariate statistical analyses to evaluate the role of political culture relative to other factors, such as ethnicity and the level of economic development. In employing such an approach, this study quantifies the role of culture compared with other factors in regional political divisions in Ukraine and Moldova. However, it is necessary to first map the character and extent of regional divisions in post-Communist Ukraine and Moldova. This is the subject of the next chapter.

3   Regional political divisions in post-Communist Ukraine and Moldova

Strong regional divisions have characterized political behaviors and attitudes in post-Communist Ukraine and Moldova. These divisions have manifested both in the results of national and regional elections and referendums held since 1991 and in regional conflicts in Transdniestria, Gagauzia, and Crimea. These divisions have transcended administrative territorial divisions and changes in electoral systems, as well as the emergence and decline of parties and politicians.

Ukraine is administratively divided into 24 regions (*oblasts*), the Autonomous Republic of Crimea, and the cities of Kyiv and Sevastopol.[17] However, the main line of division has cut between historical regions. During different historical periods, Western regions of Ukraine belonged to the Austro-Hungarian Monarchy, Poland, Romania, and Czechoslovakia; these regions became part of Soviet Ukraine as a result of the 1939 Soviet-Nazi pact and World War II. Western Ukraine includes the Lviv, Ternopil, Ivano-Frankivsk, Chernivtsi, Transcarpathia, Volyn, and Rivne regions.[18] The Lviv, Ternopil, and Ivano-Frankivsk regions are collectively known as Galicia. About 20 percent of the population of Ukraine lives in Western Ukraine. All of the other regions make up Eastern Ukraine, which was part of Russia and then the Soviet Union for several hundred years. In contrast to other Eastern Ukraine regions, Crimea was not part of Soviet Ukraine until 1954, when Nikita Khrushchev transferred the region into Soviet Ukraine from the Russian Republic.

---

[17]   Sevastopol is treated in this study as part of Crimea for purposes of statistical analysis because the city's population is several times smaller than the population of other regions in Ukraine. Sevastopol owes its special administrative status to the Black Sea Fleet's main base, which is located there. The Fleet was divided between Ukraine and Russia in the mid-1990s. The Russian part of the fleet is stationed in Sevastopol.

[18]   Southern Bessarabia, located in the Southwest of the Odesa region in Ukraine, was part of Romania in the inter-war period. However, it was given to Ukraine in 1940 (see Forsberg, 1995). The Izmail region formed from Southern Bessarabia was included in the Odesa region in the mid-1950s.

The new administrative-territorial system adopted in Moldova in 1999 divided the country into nine counties, one municipality (Chishinau), and two autonomous regions (Gagauzia (Gagauz Yeri) and Transdniestria [Transnistria]). Special status was granted to Transdniestria and Gagauzia, in recognition of significant divisions between these regions and the rest of Moldova. In contrast to Western Moldova, which was part of Romania in the period between World War I and II, Transdniestria remained under Soviet rule. The Gagauz autonomous region was created in place of several Southern districts populated by the Gagauz, Turkic Orthodox Christian people, whose ancestors had fled religious persecution in the Ottoman Empire in the nineteenth century.

Ukraine and Moldova shared the Soviet political system before their independence. The Soviet Union was a one-party state until Mikhail Gorbachev initiated policies of *perestroika* and *glasnost*. The Communist Party of the Soviet Union (CPSU) held the monopoly of power. The Communist Party of Soviet Ukraine and the Communist Party of Soviet Moldova were integral parts of the CPSU. The existence of other parties was prohibited; political opposition and dissent led to prosecution. However, political reforms initiated by Michail Gorbachev, then General Secretary of the CPSU, began a period of political liberalization in the late 1980s that resulted in the emergence of multiparty systems and the abolition of the Communist party monopoly of power.

Both Ukraine and Moldova adopted presidential-parliamentary systems of government and multiparty political systems after the collapse of Soviet Communism. Presidents of both countries had the power to nominate the prime minister and key members of the government. However, the presidential-parliamentary systems were unstable in both Ukraine and Moldova. There were frequent attempts to redraw the balance of power in the two countries.

In 2000, Leonid Kuchma, who had been re-elected president of Ukraine in November 1999, initiated a referendum along with other steps aimed at reducing the power of parliament. The provisions approved by the referendum included lifting deputies' immunity from prosecution, reducing the number of the seats in parliament, introducing a second chamber of parliament composed of regional officials – who were appointed by the president, and granting the president the right to dissolve parliament if it could not pass a budget or form a working majority (Maksymiuk, 2000). These provisions led to a political crisis in Ukraine, and the amendments were not implemented because of the opposition of parliament.

However, a different version of political reform was more successful in Ukraine. This political reform was backed by Leonid Kuchma, his political allies, and by the Socialist Party. As the result of an agreement between key political players, aimed at solving the political crisis during the 2004 presidential elections, the parliament approved changes that would decrease the powers of the president and increase powers of the parliament and prime minister. With the political reform that came into effect in 2006 Ukraine became a parliamentary-presidential republic.

Petru Lucinschi, president of Moldova, made similar attempts to use referendums to change the Constitution and increase presidential power in 1999. However, the Election Commission declared that the results of the 1999 referendum were invalid because the number of voters who took part in the referendum (55 percent) was smaller than required (60 percent).[19] In 2000, the Moldovan parliament approved, by a veto prove majority, a law that instituted election of the president by the parliament instead of through the former system of direct presidential elections.

Several dozen political parties have taken part in national elections since Ukraine and Moldova became independent states. However, in both countries, as in many other former Soviet Republics, parties have been weak. With the exception of the Communists, party membership has been limited. Parties often suffered internal splits. As a result, several parties advocated pro-Communist or nationalist programs and competed among themselves. (See Wilson, 1997a and 1997b).

A number of successor Communist parties emerged when the Communist Party was banned in both Ukraine and Moldova after the failed coup attempt in August of 1991. The Communist political spectrum included these new Communist parties as well as the old parties, which were restored after the ban was lifted in 1993 in Ukraine and in 1994 in Moldova. The Communist Party of Ukraine advocated restoring state control over the economy, estab-

---

[19]   However, the Constitutional Court of Moldova ruled that the election result was valid, but not judicially binding. Sixty percent of the voters supported the president's proposals.

lishing a loose union of the former Soviet republics and limiting Western involvement in Ukraine. Petro Symonenko, the leader of the Communist Party of Ukraine, stated that the union could take one of many possible forms, including confederation.[20] The Communists advocated giving Russian the status of the second state language of Ukraine.

The Socialist and Peasant Parties had more moderate stances on both economic policy and restoring ties with Russia and other former Soviet republics than did the Communist Party of Ukraine. The Socialist Party (SPU) was organized by some of the former functionaries of the Communist Party of the Soviet Union. Oleksandr Moroz, the former leader of the Communist majority in the parliament of Soviet Ukraine, became the head of the Socialist Party. The party gradually moved towards social-democratic ideology, and it even allied with several nationalist and centrist parties in an attempt to oust President Leonid Kuchma after Oleksandr Moroz made public highly incriminating recordings of the president's conversations. However, the SPU has not become a social-democratic party.[21] The Progressive Socialist Party was formed by a pro-Russian faction that split from the Socialist Party. Kuchma's administration supported Progressive Socialists as a counterweight to other pro-Communist parties. (See Solchanyk, 1998). The Peasant Party represented collective farm chairmen. Despite their differences, all of these parties supported Petro Symonenko, the leader of the Communist Party, in the second round of the presidential elections in 1999. However, in contrast to the Communist Party and the Progressive Socialist Party, the Socialist Party backed Viktor Yushchenko in the second round of the 2004 presidential elections.

Similarly, several parties emerged as successors of the Soviet Communist Party in Moldova. The Party of Moldovan Communists was the largest and best organized among these parties. Vladimir Voronin, its chairman, was elected the president of Moldova in 2001. In addition, a number of pro-

---

[20]   See Symonenko, 1996.

[21]   For example, during the 2006 parliamentary elections, more than one fourth of the SPU's parliamentary candidates were managers and businessmen, while none were workers. The SPU received strong support in many rural areas of Central Ukraine; *Silski Visti*, the main newspaper read by rural residents, backed the SPU.

Communist parties were active in Transdniestria but not in the rest of Moldova. (King, 2000).

As noted, regional cleavages in post-Communist Ukraine and Moldova manifested in a number of ways, including significant variation in votes in parliamentary and presidential elections and referendums, and the emergence of regional-based movements and regional conflicts. Although a great number of political parties and leaders changed their programs and alliances from one election to another, regional divisions remained a permanent feature of Ukrainian and Moldovan politics.

3.1 Party vote

The Communist/pro-Russian vs. nationalist/pro-Western cleavage became a principal ideological cleavage in Ukraine and Moldova after the establishment of multi-party systems and democratic elections in 1990. Communists and nationalists opposed each other on such key political issues as the independence of Ukraine and Moldova, foreign policy orientation, and language and privatization policies. Although several parties in Ukraine and Moldova that claimed to be successors of the Soviet Communist Party disagreed on many issues, generally they favored closer cooperation with, or some form of political union with, Russia and other former Soviet republics.

Nationalist parties and movements emerged as the main opposition force in Ukraine and Moldova as soon as non-Communist parties were allowed to function during Gorbachev's reform period. The independence goal advocated by nationalists for Ukraine and Moldova was achieved in 1991, and nationalist politicians occupied many leading positions in both countries. However, nationalist political movements, which had once been united in their opposition to the Soviet Union, suffered organizational splits. *Rukh* (People's Movement of Ukraine) became split into two competing parties. Another *Rukh* party was formed with the support of Kuchma's administration as a counterweight to nationalist parties, but this party did poorly in the 2002 parliamentary elections.

Picture 1 The coat of arms of independent Moldova is influenced by the Romanian coat of arms

Similarly, the Popular Front in Moldova, the main nationalist organiza-tion, split into several parties. The Christian Democratic People's Party emerged as the main successor of the Popular Front. However, the activity of this and other nationalist organizations was limited to the Bessarabian part of Moldova. Authorities of the self-declared Transdniestrian Republic prohibited nationalist pro-Moldovan parties.

The nationalist political spectrum in post-Communist Moldova ranged from moderate civic forms of nationalism to radical ethnic nationalism. Mod-erate nationalists in Ukraine favored an independent foreign policy, member-ship in NATO and the European Union, and the Ukrainization of education and mass media, but defined the Ukrainian nation in civic rather than ethnic terms. Many Ukrainian radical nationalists claimed to be followers of the Or-ganization of Ukrainian Nationalists (OUN), which came to prominence during World War II. Moderate nationalists in Moldova favored the preservation of their country as an independent state and pro-Western orientation in foreign policy that included membership in NATO and the EU, while radical national-ists advocated unification of Moldova with Romania. All Moldovan nationalist parties opposed the secession of Transdniestria and Gagauzia.

Similar divisions existed between Communist parties and nationalist parties on the issue of privatization and market reform. Although Communist parties in both Ukraine and Moldova accepted in principle the existence of private property and the market economy, they opposed large-scale privatiza-tion and comprehensive market reforms. Nationalists were much more sup-portive of privatization and pro-market than were Communists. Parties that were liberal in the classical European sense were the most ardent advocates of privatization and free market, but they had limited support in post-Communist Ukraine and Moldova.

The results of parliamentary elections since 1990 have demonstrated that Communist parties were much more successful in Eastern Ukraine than in Western Ukraine. For instance, in the 1998 elections, the four pro-Communist parties that cleared a 4 percent vote threshold (the Communist Party, the coalition of the Socialist and Peasant parties, and the Progressive Socialist Party), gained significantly less support in Western Ukraine than in Eastern Ukraine, with the exception of Ukraine's capital, Kyiv. The pro-Communist vote was lowest in three regions of the former Austro-Hungarian province of Galicia, at around 6 percent. In Transcarpathia, another former Austro-Hungarian region also known as Carpatho-Ukraine, the pro-Communist parties received 10 percent of the vote. In two West Ukrainian *oblasts* of the former Russian and Polish province of Volhynia, the pro-Communist vote was 15 to 16 percent. The Communist parties gained the relative majority of votes (about 29 percent) in only one region of Western Ukraine, Chernivtsi oblast, also referred to by its historical name, Bukovyna. However, their support in this region, which belonged to Romania during the inter-war period and was mostly a part of the Austro-Hungarian Monarchy before that, was still lower than the national average. (See Figure 3.1.)

In contrast, Ukrainian nationalists led the party vote in Western regions in the 1998 elections, although their vote was split among several parties. *Rukh*, the main nationalist party, won in 5 of 7 regions in Western Ukraine. *Rukh* received 32 percent of the vote in the Lviv region, 29 percent in the Rivne region, 28 percent in the Ivano-Frankivsk region, 17 percent in the Volyn region, 15 percent in the Chernivtsi region, and 7 percent in Transcarpathia, compared with 10 percent of the national vote. Other nationalist parties also gained the highest level of support in Western regions of Ukraine. However, their poor performance in the numerous and populous regions of Eastern Ukraine did not allow them to cross the 4 percent barrier of the national vote.

The 2002 parliamentary elections showed similar regional divisions in Ukraine. The Yushchenko-led "Our Ukraine" bloc, which included some liberal parties, big businessmen, and leading nationalist parties such as the Congress of Ukrainian Nationalists and two main successor parties of *Rukh*, won 64 to 75 percent of the vote in the regions of Galicia, 55 to 58 percent in Volhynia, 46 percent in Bukovyna, and 37 percent in Transcarpathia, compared to 3 to 35 percent in Eastern Ukraine. In contrast, support for the Communist Party of Ukraine ranged between 2 and 8 percent in the historical West and 9 and 40 percent in Eastern regions. (Figure 3.2.)

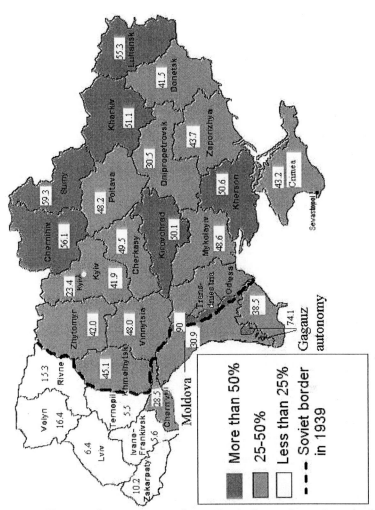

Figure 3.1 The vote for pro-Communist parties in the parliamentary elections in Ukraine and Moldova in March 1998 and the local elections in Transdniestria in 1995

Note: The result in the Crimean autonomy does not include the vote for the Union Party, a Pro-Russian party in the region. It received about 11 percent of the vote in Crimea in the 1998 parliamentary elections.

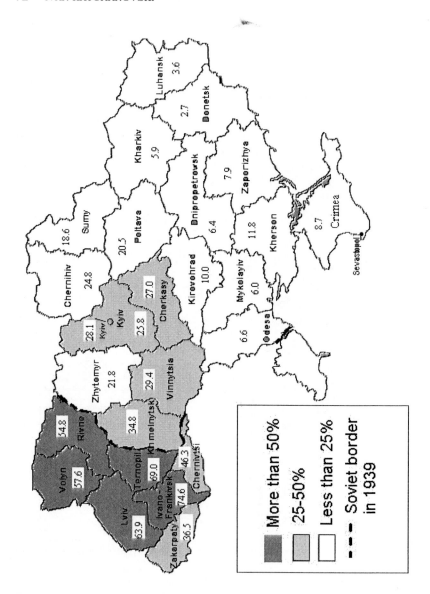

Figure 3.2 The vote for the "Our Ukraine" bloc in the parliamentary elections in Ukraine in March 2002

The results of the parliamentary elections in majoritarian districts showed the same pattern of regional division in Ukraine, although the difference was smaller than in the case of the party-based national constituency. Communist candidates were much more successful in Eastern Ukraine than in Western Ukraine, while just the opposite was true of nationalist candidates. For example, in the 1994 elections, based entirely on the majoritarian district system, Communist candidates won almost all of their seats in Eastern Ukraine. (See Arel and Wilson, 1994; Bojcun, 1995).

Other political cleavages existed in Ukraine in addition to the Communist/pro-Russian-nationalist/pro-Western cleavage. A division between pro-Kuchma and anti-Kuchma parties emerged after the 2000 tape scandal. Important differences manifested on this issue within the nationalist and Communist political spectra. After the political crisis of 2000, several Communist, nationalist, and centrist parties – among them the SPU and a bloc that included both centrists and nationalists and was headed by former oligarch Yulia Tymoshenko – led the anti-Kuchma opposition. Other centrist and oligarchic parties, as well as parties that had split from the SPU and *Rukh*, adopted pro-Kuchma positions; they formed a parliamentary majority. However, such coalitions represented tactical alliances that were unlikely to survive in the long run. The pro-Kuchma majority in parliament disintegrated when their candidate suffered defeat in the 2004 presidential elections.

The major realignment of parties in Ukraine that resulted from the "Orange Revolution" in late 2004 and a significant decline in public support for the Communist Party of Ukraine failed to end the regional political divide. For example, a poll conducted by the Democratic Initiatives Foundation at the end of December 2005 showed that the Yushchenko bloc "Our Ukraine," which included the Yushchenko-led People's Union "Our Ukraine," the People's Movement of Ukraine (a successor of *Rukh*), and the Congress of Ukrainian Nationalists, received a much higher level of support in Western Ukraine (39 percent) than in the Center (16 percent), the South (9 percent), the East (6 percent), and Donbas (1 percent).[22] (See Table 3.1).

---

[22]   The East in this survey included the Kharkiv region, the Dnipropetrovsk region, and the Zaporizhzhia region.

The Tymoshenko Bloc, which included some former nationalist leaders of the Ukrainian National Assembly and the Ukrainian Republican Party and was led by the former oligarch Yulia Tymoshenko, was much more popular in historical regions of Western Ukraine (29 percent) than in the South (11 percent), the East (11 percent), and Donbas (0 percent). The Yulia Tymoshenko Bloc was the leading political force in the Center (31 percent). Another poll, conducted by the Democratic Initiatives Foundation in December 2005, showed that the Tymoshenko Bloc was most popular in Kyiv city. Thirty-seven percent of the respondents in Kyiv city supported this Bloc compared to 18 percent in support of the Yushchenko Bloc "Our Ukraine." The Socialist Party and the Party of Regions each enjoyed backing of 10 percent from the residents of Kyiv city.

Table 3.1 Regional differences in support for political parties in Ukraine in December 2005 (%). (Democratic Initiatives Foundation Survey)

	Regions				
	West	Center	South	East	Donbas
Yushchenko Bloc "Our Ukraine"	39	16	9	6	1
Yulia Tymoshenko Bloc	29	31	11	11	0
Socialist Party	7	11	5	3	0
People's Bloc of Volodymyr Lytvyn	5	8	7	3	1
Party of Regions	5	16	30	51	81
Communist Party	4	3	6	6	4
"People's Opposition" Bloc of Nataliia Vitrenko	2	4	7	4	7
Other parties	6	8	23	8	4
Against all	3	3	2	8	2
Total (%)	100	100	100	100	100

After the 2004 presidential elections, the pro-Russian Party of Regions – which was led by Viktor Yanukovych and backed by Ukraine's wealthiest oligarch, Renat Akhmetov, who, like Yanukovych, is from Donbas

– displaced the Communist Party as the leading party in most regions of historically Eastern Ukraine. The 2005 Democratic Initiatives Foundation Survey showed that the Party of Regions enjoyed the support of 81 percent of likely voters, excluding undecided respondents, in Donbas (the Donetsk and Luhansk regions), 51 percent in other geographically Eastern regions, 30 percent in the South, and 16 percent in the Center, compared to 5 percent in Western Ukraine (Table 3.1). The popularity of the Party of Regions was artificially boosted through the use of administrative resources by then prime minister Viktor Yanukovych during the presidential elections in 2004. For example, such administrative methods as *temnyky* (detailed coverage guidelines issued by the administration of President Kuchma) ensured favorable and free-of-charge television coverage for Viktor Yanukovych during the 2004 presidential election campaign.

Public support for the Communist Party varied from 3 to 4 percent in the Center, Western Ukraine, and Donbas to 6 percent in the South and the East. This party lost support before the 2004 presidential elections, in great part because of a generational change and because of the switch by some of its deputies and supporters to the Party of Regions, which combined a pro-Russian orientation with populist policies such as a significant increase in the minimum pension. The Nataliia Vitrenko Bloc, which included the Progressive Socialist Party, had a higher level of support in regions of Eastern Ukraine (4 to 7 percent) than in Western Ukraine (2 percent). (Table 3.1.)

The Socialist Party, which had distanced itself from the other ex-Communist parties through its drift towards social-democratic ideology and its support for Viktor Yushchenko in the final round of the 2004 presidential elections, continued to enjoy its strongest support in the Center (11 percent). Its popularity was lower in other regions of Eastern Ukraine (0 to 5 percent) and in Western Ukraine (7 percent) (Table 3.1).

A poll conducted by the Kyiv International Institute of Sociology (KIIS) in December 2005 showed similar regional divisions in party support even though it used a classification of regions that was not directly comparable with the classification employed by the Democratic Initiatives Foundation. The Yushchenko bloc "Our Ukraine" was most popular (42 percent) in the geographic West of the country – that is, in regions of historical Western Ukraine and the Khmelnytsky region. Support among likely voters for this bloc declined to 20 percent in the Center, 12 percent in the South, and 3 percent in the East. The Party of Regions had the support of 72 percent of the respondents in the geographic East of Ukraine (the Donetsk region, the Luhansk region, and the Kharkiv region), 47 percent of the respondents in the South, 12 percent in the Center, and just 6 percent in the West.

The popularity of individual parties changed somewhat by the time of the parliamentary elections in March of 2006. However, these elections, which for the first time were contested only by political parties at the national level, again produced a regional divide – and they could generate a new political crisis. (See pp. 125-126 of this book). As noted, a political and legal deal, brokered in December 2004 to solve a political crisis, transformed Ukraine into a parliamentary-presidential republic. This transformation decreased presidential powers, and increased the powers of parliament and consequently the influence of political parties. In this sense, the political system in Ukraine moved closer to the system that existed in Moldova, with the exception of the self-declared Transdniestrian Republic.

A direct comparison of election results in the historical regions of Moldova is not possible, because the Transdniestrian authorities effectively prevented voters in their region from taking part in the national elections. Only a limited number of eligible Transdniestria voters traveled to the Central-government-controlled Moldovan territory to cast their ballots. (See *Report*, 1998). However, a comparison of separately held elections in Western Moldova and Transdniestria shows that pro-Communist and pro-Russian parties were stronger in the Transdniestria region than in the rest of Moldova, with the notable exception of the Gagauz region.

In the 1995 local elections in Transdniestria, the pro-Communist and pro-Russian Union of Patriotic Forces, which had been the leading political party in Transdniestria since the region de facto seceded from Moldova in 1991, took more than 90 percent of the vote. In contrast, in the separately held Moldova local elections, the Communist Party and the coalition of the Socialist Party of Moldova and *Edinstvo* (Unity) together scored 23 percent of the vote (King, 2000, p. 158). In the 1994 parliamentary elections in Moldova, the bloc of the Socialist Party – which had emerged in place of the banned Communist Party – and the *Edinstvo* (Unity) movement – which advocated the interests of Russian-speaking minorities in Moldova and initially supported

Transdniestrian separatists – received 22 percent of the vote (Crowther, 1997b, p. 327).

Preliminary results of the parliamentary elections in the Transdniestrian Republic in December 2005 again indicated significant support for pro-Russian/pro-secessionist parties. Candidates from the pro-presidential movement "*Respublika*" won about one-third of the seats (13 of 43 seats). The "Renewal" movement, which included some local oligarchs, received the majority of parliamentary seats (23 of 43). Both political organizations backed a pro-Russian orientation and the independence of the region from Moldova.

In the 1998 parliamentary elections, the Party of Moldovan Communists, along with two smaller pro-Communist parties, garnered less than one-third (31 percent) of the vote in Moldova, excluding Gagauzia and Transdniestria. Almost two and a half times (74 percent) more voters in the Gagauz autonomy voted for the Communist parties in the same elections (Figure 3.1). A similar pattern was repeated in the 1999 local elections, when more than half (53 percent) of voters in the Gagauz region supported the Communist parties, compared to a third (33 percent) in the rest of Moldova, excluding Transdniestria. Similarly, in the 2001 parliamentary elections, the Party of Moldovan Communists earned 81 percent of the vote in Gagauzia, compared to 49 percent in the rest of Bessarabia. (See *Electorala,* 1998; *IFES,* 1998, 2001a).

The results of the parliamentary elections in Moldova in March 2005 provided fresh evidence of pro-Russian and pro-Communist political values among the Gagauz. The "*Patria-Rodina*" bloc received the majority (51 percent) of votes in the Gagauz autonomy, while it scored only 5 percent of the national vote in Moldova. The Socialist Party and the splinter Party of Socialists established this electoral bloc. These parties, which had once been allied with the Party of Moldovan Communists, offered a pro-Russian electoral program that included Moldova's integration in the Common Economic Space, a union of ex-Soviet republics led by Russia, and support for a Russian plan to resolve the Transdniestrian conflict. The movement "*Ravnopravie*," which also favored a union with Russia, received the support of more than 5 percent of Gagauz voters, compared to less than 3 percent in Moldova overall.[23]

---

[23]   See "Preliminary Results," 2005.

In spite of the administrative resources used by the ruling Party of Moldovan Communists, support for this party in Gagauzia in the 2005 parliamentary elections dropped by more than 200 percent compared to the 2001 parliamentary elections. Vladimir Voronin, the leader of this party and president of Moldova, did not accept the Russian plan for Transdniestria, and changed his orientation from the Commonwealth of Independent States (CIS) towards European integration in order to stay in power. The Party of Moldovan Communists received about one-third (31 percent) of the vote in Gagauzia compared with about one half of the vote in the rest of Moldova, excluding the Transdniestrian Republic.[24]

Nationalist pro-Western parties were weaker in the Gagauz autonomy and Transdniestria region than in the rest of Moldova. For instance, parties that formed a coalition in the aftermath of the 1998 parliamentary elections, in order to prevent the Communists from heading the government, won 11 percent of the vote in Gagauzia, compared with their total vote of 46 percent in Moldova. This coalition included the For Democratic and Prosperous Moldova bloc organized by supporters of President Petru Lucinschi, the Democratic Convention bloc led by the former President Snegur, and the Party of Democratic Forces, which had backed Mircea Snegur in the second round of the 1996 presidential elections.

Like previous elections, the 2005 parliamentary elections showed a low level of support for Moldovan nationalist and pro-Romanian parties in Gagauz Yeri. Only about 1 percent of voters in this autonomous region backed the Christian Democratic People's Party. In comparison, this main nationalist party received about 10 percent of the national vote in Moldova, excluding the Transdniestrian Republic.[25]

The political influence of Transdniestrian parties, which opposed the region's separation from Moldova, was limited (Kolsto and Malgin, 1998, p. 115). However, one has to take into account that the election results in Transdniestria were biased because parties representing Moldovan nationalists were not allowed to operate in the region or participate in elections. In 1993, a nationalist deputy of the Moldovan parliament was sentenced to

---

[24]   Ibid.
[25]   Ibid.

death,[26] and several other nationalist leaders received prison sentences in Transdniestria for taking part in the military conflict between Transdniestria and the Central government of Moldova (Crowther, 1997b, p. 347).

3.2 Presidential elections

The results of several presidential elections in Ukraine and Moldova showed a similar regional divide. Nationalist and pro-Western candidates received much stronger support in Western Ukraine than in Eastern Ukraine. In the December 1991 Ukrainian presidential elections, three nationalist candidates received the majority of the vote in four Western Ukraine regions. In the other three regions of Western Ukraine, the vote for the nationalist candidates was only slightly behind the vote for Leonid Kravchuk (See Kuzio and Wilson, 1994). Leonid Kravchuk, the head of parliament and the former second secretary and ideology chief of the Communist Party of Soviet Ukraine, ran as an independent and received his highest level of electoral support in the Eastern Ukrainian regions. He argued that an independent Ukraine would reach the level of economic development found in advanced Western countries. Kravchuk also promised to protect the rights of ethnic minorities, mainly Russians, and maintain close links to Russia.

In the second round of the 1994 presidential elections, Leonid Kravchuk, who adopted a nationalist program while in office, won the majority of votes in all regions of Western Ukraine. His support was highest in Galicia (94 to 95 percent), followed by the historical Volhynia province (84 to 87 percent), Carpatho-Ukraine (71 percent) and Bukovyna (62 percent). In comparison, Kravchuk's vote in regions of Eastern Ukraine ranged from 9 percent (Crimea) to 60 percent (Kyiv city). (See Huntington, 1996, p. 166).

Such a degree of regional division, which was remarkable in itself, also signified the reversal of the regional vote pattern in the December 1991 elections. Leonid Kravchuk campaigned on a pro-Russian platform and subsequently received his highest electoral support in Eastern Ukrainian regions.

---

[26]   The death sentence against Ilie Ilascu was not carried out. He was reelected to the Moldovan parliament, but remained in a Transdniestrian prison until his release in 2001.

(See Kuzio and Wilson, 1994). The correlation between the proportion of the vote cast for Kravchuk in 1991 and 1994 in 26 regions of Ukraine is strongly negative (-0.74).[27]

The same pattern was repeated in the 1999 presidential elections. Leonid Kuchma won in 1994 by campaigning on a platform that favored forging close economic links with Russia and giving Russian the status of an official language. Kuchma was supported by the Communists in the second round of the 1994 elections. However, both his policy as the president of Ukraine and his 1999 campaign platform shifted towards support for the independence of Ukraine. Leonid Kuchma did not make Russian the second official language in Ukraine, and he opposed joining a union signed by Russia and Belarus.[28] In the second round of the 1999 elections, Kuchma received from 73 to 92 percent of the vote in the Western regions of Ukraine, compared to 4 to 35 percent five years earlier (see Figures 3.3 and 3.4). Support for him declined significantly in Eastern Ukraine during this period. The correlation between the proportions of the vote for Kuchma in 1999 and in 1994 in 26 regions of Ukraine is strongly negative (-0.81). (Table A.2, Appendix.)

The results of presidential elections in post-Communist Ukraine showed that pro-Communist and pro-Russian candidates were much more successful in Eastern regions than in historically Western regions, especially in the oblasts of the former Austro-Hungarian province of Galicia. For example, in the second round of the 1999 elections, Petro Symonenko, leader of the Communist Party of Ukraine, received about 5 percent of the vote in Galicia, 10 percent in Carpatho-Ukraine, 17 to 19 percent in two oblasts of the former Volhynia province, and 21 percent in Bukovyna, as opposed to a much higher proportion of the vote in Eastern Ukraine, where it ranged from 26 percent in Kyiv city to 59 percent in the Vinnytsia region. (Figure 3.4.)

---

[27]   The correlation coefficient measures strength and direction of association from completely negative (-1) to perfectly positive (1).

[28]   The fact that Leonid Kravchuk, defeated by Leonid Kuchma in the 1994 elections, became a Kuchma supporter during the 1999 elections was another indication of the significant shift in Kuchma's political orientation.

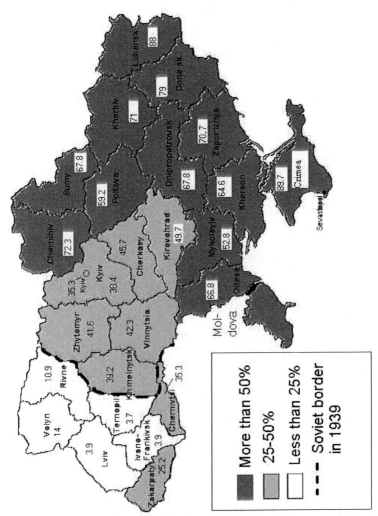

Figure 3.3 The vote for Leonid Kuchma in the second round of the 1994 presidential elections in Ukraine

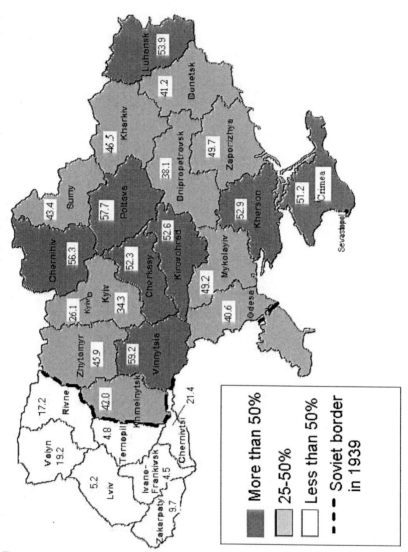

Figure 3.4 The vote for Petro Symonenko in the second round of the 1999 presidential elections in Ukraine

Table 3.2 Regional voting results in Ukraine, 1991-2004 (%)

Region	Referen-dum Dec. 1991	Kravchuk 1991	Nationa-list 1991	Commu-nist 1994	Nationa-list 1994
Chernivtsi	92.8	43.6	49.0	6.1	25
Ivano-Frankivsk	98.4	13.7	82.1	17.6	58.3
Lviv	97.5	11.6	85.0	2.9	60.9
Rivne	96.8	53.1	42.5	8.1	70.0
Ternopil	98.7	16.8	80.2	1.0	70.0
Volyn	96.3	51.9	43.5	11.2	22.2
Transcarpathia	92.6	58.0	35.4	2.3	0
Cherkassy	96.0	67.1	28.0	27.0	0
Chernihiv	93.7	74.2	19.9	24.0	0
Kyiv region	95.5	65.6	28.4	15.4	35.3
Kirovohrad	93.9	75.8	18.2	31.9	9.1
Khmelnytsky	96.3	75.5	20.3	27.1	15.4
Poltava	94.9	75.1	19.1	26.3	12.5
Sumy	92.6	72.4	20.4	39.0	7.7
Vinnytsia	95.4	72.3	23.1	9.8	5.9
Zhytomyr	95.1	77.6	18.3	16.1	0
Donetsk	83.9	71.5	13.7	38.8	0
Kharkiv	86.3	60.9	22.7	24.1	0
Zaporizhzhia	90.7	74.7	17.4	36.5	0
Luhansk	83.9	76.2	12.7	43.3	0
Kherson	90.1	70.2	16.7	31.7	0
Mykolayiv	89.5	72.3	21.3	27.7	0
Odesa	85.4	70.7	18.0	23.2	0
Crimea	54.6	56.3	7.9	19.5	0
Dnipropetrovsk	90.4	69.7	21.8	18.2	0
Kyiv city	92.7	56.1	36.6	11.6	13.0

Table 3.2 Cont.

Region	Kravchuk 1994	Nationalist 1998	Kuchma 1999	Commu- nist 2002	Yanuko- vych 2004
Chernivtsi	61.8	23.9	73.2	12.3	16.4
Ivano-Frankivsk	94.5	57.6	92.3	3.3	2.9
Lviv	93.8	47.2	91.6	4.1	4.7
Rivne	87.3	39.2	76.5	9.5	12.3
Ternopil	94.8	56.9	92.2	2.7	2.7
Volyn	83.9	27.0	75.4	7.8	7.0
Transcarpathia	70.5	15.4	84.5	9.1	27.6
Cherkassy	50.8	13.0	40.0	34.4	17.4
Chernihiv	25.1	9.4	37.5	33.8	24.2
Kyiv region	58.3	14.3	58.5	25.0	13.8
Kirovohrad	45.7	8.3	40.9	39.8	31.7
Khmelnytsky	57.2	14.3	51.0	24.4	16.0
Poltava	37.4	10.7	35.2	42.2	29.2
Sumy	28.9	6.9	48.5	33.6	16.9
Vinnytsia	54.3	8.7	33.9	35.0	12.9
Zhytomyr	55.6	17.7	48.1	32.6	28.9
Donetsk	18.5	4.7	52.9	33.9	93.5
Kharkiv	26.0	5.9	46.6	38.2	68.1
Zaporizhzhia	26.8	6.5	44.8	39.9	70.1
Luhansk	10.1	4.1	40.7	45.9	91.2
Kherson	32.1	9.9	41.9	42.9	51.3
Mykolayiv	44.7	9.3	45.9	37.7	67.1
Odesa	29.3	7.9	52.8	37.1	66.6
Crimea	8.9	8.5	44	38.7	83.0
Dnipropetrovsk	29.7	7.6	56.4	39.8	61.1
Kyiv city	59.7	19	64.8	14.5	17.5

Sources: CVK (2000, 2002, 2004); Holdar (1995); Kuzio and Wilson (1994); Wilson (1997a).

Note: See the Appendix for definitions. Results for Crimea include Sevastopol city.

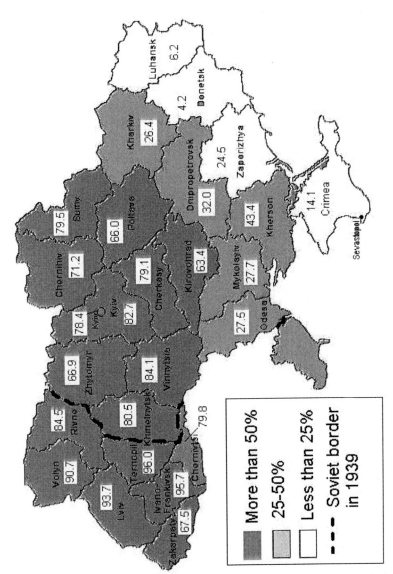

Figure 3.5 The vote for Viktor Yushchenko in the repeat second round of the 2004 presidential elections in Ukraine

Similarly, official results of the repeat second round of the presidential elections in December 2004 showed that Viktor Yanukovych, a pro-Russian candidate, received the majority of votes in Donetsk and Luhansk regions, the Crimea including Sevastopol city, and six other Eastern regions. Support for him was less than 5 percent in Galicia regions. (See Table 3.2.)

Support for Viktor Yushchenko showed the reverse regional pattern. His greatest level of support was in the historical regions of Western Ukraine, especially in Galicia (Figure 3.5). Yushchenko advocated a pro-Western foreign orientation for Ukraine, including membership in NATO and the European Union.

A comparison of separately held elections in Transdniestria and the rest of Moldova showed that nationalist pro-Western candidates were favored in the West, while pro-Communist and pro-Russian candidates were favored in Transdniestria and Gagauzia. Mirchea Snegur, who turned towards nationalism after serving as secretary of agriculture in the Moldovan Communist Party, won the presidential elections in Moldova in December 1991 with 98 percent of the vote[29] (Crowther, 1997b, p. 322). In separate elections held in the Transdniestria region, Igor Smirnov, a factory director and leader of a pro-Communist and pro-Soviet movement, was elected president of Transdniestria with 65 percent of the vote (Ozhiganov, 1997, p. 172).

In the second round of the 1996 presidential elections, Petru Lucinschi, who had been head of the Communist Party in Moldova during the Gorbachev period, received about 93 percent of the vote in the Gagauz region compared with the 54 percent he received in all of Western Moldova (see *IFES*, 1996; *Minorities at Risk*, 2000). He ran against the nationalist incumbent on a more pro-Russian platform and was backed by the Moldovan Communist Party in the second round.[30] (Crowther, 1997a, p. 320). Igor Smirnov, who was reelected president of the Transdniestrian Republic in 1996, received about 70 percent of the vote in the break-away region.

---

[29]   Snegur ran unopposed.
[30]   Petru Lucinschi favored closer relations with Russia and negotiated a solution of sorts to the conflict with Transdniestria.

The Taraclia district, which has a large proportion of ethnic Bulgarians, voted similarly to Gagauzia in the national elections in Moldova. (*IFES*, 1996, 1998). In the 1998 parliamentary elections, the Communist parties received 58 percent of the vote in the Taraclia district, almost two times more than in the rest of Moldova. Petru Lucinschi received overwhelming support (90 percent) in the Taraclia district during the 1996 presidential elections.

The regional divisions in Ukraine and Moldova also manifested in mass protests over political issues. For example, traditional historical divisions were evident during mass actions in support of Viktor Yushchenko after the official results of the second round of the 2004 presidential elections were falsified in favor of Viktor Yanukovych. More than one million people took to the streets to protest the falsification and support Viktor Yushchenko. Media reports and personal observations showed that the absolute and relative size of pro-Yushchenko demonstrations and rallies in Western Ukrainian cities and towns significantly exceeded their size in Eastern Ukraine, with the notable exception of Kyiv city.

More than half of the signs displayed by participants of a mass rally, which lasted for several weeks, in support of Viktor Yushchenko in Kyiv indicated that they came from localities in Western Ukraine. Similarly, at least half of more than 400 signatures on the facade of a post office building located near the center of *Maidan* in Kyiv were left by Western Ukrainian participants of the rally. It is noteworthy that special police units were brought in from Crimea and Donbas to guard the headquarters of President Leonid Kuchma during the "Orange Revolution."

After the second round of presidential elections in November 2004, Ukraine came close to a violent conflict that could have spiraled into civil war and led to the break-up of the country, as had happened in Moldova in the beginning of the 1990s. Local authorities, predominantly in Western Ukraine, recognized Viktor Yushchenko as president, while local authorities in a number of Eastern regions backed Viktor Yanukovych as the legally elected president of Ukraine. Local council deputies from pro-Yanukovych regions held a congress in Severodonetsk in the Luhansk region in Eastern Ukraine; and they threatened to declare an autonomous republic in the Eastern and Southern regions of Ukraine unless Viktor Yanukovych was recognized as the president of Ukraine.

The Kuchma administration came very close to using military force against Yushchenko supporters, some of whom also wanted to seize power by force. On November 28, 2004, the commander of the Internal Troops of the Ministry of Internal Affairs ordered his units, which had been brought into the vicinity of Kyiv city from other regions of Eastern Ukraine, to disband the pro-Yushchenko demonstrators at the center of Kyiv city. The Internal Troops units received assault rifles and bullets, and started their march to Kyiv city. Many top commanders and servicemen from the Ukrainian Army, the Military Intelligence, the Security Service, and the Ministry of Internal Affairs, and some leaders and supporters of the Yushchenko camp, were ready to mobilize forces and weapons to stop the advancing units of internal troops, which numbered more than ten thousand men. The order that had been issued to internal troops was rescinded at the last minute. The acts of a number of political and military leaders helped to avoid the violent conflict. (See Chapter 5 of this book and Chivers, 2005; Leonov, 2005; Lykhovii, 2005; "Oleksandr Turchynov," 2005; Solohubenko, 2005; Wagstyl, Freeland, and Warner, 2004).

A KIIS survey conducted in October and November of 2005 showed that Western Ukrainians expressed far more support for mass actions in celebration of the first anniversary of the "Orange Revolution" in Kyiv than residents of other regions did. Only 28 percent of the respondents in Western regions, compared to 56 percent in Central regions including Kyiv city, 65 percent in the South, and 84 percent in the East, opposed festive rallies on Maidan to celebrate the first anniversary. (See Mostova and Rakhmanin, 2005).

Similar regional differences manifested in Ukraine over the opposition to President Leonid Kuchma, who was accused at the end of 2000 of being involved with the kidnapping and murder of a journalist who had exposed corruption among the political leadership of Ukraine. Western Ukrainian regions witnessed much larger actions of mass protest against Leonid Kuchma than did Eastern regions, with the exception of Ukraine's capital.

Picture 2 Pro-Yushchenko demonstrators from the Rivne region and the Volyn region during an "Orange Revolution" rally on Maidan in Kyiv city in the end of 2004. Photo by A. Cheban. Reproduced with permission from "The Orange Revolution" CD (Kyiv, 2005), Oleksandr Sparinsky ©.

Among pro-Yushchenko demonstrators, residents of Kyiv city were disproportionately represented compared to other regions of Eastern Ukraine, in particular the Central part of Ukraine. Kyiv city, as the capital city and the largest urban center of Ukraine, has a significant concentration of Ukrainian intelligentsia and students, many of whom are from Western Ukraine. This concentration of intelligentsia, students, and migrants from Western Ukraine provided support for the development of nationalist parties and organizations in Kyiv during Gorbachev's reforms. The results of elections and referendums held betwee 1991 and 2004 show that Kyiv city is closest among Eastern Ukrainian regions in its political orientation to regions of Western Ukraine. (Table 3.2.)

The popular support for Viktor Yushchenko in the presidential elections did not necessarily mean a significant change in the political culture. Media reports and personal observations reveal that young people were over-represented among pro-Yushchenko demonstrators. The political cultures of Ukrainians who had grown up in different historical regions during the post-Communist period were to some extent drawn together through shared experiences, such as the socialization of the younger generation through a common school and university education in independent Ukraine. However, results of the exit polls conducted during the 2004 presidential elections showed similar levels of support for Viktor Yushchenko among the younger generation and the older generation.

In Moldova, tens of thousands of people took part in demonstrations in the capital, Chishinau, in the beginning of 2002 to oppose the Communist government's plans to reintroduce Russian as a mandatory subject in the school curriculum, and to replace the teaching of the history of Romanians with the history of Moldova. These demonstrations were led by the nationalist Christian Democratic People's Party (CDPP).[31] In response to these mass demonstrations of protest, the Moldovan Communist government dropped the proposed changes, which had been based on campaign promises. Even though the Party of Moldovan Communists had received half of the vote in the 2001 parliamentary elections, an opinion poll conducted that same year indicated that only about one-third of respondents, including 65 percent of ethnic Russians and 53 percent of Ukrainians, supported the Communist's proposals. Fifty-eight percent, including 69 percent of ethnic Moldovans, opposed these proposals.

In contrast, as in the Soviet times, the Russian language remained a mandatory subject of instruction in Transdniestria, and history curriculums emphasized Moldovans' close ties with Russia as well as differences between Moldovans and Romanians. However, even considering the authoritarian nature of the Transdniestrian political system, it is noteworthy that these issues did not lead to mass protests among the local Moldovans, who are the largest ethnic group in the region. The 1998 Laitin/Hough survey showed that

---

[31]   Because of its role in the demonstrations, the CDPP was suspended in January 2002 by Moldova's Communist-controlled parliament, but the ban was later lifted.

just 3 percent of respondents in the Transdniestrian Republic, including 4 percent of ethnic Moldovans, took part in the meetings and demonstrations against the separatism of Tiraspol. In contrast, 9 percent of respondents from the rest of Moldova, including 11 percent of ethnic Moldovans, said they had participated in such actions.

The issue of Romanization, or granting Romanian the status of an official language of the government and education system, produced similar regional divisions in Moldova. One-third (34 percent) of respondents from Transdniestria, compared to 9 percent in the rest of Moldova, claimed in the 1998 Laitin/Hough survey that they had taken part in meetings and demonstrations against Romanization. Ethnic Moldovans exhibited the same regional differences on this issue. One fifth (22 percent) of Moldovans in the Transdniestrian Republic, compared to 4 percent in Bessarabia, said that they had participated in actions of protest against Romanization.

The 1998 Laitin/Hough survey indicated that 23 percent of the Gagauz took part in meetings and demonstrations against Romanization, while only 2 percent of the Gagauz participated in such actions of protest against Transdniestrian separatism.[32] In Gagauzia, Russian remained the main language of instruction in schools and college. Although instruction in the Gagauz language expanded, it occupied a secondary role compared to Russian. This reflected language preferences of the majority of the Gagauz, who speak Russian.

3.3   Separatism in Transdniestria

In contrast to Ukraine, regional political cleavages in Moldova erupted in violent conflict. Moldova became split along regional lines after Eastern districts de facto seceded in September of 1990 and proclaimed the creation of the Transdniestrian Moldovan Soviet Socialist Republic, with its capital in Tiraspol. According to the official results of the referendum held in Transdniestria in December 2001, 98 percent of the voters supported its independ-

---

[32]   Laitin/Hough survey respondents who considered themselves at least 50 percent Gagauz are classified as Gagauz in this study.

ence.[33] ("Moldavia's Minorities Vote to Quit," 1991). In 1992, a military confrontation between Transdniestrian separatists and the forces of the Central Moldovan government took place. As a result of clashes in the town of Bendery (Tighina), located on the right bank of Dniester (Nistru) and very close to Tiraspol, several hundred people lost their lives. (See Selivanova, 1996).

One of the factors leading to the success of Transdniestrian separatists was the support they received from the Russian troops. The Fourteenth Army stationed in the region de facto supported Transdniestrian separatists in their conflict with the forces of the Central government of Moldova. Top commanders, junior officers, and some units of the Fourteenth Army joined the Transdniestrian separatists, who received a significant proportion of their weapons from the army (King, 2000, pp. 191-194).

Even though Alexander Lebed, who became a commander of the Fourteenth Army after the major clashes occurred in 1992, proclaimed his neutrality in the conflict, the presence and actions of several thousand Russian troops in the region guaranteed the existence of the Transdniestrian Republic.[34] Lebed threatened the use of force against Moldova and ordered the bombardment of Moldovan troops in order to stop their advance on Transdniestria. His stance and actions helped to stop the violent conflict in the region. However, these actions also amounted to de facto support for the Transdniestrian secession, even though Lebed criticized the unwillingness of the Transdniestrian leadership to settle the conflict with the Moldovan government. (See Dunlop, 1997; Ozhiganov, 1997).

The territory of the Transdniestrian Republic almost exactly coincided with the historical divisions in Moldova. With the exception of the city of Bendery (Tighina), which was located on the Western bank, the self-declared Transdniestrian Republic contained districts on the Eastern bank of Dniester

---

[33] The turnout was 78 percent.

[34] The Russian Army in Transdniestria was staffed by local conscripts to a significant extent. In addition to the Fourteenth Army, a separate contingent of Russian troops was deployed in the region to separate the conflicting sides. Lebed became a major figure in Russian politics after he was dismissed from his post as commander of the Russian troops in Transdniestria. He placed third in the 1996 presidential campaign and headed the Security Council in Russia.

(Nistru) that had never been part of Romania, in contrast to the districts on the Western bank.[35]

The Transdniestrian Republic had its own government and currency, but was unrecognized by other countries. The legal status of Transdniestria has not yet been settled. Several meetings about Transdniestria, which were attended by leaders of the Transdniestria Republic and presidents of Moldova, Ukraine, and Russia, failed to produce any binding agreement on the status of the region. The Transdniestrian Moldovan Republic, like the Turkish Republic of Northern Cyprus in Cyprus, the Abhkazian Republic in Georgia, and the Republic of Nagorno-Karabakh in Azerbaijan, remain unrecognized in the international arena (Kolossov and O'Loughlin, 1999).

Vladimir Voronin, who was elected Moldova's Communist president in 2001, proposed a federal status for Transdniestria as a way to solve the regional conflict. Presidents of Russia and Ukraine and governments of Romania and the United States, as well as international organizations such as the Organization for Security and Cooperation in Europe (OSCE), were involved in negotiations with Moldovan and Transdniestrian leaders over the settlement of the Transdniestrian conflict. However, these negotiations encountered significant problems, stemming from disagreements over the status of Transdniestria and the regional distribution of power in a unified Moldova as well as from differences between the presidents of Moldova and the Transdniestrian Republic.

---

[35]   These districts formed the main part of the Autonomous Moldovan Republic, which existed in Soviet Ukraine from 1924 to 1940.

Picture 3 The coat of arms of the unrecognized Transdniestrian Republic is based on the Soviet coat of arms

3.4   Separatism in Gagauzia (Gagauz Yeri)

Several districts in the South of Moldova, which were populated by the Gagauz, declared the creation of the Gagauz Soviet Socialist Republic in August

1990.[36] In the December 1991 referendum in the Gagauz region, about 95 percent of the voters voted in favor of the independence of Gagauzia. The participation rate was 85 percent. ("Moldavia's Minorities Vote to Quit," 1991). The regional authorities boycotted the 1991 presidential elections in Moldova. In elections that were separately held in the Gagauz region, Stefan Topal, a leader of a Gagauz secessionist movement, won over 90 percent of the vote and became president of the unrecognized Gagauz Republic in 1991.

The Central government of Moldova initially opposed the creation of the Gagauz Republic, and declared martial law in the region. However, an agreement on autonomy of the Gagauz region, which was approved by the Moldovan parliament in 1994, reduced tensions. The Gagauz autonomy, also called Gagauzia or Gagauz Yeri, consists of the districts and villages that voted to be included in the autonomous region (see Chinn and Roper, 1998). The Gagauz autonomy has the right to decide its own status if Moldova re-unites with Romania (See King, 1997, p. 750).

It is noteworthy that the Gagauz, in contrast to many other Turkic minorities in countries of the former Soviet Union, demonstrated pro-Communist and pro-Russian political orientation (see Katchanovski, 2005). Gheorghe Tabunshchik, the former First Secretary of the Communist Party of Soviet Moldova in the Gagauz region, was elected governor of the Gagauz autonomy in 1995 (Chinn and Roper, 1998). In October 2002, he ran for governor as a Party of Moldovan Communists candidate and won in Gagauzia for a second time. Tabunshchik received 51 percent of the vote in the second round of the elections in the autonomous region.

In the 1995 Gagauzia parliament elections, *Vatan,* a Gagauz party headed by Stefan Topal, received 15 percent of the vote, and the Communist Party of Moldova received 14 percent. The Gagauz People's Party, which opposed Gagauzian secessionism, had only 4 percent of the vote. The Agrarian Democratic Party, which received 47 percent of the vote in the 1995 local elections in Moldova, obtained just 12 percent of the vote in Gagauzia. Non-party candidates received more than half of the vote (55 percent). (*IFES,* 1995).

---

[36]   Moldova is the principal place where the Gagauz live. There are about 153 thousand Gagauz in Moldova. They constitute approximately 4 percent of the population.

Picture 4 The coat of arms of the Gagauz Autonomy is influenced by the Soviet coat of arms

Gagauz separatists received support from the Transdniestrian authorities in their conflict with the Moldovan nationalists (King, 1997).[37] The

---

[37]   Gagauz and Transdniestrian separatist leaders, including Topal and Smirnov, were arrested by the Central authorities in Moldova for expressing support for the coup at-

Gagauz authorities maintained political ties with the Transdniestrian government in spite of its conflict with Chishinau. In contrast, links between the Gagauz autonomy and Turkey were mostly confined to cultural, educational, and economic areas.

Gagauz leaders wanted to elevate the region's constitutional status in the federal system arrangement that was discussed between authorities of Moldova and the Transdniestrian Republic after the victory of the Moldovan Communist Party in the 2001 elections. Some of Gagauz leaders in the regional administration and in parliament expressed dissatisfaction with the Central government's treatment of the autonomous region in political and economic areas. These actions indicated the persistence of the political divisions between Gagauzia and Bessarabian Moldova.

3.5 Separatism in Crimea

In post-Communist Ukraine, a significant secessionist political movement emerged in Crimea. Crimea gained the status of autonomous republic in February 1991, following a regional referendum in which 93 percent of the voters supported the restoration of Crimean autonomy. (See Drohobycky, 1995). Even though more than half (54 percent) of Crimean voters voted for the independence of Ukraine in the December 1991 referendum, political leaders and organizations that advocated for the separation of Crimea from Ukraine received the majority of the vote in local parliamentary and presidential elections in 1994. The Russia Bloc received two thirds (67 percent) of the vote in the parliamentary elections. The bloc favored the creation of an independent Crimean Republic or the region's reunification with Russia. Yurii Meshkov, the candidate for the Russia Bloc, won the 1994 presidential elections in the second round with 73 percent of the vote (Wilson 1995, p. 113). However, the bloc lost its positions, including the presidency, which was abolished by the Ukrainian parliament in 1995 following internal splits and pressure from the Ukrainian authorities (Solchanyk, 1995).

---

tempt led by conservatives opposed to Gorbachev's reforms in the Soviet Union in August 1991.

After the disintegration of the Russia Bloc in the mid-1990s, the Communist Party of Crimea, affiliated with the Communist Party of Ukraine, became the leading political force in the region. The party received the largest proportion of votes in the 1998 Crimean Republic parliament elections, and its leader was elected parliamentary speaker.

Crimean Tatars established, and overwhelmingly supported in elections in the Crimean autonomy, their own ethnically based political organizations. For example, the *Mejlis* won all fourteen of the seats reserved for the Tatars in the 1994 elections to the Crimean parliament. A 2001 poll, conducted by the Ukrainian Center for Economic and Political Studies (Razumkov Center) in Crimea, showed that 11 percent of the respondents supported the *Mejlis*. Since the percentage of Crimean Tatars in the population of Crimea is of similar magnitude, this poll result indicates that the absolute majority of Crimean Tatars supported the *Mejlis* ("Krym na politychnii karti Ukrainy," 2001). The *Mejlis* and other Crimean Tatar organizations consistently opposed Russian separatism in Crimea.

The *Mejlis* and nationalist/pro-Ukrainian politicians often supported each other in order to counter the pro-Russian movement in Crimea. The chairman of the *Mejlis* ran on the *Rukh* list in the 1998 parliamentary elections. Such cooperation allowed *Rukh* to receive about 7 percent of the vote in Crimea and rank third place among political parties. Crimean Tatar voters gave *Rukh* about two thirds of their votes in the region. Similarly, in the 2002 parliamentary elections, the *Nasha Ukraina* ("Our Ukraine") bloc received, with support from Crimean Tatars, 10 percent of the vote in Crimea.

Similarly, the *Mejlis* and other major organizations of Crimean Tatars backed Victor Yushchenko, the leader of the "Our Ukraine" bloc, in all rounds of the 2004 presidential elections in Ukraine.[38] The Crimean Tatars contributed a significant proportion of 14 percent of the vote that Yushchenko received in the repeat second round of the presidential elections in Crimea. In contrast, Viktor Yanukovych, a pro-Russian presidential candidate, obtained 83 percent of the vote in Crimea, including Sevastopol city.

However, this cooperation between the *Mejlis* and nationalist/pro-Ukrainian organizations was a marriage of convenience that resulted from a

---

[38]   See "Zaiava," 2005.

mutual anti-Communist and anti-Russian orientation. Some Crimean Tatars' organizations, which were much less influential than the *Mejlis*, advocated separation from Ukraine. For example, the Union of Crimean Turks (*Azat Kyyrim*) declared the establishment of the independent state of Crimean Tatars as its main goal. The Crimean Tatar National Movement initiated in 1999 a collection of signatures for an international tribunal to investigate genocide and ethnocide against Crimean Tatars. The statement named Ukraine as the main defendant because it controlled territory belonging to the Crimean Tatar people.[39]

Support for pro-Russian and pro-Communist political leaders and organizations that advocated for the separation of Crimea from Ukraine was low among Crimean Tatars. Their political orientation differentiated Crimean Tatars not only from the majority of ethnic Russians but also from a significant proportion of ethnic Ukrainians who supported pro-Russian and pro-Communist parties and politicians in Crimea.

3.6 Separatism in Donbas and neighboring regions

Attempts, made by some local politicians in the early 1990s, to raise the issue of allowing Donbas and neighboring regions in Eastern and Southern Ukraine to separate or granting them autonomy were unsuccessful. However, this issue came to the forefront of Ukrainian politics after the disputed second round of the 2004 presidential elections. As noted, on November 28, 2004 in Severodonetsk in the Luhansk region, during a congress of several thousands of regional officials and local deputies primarily from regions that backed Viktor Yanukovych during the presidential elections, many politicians voiced separatist slogans. They threatened to declare an autonomous republic in Eastern and Southern regions of Ukraine unless their candidate was recognized as a winner of the elections.

Politicians from the Donetsk and Luhansk regions, which together are called Donbas, played the leading role in this congress. For example, Viktor Yanukovych, who was born in the Donetsk region and served as the head of

---

[39]   See "Krym," 2001.

the regional administration before he became prime minister of Ukraine, attended this meeting. On the day of the congress, the Donetsk region Council voted 155 to 1 to hold a regional referendum on transforming Ukraine into a federal state and granting this region an autonomous status.

Demands for the creation of the autonomous republic were dropped and the Donetsk referendum cancelled after their proponents were threatened with criminal prosecution for violating the territorial integrity of Ukraine; Yanukovych and other leading politicians from his camp accepted a compromise on holding the repeat second round of the presidential elections. Viktor Yushchenko and his allies, who formed the new government, dismissed the separatist demands as an election-time ploy, initiated the criminal prosecution of several regional officials who had voiced the demands, and rejected calls for the federalization of Ukraine.

The sudden nature of the separatist calls and their reversal indicate that they were artificial to a significant extent. However, separatism in Donbas and the neighboring regions continues to exist in different forms, such as in calls for the federalization of Ukraine. Such calls and the collection of signatures for a referendum on federalization of Ukraine were supported by Viktor Yanukovych, leader of the Party of Regions; Nataliia Vitrenko, leader of the Progressive Socialist Party of Ukraine; Evhen Kushnarev, leader of the New Democracy Party and the former head of the state administration of the Kharkiv region as well as some leaders of other parties. A survey conducted in May 2005 by the Kyiv International Institute of Sociology and the Razumkov Center showed that the majority (61 percent) of respondents who had an opinion on this issue in the Donetsk, Luhansk, and Kharkiv regions supported the federalization of Ukraine. Forty two percent of Ukrainians in Southern regions, 31 percent in Central regions, and 26 percent in eight geographically Western regions favored the transformation of Ukraine into a federal state.

3.7   Referendums: Regional patterns

The regional voting pattern in several referendums held in post-Communist Moldova was similar to that produced by the elections. In the March 1991 All-Union referendum on the future of the Soviet Union, the

overwhelming majority (about 82 percent) of those who took part in the Gagauz region referendum voted for the preservation of the Soviet Union. In
Transdniestria, the vote for the preservation of the Soviet Union was more
than 93 percent. (See Babilunga and Bomeshko, 1998, pp. 30-31; Chinn and
Roper, 1998, p. 95; Kolsto, Edemsky and Kalashnikova, 1993, p. 984).[40]

The March 1991 referendum was not held in other regions of
Moldova. The nationalist Popular Front, whose supporters were a dominant
force in the parliament of Moldova, was opposed to the referendum. However, in the March 1994 referendum, more than 90 percent of voters supported independence and 5 percent supported the unification of Moldova with
Romania (Crowther, 1997b). In contrast, in a separately held regional referendum in Transdniestria in December 1994, about 90 percent of voters favored joining the Commonwealth of Independent States (CIS) as a sovereign
state. The Commonwealth includes non-Baltic republics of the former Soviet
Union.

Referendums held in Ukraine produced a more mixed picture. The
March 1991 All-Union referendum on the future of the Soviet Union indicated
strong regional divisions in Ukraine. The vote in favor of the Union in all
seven Western Ukrainian regions was much lower than the Ukrainian average of 71 percent. However, the results varied from a "yes" vote of 16 to 19
percent in the former Austro-Hungarian province of Galicia to a "yes" of 54
percent in the former Polish province of Volhynia, with 60 percent in the formerly Austro-Hungarian and Czechoslovak region of Carpatho-Ukraine, and
61 percent in the formerly Austro-Hungarian and Romanian Bukovyna. It is
noteworthy that the vote in favor of preservation of the Soviet Union in the
March 1991 referendum was highest in Crimea (87 percent).

A separate referendum held in Galicia in March 1991 showed that
opposition to the Soviet Union and support for the independence of Ukraine
were strongest in this former Austrian province. Eighty-eight percent of voters
in Galicia voted for Ukrainian independence in this referendum. (Solchanyk,
1991).

---

[40]   The participation rate ranged from 71 to 95 percent in various cities and districts of
the region. (Babilunga and Bomeshko, 1998, pp. 30-31).

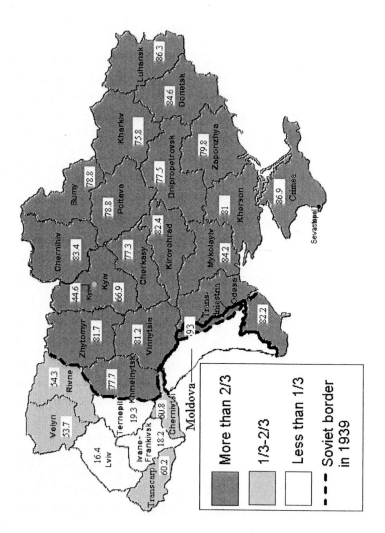

Figure 3.6 The vote for the preservation of the Soviet Union in the Soviet referendum of March 1991

Note: In Moldova, the referendum was held only in the Transdniestria region and in the Gagauz region.

The December 1991 referendum on Ukraine's independence did not show the same extent of regional cleavage as did the March 1991 referendum and various national elections. Ninety percent of the voters in Ukraine cast their votes for the independence of Ukraine. All regions, including Crimea, expressed support for Ukraine's independence. In most regions of Eastern Ukraine, more than 80 percent of the voters supported independence, a sharp reversal from the results of the referendum held less than a year earlier. The correlation between the regional vote in favor of independence of Ukraine in the December 1991 referendum and the regional vote in favor of the preservation of the Soviet Union in the March 1991 referendum is -0.44. (See Table A.2 in the Appendix). Even though the correlation is in the expected negative direction, its moderate coefficient signifies a swift shift in attitudes on this principal issue during a period of less than nine months.

The results of the December 1991 referendum reflected to a significant extent changes in attitudes in Eastern regions, rather than changes in deeply held values. Attitudes are much more volatile than are values. In contrast to values, which are rooted in political culture, attitudes are influenced by many temporary factors such as the economic situation. (Almond, 1990, pp. 149-150; Lipset, 1996, p. 24). An August 1991 coup attempt in the Soviet Union affected the outcome of the December 2001 vote in Eastern Ukraine. The failed coup, organized by the opponents of Gorbachev's reforms and a new Union treaty in the Soviet leadership, was followed by declarations of the independence of Ukraine and other Soviet republics. The failure of the coup led to the rapid reversal of pro-Union positions held by a great number of Communist leaders and voters in Eastern Ukraine. For example, almost all members of the Communist faction in the Ukrainian parliament voted for the declaration of Ukraine's independence on August 24th, 1991. Organized opposition to independence was practically absent on the national level (Pritzel, 1997, 342-344). The Communist Party of Ukraine, the major political force to oppose the independence of Ukraine, had been banned after the failed attempted coup of August 1991. As a result, all major political organizations and political leaders in Ukraine campaigned for independence. They argued that independence would bring immediate economic prosperity to Ukraine (Motyl and Krawtchenko, 1997, pp. 245-246).

Post-1991 survey data support the argument that the vote in favor of Ukrainian independence in Eastern regions of Ukraine reflected a shift in attitudes. The Razumkov Center poll conducted in August 2002 showed that an overwhelming majority of respondents who gave a definite answer in Western Ukraine (94 percent), the Center (83 percent), the East (73 percent), and the South (68 percent) confirmed that they had supported the independence of Ukraine in the December 1991 referendum. However, when asked how they would vote if such a referendum were to be held again, a significantly lower proportion of Ukrainians in Central regions (64 percent), and especially Southern and Eastern regions (42 percent), declared their intention to vote in favor of the independence of Ukraine. The slight decline in support for independence among Western Ukrainians (89 percent) was within a statistical margin of error. (Table 3.3.)

A deep economic crisis after the break-up of the Soviet Union significantly weakened support for the independence of Ukraine among Eastern Ukrainians. According to the Socis-Gallup polls, support for the unification of the former Soviet republics jumped in Ukraine from 21 percent in 1992 to 47 percent in 1994. (See Kremin, Bezluda, Bondarenko, Valevski, Golovatij, Michenko, Riabov, Sitnik, and Yaremenko, 1997).

The results of the April 2000 referendum on constitutional change in Ukraine revealed a similar anomaly. At the beginning of 2000, the Communist deputies resisted President Kuchma's decision to hold a referendum on confidence in parliament and on changes to the Constitution that would significantly increase presidential power. As a result, the Ukrainian parliament split into two parts, Communist and non-Communist. Eleven non-Communist factions, threatened by the dissolution of the parliament, formed the majority and held a parallel parliament session outside the parliament building. The non-Communist majority included different political forces such as nationalists, liberals, centrists, and independents. It voted to remove the pro-Communist speaker, first-deputy speaker of the parliament, and parliament commission chairmen and chairwomen from the Communist parties. The deputies from the majority coalition took control of the parliament building and installed their own parliament leadership.

Table 3.3 Support for independence of Ukraine (Razumkov Center survey, August 2002) (%)

	Western Ukraine	Center	South	East
Vote in the December 1991 refer-endum on the independence				
Supported	94	83	68	73
Opposed	6	17	32	27
Total (%)	100	100	100	100
Vote if such a referendum on inde-pendence were held today				
Support	89	64	42	42
Oppose	11	36	58	58
Total (%)	100	100	100	100

All questions favored by President Kuchma in the April 2000 referendum were approved with large majorities, ranging from 82 to 90 percent of the voters. The "yes" vote in all regions of Western Ukraine exceeded the national average which, depending on the question asked, ranged from 82 to 90 percent. (*CVK*, 2000). In the Transcarpathia region of Western Ukraine, the participation rate (98 percent) and the vote in favor of the president's proposals (94 to 97 percent) came close to results that were typical during Soviet rule. Both leaders of the nationalist *Rukh*, which had split into two separate parties in 1999, opposed all referendum questions with the exception of one concerning lifting deputies' immunity. The Communists urged boycotts of the referendum, but the turnout rate (79 percent) was higher than voter participation in the 1999 presidential elections. In all regions of Ukraine, the turnout rate surpassed 70 percent, and the "yes" answer exceeded 65 percent on all questions (*CVK*, 2000).[41]

The referendum results in favor of proposals on two of the four questions exceeded by approximately 30 to 40 percentage points the positive answers given to the same questions in a survey conducted several weeks earlier by the Kyiv International Institute of Sociology, a respected academic polling organization (*KIIS*, 2000). Among the factors that contributed to these results were pressure from the government on mass media and a low level of confidence in parliament. With the exception of several major newspapers and local television stations, the Ukrainian mass media gave overwhelmingly positive coverage of the president's proposals and for the most part did not air the views of the opponents of the referendum. The television broadcasts of parliament sessions were suspended before the 1999 presidential elections.

The Freedom House (1999 and 2000) score for Ukraine on a measure of press freedom, which runs from 0 – completely free – to 100 – completely unfree, changed from 50 in 1998 to 60 in 1999. This put Ukraine on the border between groups of countries whose press was either partly free (30 to 60) or non-free (61 to 100).[42]

---

[41]   Many experts in Ukraine and abroad have questioned the legality of the 2000 referendum and the parliament leadership coup. A commission set up by the Council of Europe concluded that the proposed referendum did not conform to constitutional norms and subsequently recommended a suspension of Ukraine's membership if the referendum took place and its results were implemented. The Council of Europe, which includes 41 countries, adopted similar measures against Greece (when it was run by the military dictatorship) and against Russia (for human rights violations during the war in Chechnya).
The Constitutional Court of Ukraine declared two proposed referendum questions (no-confidence vote in parliament, and the use of referendums to amend the Constitution) as in violation of the 1996 Ukrainian Constitution. However, the Constitutional Court recognized four other referendum questions as being legally binding: the lifting of deputies' immunity from prosecution, reducing the number of seats in parliament, introducing the second chamber of parliament composed of regional officials who are currently appointed by the president, and granting the president the right to dissolve parliament if it were unable to pass a budget or form a working majority (Maksymiuk, 2000).

[42]   Countries with similar scores in 1999 included Colombia and Nepal (59), Russia and Bangladesh (60), Lebanon, Kyrgyzstan and Ghana (61). The press freedom score in Moldova was similar to the score for Ukraine, 58 in 1999 and 56 in 1998. The freedom of press was most restricted by the authorities in Transdniestria. Freedom of the press in Moldova and Ukraine, compared to other post-Communist countries, was

3.8   Surveys of public opinion: regional patterns

Surveys of public opinion in Ukraine and Moldova showed significant regional cleavages. Respondents from the Western regions of Ukraine differed considerably in their political preferences from respondents from Eastern regions.[43] The distinction between Western and Eastern Ukrainians is not just an academic concept. Rather, this distinction is entrenched in public perception.

A KIIS survey conducted in October and November of 2005 showed that 42 percent of Ukrainians who had made up their minds on this issue considered the East-West division in Ukraine to be a divide between hostile sides. The response indicated significant regional differences in perceptions of the regional divisions. Twenty-nine percent of Ukrainians in geographically Western regions, 36 percent in the Center, 41 percent in the South, and 62 percent in the East agreed that the West and the East in Ukraine represented hostile sides. (See Mostova and Rakhmanin, 2005). A focus group study conducted by the US State Department Office of Research in five different Ukraine cities reported that, "while participants generally started out by agreeing that there was little conflict within their country, they often went on to detail the differences between Eastern and Western Ukrainians, frequently attributing the variance to Western Ukraine's much more recent accession to the Soviet Union." (Department of State, 2000, p. 3).

The mutual perceptions of Western and Eastern Ukrainians are to a certain degree interlaced with stereotypes and prejudices. The former are often called *banderivtsi*, a reference to the followers of the Organization of Ukrainian Nationalists (OUN),[44] while the latter are labeled as *communyaky*, or devoted Communists. As this study notes, it is a mistake to extrapolate the views of these radical political organizations to the whole population of a par-

---

significantly lower than in Poland (19), Czech Republic (20), and the Baltic States (18-24), but higher than in Belarus (80), Yugoslavia (81), Uzbekistan (83), Turkmenistan (86), and Tajikistan (94).

[43]   See Barrington, 1997; Hesli, 1995; Holovakha, 2000; Khmelko and Wilson, 1998; Kubicek, 2000; Miller, Klobucar, and Reisinger, 2000; Miller, White and Heywood, 1998; Shulman, 1999a; *USIA*, 1998; Wilson and Birch, 1999.

[44]   The OUN was split into two wings during World War II, and *banderivtsi* represented one of these wings. However, in popular perception, all followers of the OUN were called *banderivtsi*.

ticular region, because these groups occupied the extremes of the political spectrum in Ukraine and their core membership represented only a small faction of the population. The same applies to Moldova.

Most survey-based studies found that pro-Communist and pro-Russian attitudes were much stronger in the East than in the West of Ukraine. Nationalist attitudes and support for Ukrainian independence showed the reverse geographical pattern. It is noteworthy that the support for pro-Communist and pro-nationalist parties is strongly correlated with attitudes towards establishing closer links with Russia, Ukraine's membership in the Commonwealth of Independent States (CIS), and the economic union of CIS countries. (Khmelko and Wilson, 1998). Similarly, survey data show that residents of the Eastern regions of Ukraine had more positive views of Russians than did respondents from Western Ukraine. This was true even when other factors such as ethnicity, age, and education level were held constant. (See Barrington, 2001).

Survey-based studies show the existence of strong regional cleavages in Moldova. Respondents from the Transdniestrian region expressed much stronger pro-Soviet and pro-Russian attitudes than responsdents in the rest of Moldova, where support for Moldovan nationalists and the independence of Moldova was much higher. (Babilunga and Bomeshko, 1998, pp. 35-38; Crowther, 1997a; *Obshchestvennoe,* 1990; O'Loughlin, et al., 1998).

Most of these survey-based studies classified regions in Ukraine and Moldova by geographical location. For example, the surveys often divided Ukraine into four geographical regions: West, Center, South, and East. Such classifications prompt one to question why a geographic location plays such an important role in shaping political attitudes. As noted, this study argues that different historical legacies in Western Ukraine and Western Moldova have made these regions politically distinct from other regions of these two countries.

The 1996 World Values Survey data on party support (categorized by ideological orientation and major historical region, and capital cities in Ukraine and Moldova) show that respondents from different historical regions differed significantly in their political orientations. Much higher percentages of respondents in the Western regions of Ukraine (from 43 percent in the former Carpatho-Ukraine to 77 percent in the former Galicia) than in Eastern Ukraine (from 11 percent in Crimea to 35 percent in Kyiv) expressed a desire to vote for various nationalist parties. Support for the Communist parties had a reverse regional pattern (Table 3.4).

Table 3.4 Party support and attitude towards the Communist system in regions of Ukraine (%). (1996 World Values Survey)

	Eastern Ukraine			Western Ukraine			
	Crimea	Kyiv city	Other	Galicia	Volhynia	Carpatho-Ukraine	Bukovyna
Party support							
Nationalist	11	35	29	77	52	43	62
Centrist	60	34	40	17	31	52	29
Communist	29	31	32	5	16	6	10
Total	100	100	100	100	100	100	100
N	82	71	1477	206	141	54	42
Rating of Communist system							
Bad	34	36	37	76	57	47	73
In the middle	25	30	26	19	26	38	18
Good	41	34	38	5	17	16	9
Total (%)	100	100	100	100	100	100	100
N	111	76	1826	245	147	58	44

Note: The survey questions are: "If there were a general election tomorrow, which party would you vote for? If don't know: Which party appeals to you most?" (Excludes don't know and other) and "People have different views about the system for governing this country. Here is a scale for rating how well things are going: 1 means very bad and 10 means very good. Where on this scale would you put the political system as it was in communist times?"

According to the 1996 World Values Survey in Moldova, support for various nationalist and pro-Moldova parties was lowest in Gagauzia (0 percent), compared with 29 percent in the capital and 34 percent in the rest of Moldova. However, contrary to the election results, an absolute majority of respondents in Gagauzia (85 percent) expressed the desire to vote for centrist parties and not for Communists (15 percent). (Table 3.5.) This major discrepancy concerned the Agrarian Democratic Party, which was supported by 55 percent of the respondents in the region but received 12 percent of the vote in the 1995 Gagauzia regional assembly elections. (IFES, 1995.)

Table 3.5 Party support and attitude towards the Communist system in regions of Moldova (%). (1996 World Values Survey)

	Gagauzia	Chishinau city	Rest of Moldova
Party support			
Nationalist	0	29	34
Centrist	85	42	52
Communist	15	29	14
Total (%)	100	100	100
N	40	170	701
Rating of Communist system			
Bad	18	21	30
In the middle	3	38	30
Good	80	41	41
Total (%)	100	100	100
N	40	170	738

Note: The survey questions are: "If there were a general election tomorrow, which party would you vote for? If don't know: Which party appeals to you most?" (Excludes don't know and other) and "People have different views about the system for governing this country. Here is a scale for rating how well things are going: 1 means very bad and 10 means very good. Where on this scale would you put the political system as it was in communist times?"

Table 3.6 Proportion of respondents giving a positive evaluation of political movements in different regions of Moldova in December 1989-February 1990 (%).

	Transdni-estrian Republic: (Bendery-Tighina)	Gagauzia	Chishinau city	Rest of Moldova (unweighted average)
Popular Front of Moldova	19	21	42	32
Edinstvo (Unity Movement)	13	24	8	3
Gagauz People Movement	10	25	5	4

Note: N=1795. Source: Survey conducted by the Department for Study of Public Opinion, the Academy of Sciences of Moldova (See Obshchestvennoe, 1990, p. 109).

A 1990 poll showed a pattern of the regional differentiation in Moldova that was more consistent with the election results (Table 3.6). Support for the Popular Front, a nationalist Moldovan movement, was much stronger in the capital (42 percent) and other districts of Western Moldova (32 percent) than in Bendery (Tighina), a city that would become part of the Transdniestrian Republic (19 percent), and in Gagauzia (21 percent). Support for the pro-Soviet, anti-independence movement in Moldova and a Gagauz separatist movement followed the reverse pattern.[45]

Attitudes towards the political system that existed during Communist rule showed a similar regional variation in both Ukraine and Moldova (Table 3.4 and 3.5). In Western Ukraine, the evaluation of the Communist system was overwhelmingly negative. Three quarters (76 percent) of respondents in Galicia regarded the Communist political system as negative, and only 5 percent of Galicians viewed it as positive. A similar distribution prevailed in Bukovyna (73 vs. 9 percent), Volhynia (57 vs. 17 percent) and Carpatho-

---

[45]   See King (1994a, pp. 293-330) on the orientation and programs of these political movements.

Ukraine (47 vs. 16 percent). In contrast, in the Eastern regions of Ukraine, the evaluation of the Communist system was relatively more positive. Slightly more than one-third (34 percent) of respondents in Crimea, 36 percent in Kyiv, and 37 percent in other regions of Eastern Ukraine, viewed the Communist political system negatively, while 41, 34, and 38 percent respectively viewed it positively.

Respondents from the Gagauzia and Transdniestria regions of Moldova were much more favorable in their evaluation of the Soviet system than were respondents from the Bessarabia region. Eighty percent of the respondents in Gagauzia gave Communist political systems a positive rating, compared to 41 percent in Chishinau and other districts of Western Moldova. A negative rating was registered by 18 percent of the respondents in Gagauzia, 21 percent in Chishinau city, and 30 percent in the rest of the Bessarabian part of Moldova. (Table 3.5.) The 1998 Laitin/Hough survey showed that three quarters (74 percent) of respondents in Transdniestria, compared to 52 percent in the rest of Moldova, felt that the fall of the Soviet Union was harmful. Fifteen percent of Transdniestrians and 33 percent of Bessarabians regarded the collapse of the Soviet Union as good. Among these respondents, 72 percent of ethnic Gagauz expressed regret for the break-up of the Soviet Union, while only 19 percent viewed the collapse of the USSR in a positive light.

The 1996 Socis-Gallup poll showed that support for the unification of Ukraine and other former Soviet Republics was highest among respondents from Crimea (70 percent) and other regions of Eastern Ukraine, excluding Kyiv (50 percent), and lowest in Galicia (3 percent) and Volhynia (15 percent) (Table 3.7). The 1997 United States Information Agency opinion poll showed that almost half (46 percent) of the respondents in Eastern Ukrainian regions fully agreed that it was "a great misfortune that the Soviet Union no longer exists." In Western Ukrainian regions, only 15 percent of the respondents fully agreed with this assertion. More than half of the respondents in Eastern Ukrainian regions (54 percent), compared to one fourth (24 percent) in Western Ukrainian regions, fully agreed that "Ukraine should try to join a union with Russia." (*USIA*, 1998, p. 5).

Table 3.7 Preferences regarding foreign orientation in major regions of Ukraine (%). (1996 Socis-Gallup Survey)

	Crimea	Kyiv city	Other Eastern regions (un-weighted average)	Galicia	Volhynia
Unification of the CIS republics into one state	70	20	50	3	15
Ukraine's departure from the CIS and conduct of the independent policy	5	27	12	41	40
Ukraine's departure from the CIS and its orientation on political union with other countries	7	22	10	26	8
Preservation of the current state (CIS membership)	9	20	15	14	15
Difficult to answer	9	12	14	16	21
Total (%)	100	100	100	100	100

Note: The survey question is "Which specified option of the foreign policy direction is best for Ukraine in your opinion? "Source: Kremin, et. al., 1997.

A 2002 poll indicated that 34 percent of Lviv residents expressed a desire to fight for an independent Galician state if Ukraine joined the Union of Belarus and Russia. Only 5 percent of the respondents would welcome such a union. Another 11 percent would demand the autonomy of Galicia. (See Gryb, 2003). The results had been similar when this question was asked in

2000: 29 percent of the Lviv respondents said that they would fight for an independent Galician state, 8 percent would welcome a merger with Russia and Belarus, and 11 percent would demand the autonomy of Galicia (Sadovyi, 2002, p. 162). In contrast, 45 percent of the respondents in the Luhansk Region of Eastern Ukraine had favored a restoration of the Soviet Union in 1993 (Iurov, 1995, p. 190). According to a 1994 survey, 75 percent of the respondents in Lviv in Western Ukraine considered changes that came about after the declaration of Ukraine's independence to be generally positive, compared to 15 percent of the respondents in Donetsk in Eastern Ukraine (Romaniuk and Chernysh, 1995, pp. 104-116).

Attitudes towards Ukraine's entrance into NATO showed similar regional differences. A poll conducted by the Democratic Initiatives Foundation in late 2002 revealed that 54 percent of respondents in Galicia and 42 percent of respondents in Bukovyna and Carpatho-Ukraine, compared to 17 percent of respondents in Donetsk and Luhansk regions, supported the future membership of Ukraine in NATO. Opposed to NATO membership were 22 percent in Galicia, 25 percent in Bukovyna and Carpatho-Ukraine, and 50 percent in the Donetsk and Luhansk regions. In Crimea, 20 percent favored NATO membership, while 54 percent were opposed. (Fond "Demokratychni initsiatyvy," 2002).

While many journalists and commentators in Western media described the victory of Viktor Yushchenko and his allies in Ukraine at the end of 2004 as a pro-Western revolution, opinion poll data did not show revolutionary changes in the political values of Ukrainians in different regions. Yushchenko received the absolute majority of the vote not only in traditionally pro-Western Western Ukraine (68 to 96 percent) but also in Central regions that demonstrated a pro-Russian orientation (63 to 83 percent). It is a mistake to completely equate popular support for Viktor Yushchenko with support for the ideas that he advanced, because many of his voters were motivated not by his ideology but by his personal charisma and by their antipathy to Viktor Yanukovych due to his criminal record and his association with oligarchs.

Many Western journalists and commentators made a similar mistake in the 1990s in their assessment of the political values of Russians. Liberal democrats in Russia were hampered by a statist and authoritarian political culture and the strong influence of charismatic politicians, as later manifested in the ascendancy of Vladimir Putin. (See Katchanovski, 1995). Similarly, many Yushchenko voters in Central regions of Ukraine, in contrast to Western Ukraine, could have switched their support to a charismatic pro-Russian politician, had one been available.

For example, surveys conducted by the Institute of Sociology of the National Academy of Sciences of Ukraine showed that Vladimir Putin was more popular in Ukraine than was Viktor Yushchenko. The charismatic Russian president had favorable approval ratings of 6.7 in 2004 and 6.0 in 2005, compared to the overall approval rating of 5.6 on the 10 point scale for Yushchenko in 2005. However, Putin's visits to Ukraine during the 2004 presidential elections and his backing of Leonid Kuchma and Viktor Yanukovych failed to change the outcome of the elections, because many Ukrainians associated Yanukovych with unpopular Kuchma. Leonid Kuchma had an overall rating of 3.2 on the 10 point scale in 2004. (Panina, 2005, p. 30).

Survey data show that only Western Ukrainian regions consistently supported key aims put forward by Viktor Yushchenko during his presidential campaign, such as Ukraine's membership in NATO and the European Union, and opposition to full integration into the Russia-led Common Economic Space. In contrast, regions in Eastern Ukraine, including the geographically Central part of Ukraine, which overwhelmingly voted for Viktor Yushchenko, were more supportive of aims advanced by Viktor Yanukovych, such as opposition to NATO membership and support of Ukraine's integration into the Common Economic Space, joint efforts by Ukraine and Russia to enter the European Union in the distant future, dual citizenship with Russia, and making Russian the second state language in Ukraine.

For example, the May 2005 survey conducted by the Kyiv International Institute of Sociology and the Razumkov Center showed that support for joining NATO was 59 percent in geographically Western regions of Ukraine, compared to 35 percent in Central regions, 18 percent in Southern regions, and 7 percent in Eastern regions (Donetsk, Luhansk, and Kharkiv). Eighty-five percent of Ukrainians in Western regions, 73 percent in Central regions, 53 percent in Southern regions, and 38 percent in Eastern regions backed Ukraine's membership in the European Union. An overwhelming majority of Ukrainians in Central regions (73 percent), Southern regions (84 percent), and Eastern regions (93 percent), compared to a minority (41 percent) in Western regions, agreed that Ukraine had to join the Common Economic Space, which included Russia, Belarus, and Kazakhstan. Ukraine's withdrawal from the Commonwealth of Independent States was favored by 45 percent of the respondents in Western regions, compared to 28, 14, and 11 percent in Central, Southern, and Eastern regions respectively.[46] (Table 3.8).

If a referendum were to be held on the issue of joining a union of Russia and Belarus, Ukraine would be sharply divided along the same regional lines. The 2005 Institute of Sociology survey showed that the majority of the respondents, excluding those who were undecided, in geographic East (92 percent), South (84 percent), and Center (53 percent), compared to 31 percent in Western regions, favored such a union for Ukraine. (Panina, 2005, p. 36.)

The 2005 KIIS/Razumkov Center survey revealed similar regional differences in attitudes towards the introduction of dual citizenship with Russia and towards making Russian the second state language in Ukraine. Eighty-eight percent of the respondents in geographically Eastern regions, 78 percent in Southern regions, and 56 percent in Central regions, compared to 24 percent in Western regions, favored dual citizenship with Russia. Support for Russian as the second state language was 91 percent in the geographic East, 80 percent in the South, 50 percent in the Center, and 20 percent in the West. Because this survey classified the Khmelnytsky region as a Western region, the survey results were likely to underestimate differences between historical Western Ukraine and Eastern Ukraine. (Table 3.8.)

Similar regional divisions characterized political attitudes among the elites of Ukraine. A 1994/1995 survey of about one thousand members of elite groups, such as professors, teachers, government administrators, journalists, managers, and writers, showed that elites in Eastern and Western Ukraine differed considerably in their world views. As measured by a scale of –5 to 5, the elites in Donetsk had very positive feelings towards Russia (4.2), while the elites in Lviv expressed negative feelings (-1.3). Donetsk respondents demonstrated less positive feelings towards Western Ukraine than towards regions of Eastern Ukraine. Similar disparities characterized the perceptions

---

[46]   These results include only respondents who selected a definite answer ("yes" or "no").

of Lviv elites of Donbas (1.9), Central Ukraine (3.7), and Western Ukraine
(4.3). (Shulman, 1999b).

Table 3.8 Regional differences in political orientation in Ukraine (2005 KIIS/
Razumkov Center Survey)

	West	Center	South	East
NATO membership				
Support	59	35	18	7
Oppose	41	65	82	93
Total (%)	100	100	100	100
EU membership				
Support	85	73	53	38
Oppose	15	27	47	62
Total (%)	100	100	100	100
Joining the Common Economic Space				
Support	41	72	84	93
Oppose	59	28	16	7
Total (%)	100	100	100	100
Withdrawal from the CIS				
Support	45	28	14	11
Oppose	55	72	86	89
Total (%)	100	100	100	100
Russian as the second state language				
Support	20	50	80	91
Oppose	80	50	20	9
Total (%)	100	100	100	100
Dual citizenship with Russia				
Support	24	56	78	88
Oppose	76	44	22	12
Total (%)	100	100	100	100
Federalization of Ukraine				
Support	26	31	42	61
Oppose	74	69	58	39
Total (%)	100	100	100	100

When asked, "how alike in culture, language, and views," Ukrainians in Ukraine and Russians in Russia are, 58 percent of the respondents in Lviv, compared to just 3 percent in Donetsk, considered them completely or very dissimilar. Four percent of the elites in Lviv and 37 percent of the elites in Donetsk viewed Ukrainians in Ukraine and Russians in Russia as completely or very similar. The elites in both regions considered the culture of Western Ukraine to be Western and the culture of Eastern Ukraine to be non-Western. (See Shulman, 1999b).

The 1990 survey conducted by the Department of Sociology of the Academy of Sciences of Moldova and the Institute of Social and Political Studies showed that support for the preservation of Moldova's membership in the Soviet Union was much higher in the Transdniestria region (82 percent) and the Gagauz region (75 percent) than in the rest of Moldova (52 percent in the capital city, and 57 percent in other districts and towns in the Western part of the country). Support for the independence of Moldova showed the reverse pattern. It was highest in Western cities and districts (37 to 41 percent), and lowest in Transdniestria (13 percent) and Gagauzia (19 percent). The issue of Moldova's unification with Romania received low support (2 to 6 percent) in all regions of Moldova. (See Table 3.9.)

The 1998 Laitin/Hough survey revealed similar differences between Transdniestria and Bessarabia regarding the future state structure of Moldova. Almost half (47 percent) of the respondents in Transdniestria favored a confederative or united government with Russia, while 25 percent supported an independent government. In contrast, 28 percent of respondents in Bessarabia expressed support for a confederative or united government with Russia, while 54 percent favored the independence of Moldova, and 5 percent backed a confederation or a union with Romania. (Table 3.10.) In the sub-sample of Gagauz respondents, 58 percent favored a confederative/united government with Russia, and 9 percent favored an independent government. No Gagauz or Transdniestrian respondents supported confederation or union with Romania.

Table 3.9 Regional dimension of attitudes towards independence of Moldova, May 1990 (%)

	Transdni-estria	Gagauzia	Chishinau city	Rest of Moldova (unweighted average)
Sovereign republic within the renewed federation of the USSR	82	75	52	57
Sovereign independent Moldovan republic	13	19	41	37
Moldovan republic as part of Romania	2	3	6	2
Other	2	1	1	2
Total (%)	100	100	100	100

Source: Survey conducted by the Department of Sociology of the Academy of Sciences of Moldova and the Institute of Social and Political Studies (*Obshchestvennoe*, 1990, p. 114). Note: N =1262. The survey question is "How do you see the future of Moldavia in the near future?"

Western and Eastern Ukrainians celebrate different religious and political holidays. The Razumkov Center survey of December 2002 revealed that 56 percent of Western Ukrainians, compared to 22 percent of the residents of Central regions, 17 percent of Ukrainians in the South, and 13 percent in the East considered Christmas, which is celebrated by Orthodox Christians and Greek Catholics on January 7, to be the biggest holiday. In contrast, the New Year was more popular in regions of Eastern Ukraine (39 to 49 percent) than in Western Ukraine (11 percent). Victory Day, which marks the Soviet victory in World War II, was considered to be the biggest holiday by 2 percent of Western Ukrainians, compared to 8 to 14 percent of the respondents in the regions of Eastern Ukraine (Table 3.11).

Table 3.10 Preferences regarding the future state structure in Transdniestria and the rest of Moldova (%). (1998 Laitin/Hough survey)

	Transdniestria	Rest of Moldova
Independent of the government of the CIS	19	31
Independent government free from inter-governmental unions	6	23
Confederative/united government with Russia	47	28
Confederative/united government with Romania	0	5
Difficult to answer	27	14
Total (%)	100	100
N	407	1130

Note: The survey question is "What future state structure would you prefer to see in Moldova?"

Other political holidays, such as Independence Day and the Anniversary of Bolshevik Revolution Day, were not perceived as the most important holidays in any region of Ukraine (Table 3.11). However, attitudes to such holidays differed significantly. For example, the Razumkov Center survey conducted in August 2002 showed that 40 percent of the respondents in Western Ukraine, compared to 13 percent in the Center, 12 percent in the South, and 10 percent in the East, considered Independence Day to be an important holiday. Conversely, 23 percent of Western Ukrainians, compared to 41 percent of the residents of Central regions, and 55 percent of the residents in the South and the East, did not regard the anniversary of Ukrainian independence as a holiday. The other respondents either regarded this holiday as similar to other official holidays or were not sure on this issue.

Table 3.11 The biggest holidays in Ukrainian regions (Razumkov Center survey, December 2002)

	Western Ukraine	Center	South	East
Christmas (January 7)	56	22	17	13
New Year (January 1)	11	40	39	49
Easter	25	19	17	17
Independence Day (August 24)	1	1	0	1
Anniversary of the Bolshevik Revolution (November 7)	0	1	1	0
Victory Day (May 9)	2	8	14	8
Army Day (February 23)	1	1	1	1
International Women's Day (March 8)	1	2	2	4
May Day (May 1)	0	1	0	1
Other/Not sure	3	5	9	6
Total (%)	100	100	100	100

3.9   Attitudes towards privatization and market reform

State versus private ownership as well as state planning versus free market have been important political issues in Ukraine and Moldova since the end of the 1980s. As noted, Communist parties in these countries generally favored the preservation of government ownership and state control of the economy, while nationalist and centrist parties supported privatization and market reforms. Survey data indicated that differentiation between supporters of pro-Communist and centrist parties in Ukraine was associated with attitudes towards private ownership and private business (Khmelko and Wilson, 1998, p. 68).

Attitudes towards privatization and the transition towards a free market in Ukraine and Moldova exhibited significant regional differences. A 1998 survey conducted by the International Foundation for Election Systems (IFES) reported that support for a free market, compared with support for central planning, was weakest in Eastern regions of Ukraine, with the exception of the capital city of Kyiv, and strongest in Western regions (O'Loughlin and Bell, 1999). Central and Eastern Eurobarometer surveys, the Kyiv International Institute of Sociology survey, and the University of Iowa Post-Soviet Citizen survey, found similar regional patterns in Ukraine (Khmelko and Wilson, 1998; Kubichek, 2000a; Miller et al., 2000).

The 1996 World Values Survey showed that support for privatization was much stronger in Western regions of Ukraine than in the historical East. Sixty-nine percent of respondents in Bukovyna, 61 percent in Galicia, 54 percent in Carpatho-Ukraine, and 45 percent in Volhynia favored an increase in private ownership of business and industry. In comparison, support for privatization in Eastern Ukraine was 22 to 27 percent. Fifty-six percent of respondents in Kyiv city, 53 percent in Crimea, and 45 percent in other regions of Eastern Ukraine, compared to 14 to 29 percent in historically Western regions, favored an increase in government ownership. (Table 3.12.)

The same survey revealed that support for privatization was lower in Gagauzia (8 percent) than in Chishinau city (35 percent) and the rest of Bessarabia (18 percent). Eighty-five percent of the respondents in Gagauzia, compared to 38 percent in the capital and 59 percent in the rest of Western Moldova, favored an increase in government ownership of business and industry. (Table 3.13.) The Laitin/Hough survey showed a similar difference between Transdniestria and the rest of Moldova on attitudes towards a transition to market economy. Nineteen percent of the respondents in Transdniestria, compared to 12 percent in Bessarabia, opposed a transition to market economy. Eighteen percent of the Gagauz expressed the same view.

Table 3.12 Attitude towards privatization in regions of Ukraine (%). (1996 World Values Survey)

| | Eastern Ukraine | | | Western Ukraine | | | |
	Crimea	Kyiv city	Other regions	Galicia	Volhynia	Capatho-Ukraine	Bukovyna
Increase private ownership	27	22	26	61	45	54	69
Middle of the road	20	22	29	22	26	32	11
Increase government ownership	53	56	45	17	29	14	20
Total (%)	100	100	100	100	100	100	100
N	119	78	1881	257	153	56	45

Note: The survey question is "Private ownership of business and industry should be increased or government ownership of business and industry should be increased."

Table 3.13 Attitude towards privatization in regions of Moldova (%). (1996 World Values Survey)

	Gagauzia	Chishinau city	Rest of Moldova (excl. Transdniestria)
Increase private ownership	8	35	18
Middle of the road	8	27	23
Increase government ownership	85	38	59
Total (%)	100	100	100
N	40	177	743

Note: The survey question is "Private ownership of business and industry should be increased or government ownership of business and industry should be increased."

It is important to note that this book focuses on the political dimension of the regional differentiation of attitudes towards private ownership and market reforms. The extent and character of privatization in regions of Ukraine and Moldova was a more complex issue that was affected more by policies of the national government than by regional differences in public opinion and social capital.[47] (See Katchanovski, 2001).

Regional variations in privatization in post-Communist Ukraine and Moldova were much less significant than differences in public attitudes towards private ownership and market reforms. As of 1998, the proportion of non-state industrial enterprises was somewhat higher in the Western regions of Ukraine (85 to 91 percent) than in Eastern Ukraine (65 to 90 percent). The proportion of cooperatives, private farms, and peasant households in agricul-

---

[47]   Social capital, a central element of economic culture, refers to commonly shared values and norms that enable cooperation among individuals within different groups and organizations, including in organizing and running private businesses. (Coleman, 1988, p. 98; Fukuyama, 1995b, 1999, p. 16). Indirect indicators of social capital, such as divorce rate, crime rate, and election turnout rate, exhibited significant variation among the historical regions of Ukraine and Moldova. The divorce rate and the crime rate were significantly higher in Eastern Ukraine than in the Western regions. The average divorce rate per 1,000 members of the population in 1997 was 4.0 in Eastern regions, compared with 1.9 in Carpatho-Ukraine, 2.4 in Galicia, 2.6 in Volhynia, and 3.1 in Bukovyna. Divorce rate figures for historical regions of Moldova were not available. However, the Transdniestrian region had a much higher crime rate than the rest of Moldova. The average crime rate in the Transdniestrian districts and cities per 100,000 members of the population in 1991 was 108, compared to 74 in the other districts and cities of Moldova (*Kharakteristika*, 1993). In 1996, the regional crime rate per 100,000 members of the population was 1290 in Eastern Ukraine, 675 in Galicia, 639 in Volhynia, 563 in Bukovyna, and 559 in Carpatho-Ukraine. The election turnout rate in the first round of the 1999 presidential elections in Ukraine showed a similar pattern of variation between Western and Eastern regions, with some exceptions. The turnout rate was 79 percent in Galicia, 77 percent in Volhynia, 67 percent in Bukovyna, and 60 percent in Carpatho-Ukraine, compared with 70 percent in Eastern Ukraine. The unweighted regional average of the election turnout rate in the 1998 parliamentary elections was 77 percent in Western Ukraine, compared with 70 percent in Eastern Ukraine. (See Katchanovski, 2001). However, the 1996 World Values Survey data did not show consistent significant differences between historically Western and Eastern Ukraine on such measures of social capital as trust and membership in voluntary associations. Respondents from Gagauzia expressed much less trust in other people (3 percent) than did respondents from other parts of Moldovan Bessarabia (23 percent). However, the importance of family and friends did not differ to the same extent in this part of Moldova. Exactly the same proportions of Western and Eastern Ukrainians said that family (98 percent) and friends (89 percent) were important in their lives and that, "regardless of what the qualities and faults of one's parents are, one must always love and respect them" (90 percent).

tural production was also somewhat higher in Western Ukraine than in Eastern regions; this difference was largely due to the role of peasant households, which contributed more to agricultural production in Western regions than did their Eastern counterparts. For example, peasant households in 1994 produced on average 78 percent of all agricultural output in Carpatho-Ukraine, 58 percent in Galicia, 56 percent in Bukovyna, and 52 percent in Volhynia. The average contribution in Eastern regions was 39 percent. However, private farms were relatively more developed in Eastern Ukraine; in 1994, they had on average 2.5 percent of the farmland compared to 1.2 percent in Western regions. (See Katchanovski, 2001; *Pro khid*, 1999; Shepot'ko, Prokopa, Maksymiuk, et al., 1997, p. 78; *Silske*, 1995, p. 84; *Statystychnyi*, 1998, pp. 129, 310, 483).

In Western Moldova, most industrial enterprises were privatized. In contrast, in Transdniestria, no large-scale industrial privatization program was implemented. Corporatization carried out in 1992 involved only 12 percent of the large and medium-size industrial enterprises, which became joint-stock companies partially owned by worker collectives and managers, with some continued state ownership (*Republic*, 1998, p. 10). In Western Moldova, the proportion of industrial and agricultural output produced by non-state enterprises was higher than in Eastern regions.

Similarly, agricultural privatization in Gagauzia lagged behind, compared to other regions of Bessarabia. As of April 1998, only 5 percent of the entitled individuals in Gagauzia received land in private ownership, compared to 19 percent in all of Western Moldova. In the Transdniestrian Republic, the Soviet-type collective and state farms remained largely unreformed, and private farms did not play a significant role. In Western Moldova, the proportion of land held by private farmers in 1996 was 8 percent, while private farms did not exist in the self-declared Transdniestrian Republic. In Gagauzia, private farming was much less developed than in the rest of Western Moldova. (See Katchanovski, 2001; Lerman, et. al, 1998, pp. 15-16; *Republic*, 1998, pp. 10, 25).

Election outcomes, referendums, and opinion surveys showed significant regional differences in political behaviors and attitudes in post-Communist Ukraine and Moldova. Electoral realignments that involved the rise of new major parties, leaders, and cleavages, for instance during the

"Orange Revolution" in Ukraine, failed to eliminate the nationalist/pro-Western vs. pro-Communist/pro-Russian regional cleavage. (See Katchanovski, 2006.)

For example, the results of the March 2006 parliamentary elections, which took place while this book was in press, showed that nationalist and/or pro-Western parties and electoral blocs (the Yushchenko Bloc "Our Ukraine," the Ukrainian People's Bloc, the *Pora-PRP* Bloc, and several smaller organizations) received the support of one half (51 percent) of voters in the regions of Galicia, and one third of voters in Volhynia (33 percent), Bukovyna (31 percent), and Carpatho-Ukraine (30 percent), compared to support from only 13 percent of voters in regions of historically Eastern Ukraine, including 2 percent in Donbas, 8 percent in Crimea, and 20 percent in Kyiv city. In contrast, combined support for pro-Russian and/or pro-Communist parties and electoral blocs (the Party of Regions, the Communist Party, Nataliia Vitrenko's "People's Opposition" Bloc, and several smaller contenders) reached, on average, 3 percent in Galicia, 8 percent in Volhynia, 16 percent in Carpatho-Ukraine, and 21 percent in Bukovyna, compared to 41 percent in Eastern Ukrainian regions, including 16 percent in Kyiv city, and even greater support in Crimea (70 percent) and Donbas (84 percent). The Yulia Tymoshenko Bloc, led by a charismatic and populist political entrepreneur who managed to unite under her banner both nationalist leaders and former pro-Kuchma oligarchs, received on average 38 percent of the vote in Volhynia, 33 percent in Galicia, 30 percent in Bukovyna, 20 percent in Carpatho-Ukraine, and 23 percent in Eastern Ukraine, including 3 percent in Donbas, 7 percent in Crimea, and 39 percent in Kyiv city.

Similar differences manifested in actions of mass political protest and in support for privatization and market reforms in post-Soviet Ukraine and Moldova. This pattern, with few exceptions, coincided with historical divisions among the regions of these two countries. The next two chapters examine the role of historical, religious, ethnic, economic, and political leadership factors in regional political cleavages and conflicts in Ukraine and Moldova.

4   Evolution of regional political cultures in Ukraine and Moldova

As discussed in chapter 2, historical legacies play an important role in the evolution of political culture and contribute to the emergence of regional political divisions. This chapter examines the role of historical factors in the emergence of different cultures in regions of Ukraine and Moldova. Religious cleavages are also examined because their emergence in these two countries is closely related to the historical differences.

Although modernists and primodialists debate the origins of national identities, both groups of scholars mostly agree that nationalism and national identity have come to the forefront of politics in many European countries since the end of the eighteenth and the beginning of the nineteenth centuries (Calhoun, 1993; Gellner, 1997; Kedouri, 1961; Kohn, 1955). Before the spread of nationalism in Europe, local, religious, and status-based identities were dominant among various strata of the population, including nobility and peasants. Peasants, the most numerous stratum of the population, spoke local dialects or regional languages. Such a situation existed in France (Weber, 1976), Spain (Hobsbawm, 1990, pp. 14-15), German states (Kohn, 1944, p. 388), Central and Eastern Europe (Gellner, 1997), and the Russian Empire (Kaiser, 1994). For example, Gellner (1997, pp. 38-39) states that "the political organization of Central and Eastern Europe was originally based on dynasties, religions and territorial institutions, rather than on language and its associated culture."

With few exceptions, the political map of Europe in the seventeenth and eighteenth centuries was dominated by dynastic monarchies, such as the Habsburg Monarchy, Kingdom of Spain, Polish-Lithuanian Commonwealth, Kingdom of Prussia, the Russian Empire, and the Ottoman Empire. They often fought for control of various parts of Europe, and their territories, which included many ethnic groups, underwent numerous changes. (See Gellner, 1997, pp. 38-40.) At that time, territories of Ukraine and Moldova were divided among the Habsburg, Russian, and Ottoman Empires. This created different conditions for the rise of nationalism and the development of national identities in regions belonging to different empires.

4.1   Historical legacies of the Russian Empire and the Austro-Hungarian Monarchy

Ukraine's territory was divided between the Russian Empire and the Austro-Hungarian Monarchy during partitions of Poland at the end of the eighteenth century.[48] Present-day Lviv, Ternopil, and Ivano-Frankivsk regions became parts of the Galicia province in the Habsburg Monarchy in 1772. Except for its eastern area, the Chernivtsi region, or Bukovyna, came under Habsburg rule in 1774. Transcarpathia, or Carpatho-Ukraine, also was part of the Austro-Hungarian Monarchy. The region had been part of the Kingdom of Hungary since the Middle Ages. (See Magocsi, 1993a, pp. 70-72, 2002; Subtelny, 1988.) In contrast, Eastern Ukrainian regions and Volhynia, most of which were controlled by the Polish-Lithuanian Commonwealth, Ukrainian Cossacks, and the Ottoman Empire during medieval times, were incorporated into the Russian Empire between the sixteenth and eighteenth centuries.

The Austro-Hungarian Monarchy came to control most of the West Ukrainian lands in the end of the eighteenth century. However, it was only in the second half of the nineteenth century that these Ukrainian regions, specifically Galicia, became a center of Ukrainian nationalism. For example, in the first half of the nineteenth century, Ukrainian intellectuals in Galicia trailed Eastern Ukrainian intellectuals in their development of literary language (Subtelny, 1988, pp. 212-242, 250). At that time, class and religious identities were much more important to Ukrainian peasants in the Habsburg Monarchy and the Russian Empire than their national identity (Subtelny, 1988, p. 245). Different dialects of vernacular Ukrainian existed in different areas, and these were named after local inhabitants, e.g., Boiky, Polishuky, and Lemky. The

---

[48]   Most of Ukraine was part of Kyiv Rus between the ninth and thirteenth centuries and part of the Polish-Lithuanian Commonwealth between the sixteenth and seventeenth centuries. A quasi-independent Cossack state existed in Eastern Ukraine during the seventeenth century.

development of a Ukrainian national identity in the Habsburg Monarchy was an evolutionary process that took at least several decades.

Many scholars argue that intellectuals and cultural elites played a major role in the emergence and spread of nationalism and the development of national identities. Nationalists promoted the primacy of a national identity among other competing identities, such as class identity and individual identity. They viewed the nation-state as the primary form of the state organization, advanced a unified literary language and a national education system, and promoted folk culture and a national history. (See Gellner, 1997, Greenfeld, 1992, and Calhoun, 1993.)

The ascent of a Ukrainian nationalism in Galicia was assisted by the rise of Polish, Hungarian, German, and Czech nationalisms. Members of the fledging Ukrainian intelligentsia viewed these nationalisms both as examples to follow and as threats to oppose.[49] Galicia, especially its western part (the area of Krakow) and the provincial capital (Lviv) in the eastern part of the province, was a center of Polish nationalism. Poles constituted the majority of the population in these parts of Galicia, while Ukrainians formed the majority of population in the rest of the region (Subtelny, 1988, p. 316).

Greater political freedom in the Habsburg Monarchy and a more supportive Austrian policy compared with the Russian Empire created favorable conditions for the development of a Ukrainian national identity in Galicia and Bukovyna. The constitutional monarchy in the Austro-Hungarian Monarchy gave Ukrainian intellectuals many more opportunities for political and cultural activities than did the absolutist monarchy in the Russian Empire (Kohn, 1955, pp. 66-67). Magocsi (1993b, p. 117) assesses the differences that emerged between Ukrainian lands in the Russian Empire and in Galicia, which had a population several times smaller, as follows:[50]

> Despite continued Polish dominance in the affairs of the province and the generally underdeveloped agrarian-based economy that left the region one of the poorest in the whole

---

[49]   In the mid-nineteenth century, pro-Russian tendencies were dominant among the Ukrainian intelligentsia in Galicia. Russophils advanced a common national identity among Russians and Ukrainians, who were called Rusyns or Ruthenians in Galicia (Subtelny, 1988; Wandycz, 1974/1994.)

[50]   Ukrainians constituted the majority only in the Eastern part of the Austrian province.

Habsburg Empire, the Ukrainians of Galicia made remarkable progress in the political and especially cultural spheres. Their region, small by comparison with the Dnieper Ukraine within the Russian Empire, became the leading center for the Ukrainian national revival in the second half of the nineteenth century.

Education played an instrumental role in the cultivation of national identity (see Gellner, 1983). As Weber (1976) documents, a standardized mass education system run by the French state helped to turn the peasants, who spoke different dialects and had various local identities, into Frenchmen. Austrian educational policy was more favorable towards the Ukrainian language than was Russian policy. Even though German, and then Polish, were the main languages of education in the Galicia province, the Ukrainian language was taught in some universities and seminaries. A great number of Ukrainian educational, religious, cultural, and political organizations and associations, which were involved in promoting Ukrainian national identity, were active in Galicia. For example, the *Prosvita* society established about three thousand reading rooms and libraries in villages in this region before World War I. (Subtelny,1988, pp. 323-324.) As Subtelny (1988, p. 335) puts it:

when Ukrainians from the Russian Empire visited Galicia in the yearly years of the 20th century, they were invariably struck by the progress their western compatriots had made. In Kyiv it was still forbidden to publish a book in Ukrainian, but in Lviv one found Ukrainian learned societies, schools, headquarters of mass organizations and cooperatives, newspapers, political parties, and parliamentary representatives.

Contact between Ukrainian intelligentsia from the Austro-Hungarian Monarchy and their Ukrainian counterparts in the Russian Empire helped to advance nationalism and a Ukrainian national identity in Eastern Ukraine. For example, such contact fostered standardization of the Ukrainian literary language. (Prizel, 1998, p. 317.) However, the fact that the Austro-Hungarian Monarchy and the Russian Empire joined opposing military alliances, which eventually waged World War I, limited contact between Ukrainians in these two countries.

Nationalism became more widespread among Ukrainian intellectuals in the Austro-Hungarian Monarchy than did classical liberalism. For example, Austrian economists, such as Carl Menger, who published in Galician newspapers, Ludwig von Mises, who was born in Lviv, and Joseph Schumpeter, who taught at Chernivtsi University in Bukovyna, did not become influential among Ukrainian intellectuals in Western Ukraine. The same applies to Hungarian-born Michael Polanyi, whose parents came from Carpatho-Ukraine.[51] German romantic nationalism, and even Marxism, gained much more currency among the Ukrainian intelligentsia in Western Ukraine than did the ideas of these proponents of classical liberalism.

Because the Russian Empire was an autocratic state, Tsarist policy was a major obstacle to the development of a Ukrainian national identity in Eastern Ukraine and the Volhynia province. The Russian authorities eliminated Ukrainian regional autonomy, prohibited the activities of Ukrainian political organizations and associations, and restricted the use of the Ukrainian language in education and print. For example, in 1847, the Russian government disbanded the Brotherhood of Saints Cyril and Methodius, one of the first pro-Ukrainian organizations. Its members and supporters, including Taras Shevchenko, a popular Ukrainian poet, were arrested and sent into exile to the outskirts of the Russian Empire. The Tsarist authorities prohibited education and publishing in Ukrainian, which they regarded as a dialect of Russian, by a series of decrees in 1863 and 1876. (See Kohut, 1988; Krawchenko, 1985; Saunders, 1993; Subtelny, 1988.)

Ukrainians were called *Malorossy* (Little-Russians), while Russians were called *Velikorossy* (Great Russians). These terms fitted the Russian imperial identity. The term *Rossiane* referred to inhabitants of the empire, in contrast to the ethnicity-based term *Russkie.* The Russian government, church, cultural, military, and business elites, with few exceptions, regarded Ukrainians (Little Russians) as a regional population and not as a distinct ethnic group. (See Magocsi, 1996, pp. 333-334; Prizel, 1998, pp. 157-162.)

The Ukrainian elite was largely assimilated in the Russian Empire. Many leading writers and scholars of Ukrainian origin, such as Nikolai Gogol

---

[51] On positions held by the Austrian and Hungarian classical liberals towards nationalism, see Mises (1983/1919) and Polanyi (1997).

(Mykola Hohol) and Vladimir (Volodymyr) Vernadsky, identified with the Russian culture.[52] Greenfeld (1992, pp. 237-239) notes that, by the end of the eighteenth century, ethnic Ukrainians constituted a significant proportion of the educated class in Russia, which she characterizes as the first Russian nationalist group.

The Tsarist government and Russian nationalists emphasized a historical affinity between Russians and Ukrainians. Ukrainians and Russians had emerged from the remnants of one state, Kyiv Rus, which existed, with Kyiv city as its center, from the ninth century to the thirteenth century. Their languages had many similarities; and Orthodox Christianity was the dominant religion in the Russian Empire, including Eastern Ukraine. These factors promoted the development of a Russophile political culture in Eastern Ukraine and Volhynia.[53]

Even though the absolute majority of Ukrainians in the Austro-Hungarian Monarchy and the Russian Empire were illiterate peasants with no strong national identity, Ukrainian nationalism had deeper roots in the former, not only among the intelligentsia but also among the peasants. In addition to the crucial role played by the Greek Catholic Church, the activities of Ukrainian educational, cultural, and political organizations helped to cultivate a national identity among the Ukrainian peasants in Galicia.

Party politics and elections were more developed in Galicia than in the Ukrainian lands of the Russian Empire. Wilson (1994, p. 577) notes that "Ukrainian parties were strongest in Austrian Galicia, where political conditions were relatively free and Ukrainian national consciousness was underpinned by the local Uniate Church." Ukrainians of Galicia, Bukovyna, and Transcarpathia began to take part in the elections to provincial parliaments in

---

[52]   In contrast to many immigrants from Western Ukraine, who retained their Ukrainian identity in North America, immigrants of Ukrainian descent who came from the Russian Empire often associated themselves more closely with the Russian nationality and culture than with the Ukrainian. (See, for example, the autobiographies of Kistiakowsky, 1976; Sikorsky, 1958; Timoshenko, 1968.)

[53]   The Eastern Ukrainian intelligentsia did not play as strong a role in the development of Russian imperial nationalism after the collapse of Communism in the Soviet Union. This can be largely attributed to the legacy of Communist rule, which emphasized the common Soviet identity of both Ukrainians and Russians. At the same time, in contrast to the Russian Empire, Russians and Ukrainians in the Soviet Union were officially treated as separate, but closely related, ethnic groups with separate languages.

1861, and elections to Austrian and Hungarian parliaments in 1873 (Birch, 1995, p. 1146). Their participation in elections was initially limited by the voting system, which favored upper classes, but broader and more direct elections to the Austrian parliament were instituted in 1907. In the 1907 Austrian parliamentary elections, the National Democratic Party held the majority of the seats (17 out of 27) that were won by Ukrainians in Galicia. This party declared a united and independent Ukraine as its ultimate goal (*Encyclopedia*, 1984-1993, p. 544; Wandycz, 1974/1994, p. 306).

In contrast, in the Russian Empire, the first elections to the parliament (*Duma*) were held only in 1906. However, the Tsar dissolved the First and Second *Duma* after several months and limited the voting rights of the lower classes in subsequent elections. This affected ethnic Ukrainians disproportionately because most of them were peasants. Pro-Ukrainian parties, which emerged later than those in the Austro-Hungarian Monarchy, did not have significant representation in the Russian parliament[54] (Prizel, 1998, p. 317; Subtelny, 1988, p. 298).

A comparison between Galicia after the break-up of the Austro-Hungarian Monarchy and Ukrainian lands in the former Russian Empire after the Bolshevik Revolution produces a seeming anomaly to the historical pattern. Independent Ukrainian Republics emerged in both former empires. However, Socialist parties were more influential in the Ukrainian National Republic (UNR) in Eastern Ukraine than in the West Ukrainian Republic led by the National Democratic Party in East Galicia. (Subtelny, 1988.) For example, in the elections to the All-Russian Constituent Assembly, the Ukrainian Party of Socialist Revolutionaries won three-quarters of all votes received by Ukrainians parties, which earned 62 percent of the total votes. Although the party supported the independence of Ukraine, it emphasized socialization of land as its main goal (Borys, 1977; Pipes, 1974/1954).[55] Its Russian counter-

---

[54]   In provinces populated by Ukrainians, the absolute majority of peasant electors who choose *Duma* deputies did not belong to any party (Emmons, 1983, pp. 249-252). In the First and Second *Duma*, a significant proportion of deputies from the Ukrainian caucus belonged to the Ukrainian Democratic Radical Party, which was linked to the liberal Constitutional Democratic Party of Russia (see *Encyclopedia*, 1984-1993, p. 378).

[55]   The left wing of the Ukrainian Party of Socialist Revolutionaries, which advocated cooperation with the Bolsheviks, formed its own party in 1919. The new party, called

part, the Russian Party of Socialist Revolutionaries, and the Bolsheviks received more than a third of the vote in Ukrainian provinces (25 and 10 percent respectively) (Radkey, 1989 and *Encyclopedia,* 1984-1993, p. 52). Even though they signified the rise of Ukrainian nationalism and national identity in Eastern regions, the results of the December 1917 elections, like the vote for the independence of Ukraine in 1991, were affected by the major political events that preceded the vote, i.e. the end of the Tsarist rule in February and the Bolshevik Revolution in October of the same year.

Pre-World War I political development in Bukovyna (Chernivtsi), which also was part of Austria, resembled that in Galicia in many aspects, such as the rise of Ukrainian educational, cultural, and political organizations. Ukrainian national identity was much less developed in Carpatho-Ukraine (Transcarpathia) than in the Austrian provinces of the Empire. Subtelny (1988, pp. 334-335) attributes this to the policy of Hungarization and isolation of the region, which belonged to the Hungarian part of the Austro-Hungarian Monarchy, and to Russophilism resulting from the arrival of Russian troops who sought to suppress the Hungarian uprising in 1848. Russophilism was stronger in Carpatho-Ukraine than in Galicia and Bukovyna. A separate national identity, called Rusyn, promoted by a local group of intelligentsia, gained significant popularity in the region. The relationship of the Rusyn nationality and language to Ukrainian, Russian, and Slovak nationality and language was a subject of controversy, in large part because of its political implications.[56] For example, Ukrainian nationalists viewed Rusyns as ethnic Ukrainians, while Russian nationalists regarded them as ethnic Russians (Dyrud, 1992).

Borot'bisty party was absorbed by the Bolsheviks in 1920. Most of *Borot'bisty* leaders and ordinary members were persecuted during the Great Terror.

[56] Rusyns are also called Carpatho Rusyns, Ruthenians, Carpathians, or Lemkos. According to the 1990 US Census, close to thirteen thousand people classify themselves as Rusyns or another of the above-mentioned categories. About a quarter of a million people with Eastern Slavic backgrounds emigrated to the United States from Carpatho-Ukraine and neighboring regions in Slovakia and Poland, identified as Rusyn areas, before World War I. Andy Warhol is often mentioned as the most prominent American of Rusyn descent. (See Magocsi, 1994.)

The history of the Transdniestria region of Moldova is similar to that of Eastern Ukraine. At the end of the eighteenth century, the Russian Empire incorporated the territory of Transdniestria, Crimea, and neighboring regions, which had been controlled by the Ottoman Empire.[57] At the beginning of the nineteenth century, the Russian Empire seized from the Ottoman Empire control over the territory of the Moldovan principality located on the right bank of the Dniester (Nistru).[58] (King, 2000, pp. 11-210; Magocsi, 1993a, pp. 74-75.) This Western part of modern Moldova, along with the Southwestern part of the present-day Odesa (Odessa) region in Ukraine, was called Bessarabia. Bessarabia was under Russian rule until World War I.

In right-bank Moldova, the Russian government eliminated autonomy, imposed severe restrictions on the Romanian language and culture, and instituted Russian as the language of education and governance. This policy lasted, with a brief interruption during the 1905 revolution, for almost a century. However, in contrast to Soviet times, the Russian government viewed Romanians and Moldovans (as Romanian-speaking inhabitants of the region called themselves) as the same ethnic group.

As a result of the efforts of local Romanian-speaking intelligentsia and intelligentsia in Romania, nationalism started to develop in Moldova in the second half of the nineteenth century and the beginning of the twentieth century. Nationalist cultural and political organizations were much more widespread in right-bank Moldova, primarily in Chishinau, than in the Transdniestria region. However, compared with Romania, which gained independence from the Ottoman Empire in 1878, national identity was weaker in right-bank Moldova. (See King, 2000.)

In contrast to results from Eastern Ukraine, regional results for the elections to the All-Russian Constitutional Assembly in Moldova are not available (Radkey, 1989). However, the indirect evidence points to the emergence

---

[57]   The territory of Transdniestria belonged to the East Slavic Kyiv Rus and Galicia-Volhynia principality, which existed mostly in the lands of present Western Ukraine after Kyiv Rus was conquered by the Mongolo-Tatars. In contrast to right-bank Moldova, Transdniestria was not part of the Moldovan principality in the Middle Ages.

[58]   The territory of present-day Moldova and Romania was under control of the Roman Empire during the second and third centuries. The Moldovan principality emerged in the fourteenth century, and came under Ottoman control during the sixteenth century. (See King, 2000, pp. 13-18; Meurs, 1994.)

of territorial political divisions at that time. Pro-Romanian nationalists had stronger positions in Bessarabia than in Transdniestria. In 1918, with the support of Romanian troops, the National Council (*Sfatul Tarii*), which was formed in Western Moldova, declared the unification of Bessarabia with Romania. (King, 2000, pp. 32-35.) In contrast, the pro-Romanian movement was much weaker in Transdniestria. Only 10 representatives from this region served on the National Council, which at various times had 125 to 162 members (van Meurs, 1994, pp. 78, 355). Transdniestria even became part of the Ukrainian National Republic during its short existence.

The divergent formation of political cultures in those Ukrainian regions that belonged to the Russian Empire and the Austro-Hungarian Monarchy did not extend to the same degree to the economic culture of Ukrainians. The involvement of Ukrainians in trade, industry, and other forms of business was limited. Most landowners, merchants, artisans, and industrial enterprise owners were from other ethnic groups: Poles, Russians, Jews, Hungarians, Romanians, Germans, and Armenians (Krawchenko, 1985; Subtelny, 1988). In both empires, the absolute majority of Ukrainians were peasants. For example, in 1900, 95 percent of Ukrainians in Galicia worked in agriculture, 1 percent worked in industry, and 0.2 percent worked in trade (Subtelny, 1988, pp. 270-271, 301). Before the abolition of serfdom, which occurred earlier in the Ukrainian regions of the Habsburg Empire (1848) than in the Russian Empire (1861), agricultural work consisted mostly of subsistence farming carried out by serfs. In both Empires, few peasants became market-oriented farmers after serfdom was abolished. By the beginning of the twentieth century, 80 percent of peasants in East Galicia were poor, owning less than 12 acres of land. About the same proportion of peasants in Eastern Ukraine and Volhynia owned less than 25 acres of land and were self-sufficient or subsistence farmers (Subtelny, 1988, pp. 263, 308). The economic situation of the Moldovan population in Bessarabia and Transdniestria was similar to that of Ukrainians in the Russian Empire and Austro-Hungary. Most Moldovans were poor peasants and had limited involvement in market activity (King, 2000).

Many of the same factors that affected the emergence of different regional political cultures in Ukraine fostered significant cultural differences between Ukrainian diasporas in Canada, the United States, Australia, South America, and Western European countries compared with Ukrainian diasporas in countries of the former Soviet Union. Ukrainian immigration to the first group of countries was primarily for economic and political reasons and originated in regions of the Habsburg Empire (Galicia and Carpatho-Ukraine). As a result, members of the Ukrainian diaspora in Canada, the United States, Australia, South America, and Western European countries have maintained a much stronger Ukrainian identity and support for Ukrainian independence and nationalism than have their counterparts in countries of the former Soviet Union.

The Ukrainian diaspora in Russia and other ex-Soviet countries, such as Kazakhstan, had many more members than did the Ukrainian diaspora in the West. Ukrainians in Russia, Kazakhstan, and other post-Soviet countries came mostly from Eastern Ukraine, and they demonstrated a pro-Russian orientation and weak support for Ukrainian independence and nationalism. Because of the same factors that favored the development of pro-Russian and pro-Communist values in Eastern regions of Ukraine, most Ukrainians in Russia and other countries of the former Soviet Union had a weak national identity, and the majority of them became Russified in their political values and language. For example, at the end of the 1990s, up to a quarter of the senators (members of the upper chamber of the parliament of Russia) were of Ukrainian descent, but they did not show a distinct pro-Ukrainian orientation. Differences between immigrants from Carpatho-Ukraine and Galicia parallel to a significant extent the political differences between these regions in Ukraine.

4.2   Historical experience of Ukrainian and Moldovan regions in the Soviet Union and East-Central European countries during the period between the two world wars

In his assessment of the aftermath of World War I, Mises (1983/1919, pp. 25-26) underlined the crucial role of historical factors in the development of a stronger Ukrainian identity in the Austro-Hungarian Monarchy than in the Russian Empire. He emphasized the effect of Austrian government policy, particularly in the area of education, and the role of the Catholic Church.[59] Comparing the prospects for a Ukrainian national identity, which he defined in terms of language, in the former Austro-Hungarian Monarchy and the Russian Empire, von Mises (1983/1919, p. 26) stated:

> The most recent political and social upheavals have furthered South Russian Ukrainism so much that it is not entirely impossible that it can no longer be overcome by Great Russianism. But that is no ethnographic or linguistic problem. Not the degree of relationship of languages and races will decide whether the Ukrainian or the Russian language will win out but rather political, economic, religious, and general cultural circumstances. It is easily possible for that reason that the final outcome will be different in the former Austrian and the Hungarian parts of the Ukraine than in the part that has long been Russian.

The separation of Ukrainian regions between the Soviet Union and East-Central European countries in the period after World War I and before World War II subjected residents of these regions to very different circumstances. After the collapse of the Austro-Hungarian Monarchy, Galicia (Halychyna), along with the Volyn and Rivne regions (a Western section of the Volhynia [Volyn] province of the Russian Empire), became part of Poland; Carpatho-Ukraine (Transcarpathia) belonged to Czechoslovakia during the inter-war period; and Bukovyna (Chernivtsi region) became part of Romania after World War I (Magocsi, 1993a, pp. 125-127). Moldovan regions, divided between the Soviet Union and Romania, also experienced different circumstances during the period between World War I and World War II. In contrast to Transdniestria, right-bank Moldova became part of Romania. Volhynia and

---

[59]   At the same time, Mises (1983/1919) neglected the role of intellectuals (the intelligentsia) in the development of a Ukrainian national identity. He implied that the influence of the Ukrainian movement from Galicia was the main factor in the emergence of the national identity in Eastern Ukraine. However, as noted, the Eastern Ukrainian intelligentsia, most notably Taras Shevchenko, whose poetry was interpreted as a call for Ukrainian independence, not only were ahead of Ukrainians in Austrian Galicia in the development of a literary language, but also formed the first pro-Ukrainian organization in the first half of the nineteenth century. Even though pro-Ukrainian parties had a smaller following and were more socialist-oriented than in the former Austro-Hungarian Monarchy, they also emerged in the Russian Empire at the beginning of the twentieth century.

Galicia in Poland, Carpatho-Ukraine in Czechoslovakia, and Bukovyna and right-bank Moldova in Romania enjoyed relatively more freedom of political associations, electoral politics, and national cultural development than did regions under Soviet rule.

The interwar historical legacy particularly affected the development of a national identity in Western (Bessarabian) Moldova and Volhynia. Romanian parties absorbed Moldovan parties and played a dominant role in elections in the region. The Romanian government promoted Romanian culture, language, and other aspects of national identity through various means. However, along with a Romanian national identity, a separate regional identity became evident in right-bank Moldova. The centralized policy of the Romanian administration was viewed by some of the region's population as neglectful of local interests. For example, the introduction of the Latin script led to a negative reaction from many Moldovans and Orthodox Church leaders, who were accustomed to the Cyrillic alphabet. (King, 2000, pp. 42-45.)

In Volhynia, which along with Galicia became part of Poland, a network of Ukrainian cultural, educational, and political organizations promoting Ukrainian national identity was active during the inter-war period. Educational organizations, such as *Prosvita,* and political parties, such as the Ukrainian National Democratic Union (based on the former National Democratic Party), extended their activities from Galicia to Volhynia. The Ukrainian National Democratic Union, which favored an independent Ukraine, won the absolute majority of seats held by Ukrainian deputies in the Polish parliament (*Sejm*). The party received a higher number of votes than did other Ukrainian parties in the 1928 elections. However, the elections also showed that Ukrainian pro-Soviet parties were stronger in Volhynia than in Galicia (Polonsky, 1972, pp. 248-249; Subtelny, 1988, pp. 435-437).

By the end of the 1930s, the Ukrainophile orientation in Carpatho-Ukraine appeared to be stronger than the Russophile and Rusyn orientations. In the 1939 elections to the parliament of quasi-independent Carpatho-Ukraine, which formed after the Munich Pact had weakened Czechoslovakia, Ukrainophiles received overwhelming support. The factors that affected the rise of a Ukrainian identity in Carpatho-Ukraine included Czechoslovakia's political system, which was the most democratic among East Central European countries, the government's support of the Ukrainophile orientation, and the closeness of local spoken language and folk culture to those in other Ukrainian regions (*Encyclopedia*, 1984-1993, p. 262; Subtelny, 1988, pp. 448-450).

Policies in the Ukrainian regions of East-Central European countries differed from Soviet policy in Eastern Ukraine. The Polish and Romanian governments implemented assimilation policies aimed at Ukrainians and imposed restrictions on Ukrainian culture and language, and civic and political organizations, especially after authoritarian regimes came to power in these countries in the 1930s. (See Polonsky, 1972; Subtelny, 1988.) However, attempts at Polonization in Galicia and Volhynia in the inter-war period had limited success. As Subtelny (1995, p. 197) puts it, "Galician Ukrainians created something like a state within the Polish state. Of all Ukrainians, they came closest to functioning as a civil society."

The Romanian government instituted a Romanization policy towards the local Ukrainian population in Bukovyna. Compared with the Austrian period, Ukrainian political and cultural activity in this region became limited. However, compared with the situation in Soviet Ukraine, Ukrainian political parties had much more freedom of activity in Bukovyna.

The Soviet government initially moved in a seemingly opposite direction by conducting a policy of Ukrainization. The ideology of the Bolshevik Party, which advanced Lenin's interpretation of Marxism in the 1910s and 1920s, emphasized "proletarian internationalism." It is noteworthy that the name of the Union of the Soviet Socialist Republics (USSR), which included most of the territory of the Russian Empire, did not contain a reference to a particular territory or ethnic group. This was a deliberate decision, because the Bolsheviks anticipated that other countries would join the Union after the victory of the Communist revolution in more economically developed countries. However, the Bolshevik leaders also moved to recognize the formal equality of ethnic groups during the transition to Communism, under which not only class but also ethnic differences were to be eliminated. Ukraine, like Russia, was given the status of a Union Republic when the Soviet Union was officially founded in 1922.

However, the effect of the Ukrainization policy on the development of a national identity in Eastern Ukraine was limited for several reasons. The policy of Ukrainization did not extend to the political arena. The activities of

Ukrainian non-Communist political organizations were prohibited in the Soviet Union, which was a one-party state. Education, even when it was conducted in the Ukrainian language, emphasized Communist ideology and focused on class struggle. The policy of Ukrainization was short-lived; it was reversed approximately a decade after it had been introduced. Beginning in the 1930s, Stalin instituted a policy of Russification. A large proportion of Ukrainian intelligentsia was accused of "bourgeois nationalism," which the Soviet leadership considered to be a political crime. Many of the intelligentsia perished during the mass terror campaign that reached its peak between 1937 and 1938, when several million people, including a significant number of Ukrainians, were arrested and exiled or executed. (Conquest, 1990; Krawchenko, 1985, pp. 133-134.) Accusations of nationalism resulted in the arrest and execution of almost all of the Communist Party leaders in Ukraine during the Great Terror. Communists sent from Russia took top positions in both the party and government in Soviet Ukraine. For instance, Nikita Khrushchev, an ethnic Russian who headed the Moscow Party organization, was appointed by Stalin in early 1938 to head the Communist Party in Soviet Ukraine (Khrushchev, 1970).[60]

The Moldovization policy in the Autonomous Moldovan Republic, which had been created in Soviet Ukraine in 1924, had one important difference from the Ukrainization policy:[61] the Soviet policy aimed at creating a separate Moldovan identity and language. One of its primary motivations was to provide a basis for Soviet territorial claims towards Romania regarding right-bank Moldova. Communist Party officials and Soviet scholars in the region propagated a theory that Moldovans were a separate nationality, distinct from Romanians. The same policy applied to a language that was promoted as a distinct Moldovan language, and not a dialect of the Romanian language. A Moldovan Cyrillic-based alphabet was instituted, except for a brief period in the mid-1930s when a Latin-based alphabet was used. Other factors that limited the effects of the Moldovization policy were the same as in Ukraine. (See King, 2000.)

---

[60]   Nikita Khrushchev spent part of his earlier career in Eastern Ukraine.
[61]   The territory of the autonomy included not only the Transdniestrian region, but also neighboring districts of Soviet Ukraine.

The artificial famine (the *Holodomor*), which resulted from Soviet collectivization and industrialization policies, disproportionately affected Ukrainian peasants.[62] At least several million of them died between 1932 and 1933 (see Conquest, 1986; Krawchenko, 1985; Kulchytskyi, 1995). The fact that the famine did not affect Western Ukraine, which was not under Soviet rule at that time, confirms its artificial character.[63]

However, the artificial famine and mass terror in Eastern Ukraine in the 1930s had less impact on the political culture of Ukrainians than the Nazi occupation and terror did. Because of the totalitarian nature of the Soviet society, censorship, and propaganda, many Ukrainians were unaware of the famine and the extent of the Soviet terror. The Soviet government and media did not mention the famine until the end of the 1980s. Similarly, the extent of the mass terror against Ukrainian intelligentsia was revealed to most Ukrainians only in the early 1990s.

During World War II, historical experiences of Ukrainians varied in different regions. The Nazi policy towards the Ukrainians – which included the conscription of millions of people for forced labor in Germany, the persecution of Communists, and mass executions of the local population under pretext of the retribution for partisan activity – was conducted the most aggressively and consistently in *Reichskommisariat Ukraine*; whose territory included most of Eastern Ukraine and Volhynia, where the Nazi administration headquarters were located.

In contrast, Galicia became part of the area controlled by the Nazi-run General Government of Poland. The legacy of Austrian rule was a major factor in explaining why Ukrainians in Galicia received less harsh treatment than did Ukrainians in regions of the former Russian Empire. For example, Heinrich Himmler viewed Ukrainians in these regions as Galicians who spoke the Galician language. The SS division, which was organized by Nazis after

---

[62] For the same reason, Ukrainians were under-represented in the Soviet Communist Party in the 1920s. However, their membership in the Soviet Communist Party significantly increased in the following decades (see Krawchenko, 1985). A similar situation occurred among ethnic Moldovans in Moldova.

[63] After World War II, a famine affected both Western and Eastern parts of Ukraine and Moldova. As in Ukraine, Moldovan peasants, who constituted the majority of the rural population, were disproportionately affected by the famine that claimed more than 100,000 lives in Moldova alone (see King, 2000, p. 96).

the German Army suffered a major defeat in Stalingrad, was called "Galicia" (Kosyk, 1993, pp. 360-361).

During World War II, Bukovyna came under the control of Romania, a German ally. Hungary, another German ally, controlled Transcarpathia during the war. The experience of Ukrainians in these regions was not as harsh as in the Nazi-controlled regions, but it was much worse than that of Hungarians and Romanians. (Marples, 1992, pp. 49-53; Subtelny, 1988, pp. 465-470.)

The Nazis, who regarded Ukrainians and other Slavs as racially inferior, planned to colonize Ukraine and exterminate or expel most of the local population to Siberia. (See Kosyk, 1993, p. 246; Madajczyk, 1962.) This policy, outlined in the "Generalplan Ost," helped to legitimize to a certain extent Soviet rule in Eastern Ukraine.[64] For example, several million Soviet Army soldiers, a significant proportion of whom were Eastern Ukrainians, surrendered to the German Army at the start of the war. However, the treatment of Soviet prisoners of war, about three million of whom perished in Nazi concentration camps, significantly reduced defections and strengthened the resistance of the Red Army. Besides those killed in combat, about three to five million Ukrainians, or more than one in ten of the pre-war population, perished during World War II. (See Rummel, 1992; Subtelny, 1988, pp. 466-470.)

The historical experience during the Nazi occupation had a considerable influence on the evolution of political culture in Ukraine. A member of almost every Ukrainian family had been killed, wounded, or sent into forced labor in Germany during the war (see Reyent and Lisenko, 1995). Soviet authorities publicized the Nazi atrocities against the local population in Ukraine and branded Western Ukrainian nationalists as Nazi allies. The Soviet government and media described different groups of victims only as "Soviet citizens" and suppressed information about conflicts between radical nationalists and Nazis during the war.

---

[64]   The scale and genocidal nature of Nazi policy towards ethnic Ukrainians, several millions of whom were killed as a consequence of the Nazi occupational policy during World War II, is often overlooked in the West. The Nuremberg Trials characterized the Nazi policy towards Ukrainians as genocide. The UN Convention on Genocide, adopted shortly after the trials, reflected in its definition of genocide specific policies and plans that the Nazis had developed to deal with Ukrainians and other Slavic people. (See, for example, Trials, 1946-1949, Vol. IV, pp. 599-627, and Vol. V, pp. 30-41; Welch, 1999.)

In Moldova, the wartime policy of Nazis and their Romanian allies was harsher in the Transdniestria region, which became part of a special military district of Romania, than in Bessarabia – with the exception of Jews, who were subject to total elimination in both regions. The racial views of the Nazis and their Romanian allies were more favorable towards Moldovans than towards Ukrainians and Russians, who constituted a much larger proportion of the population in the Transdniestria region. In addition, most Soviet and Communist officials in Moldova were from Transdniestria.

Radical Ukrainian nationalist organizations assumed a leading role in West Ukrainian politics during World War II. The decline of moderate nationalist parties in Western Ukraine as a result of the authoritarian policies of Polish and Romanian governments in the 1930s, and the imposition of the Soviet and then Nazi rule contributed to the ascent of the radical Ukrainian nationalists. Underground organizations, such as the Organization of Ukrainian Nationalists (OUN), which advanced the ideology of radical nationalism, were much better suited to activity under non-democratic regimes and wartime conditions. Another factor in the rise of radical nationalist organizations was their initial support by Nazi Germany. However, a group of nationalist leaders, who attempted to declare a Ukrainian state after Germany invaded the Soviet Union in 1941, was arrested by Nazis. (See Magocsi, 1996, pp. 626-627.) Although the Organization of Ukrainian Nationalists, which split into two rival factions, attempted to expand its influence in Eastern Ukraine during World War II, Western Ukraine remained the main stronghold of the OUN. Western regions, especially forested parts of Volhynia and Galicia, contained the main bases of Ukrainian nationalist partisans, who called themselves the Ukrainian Insurgent Army (UPA), and mainly fought against the Polish and Soviet presence until the early 1950s.

In contrast, the majority of Soviet partisan groups emerged in Eastern Ukraine with the direct assistance of Soviet authorities. Several of the Soviet partisan groups moved into Western Ukraine, mainly forested parts of Volhynia and Galicia, but they did not find the same support among local Ukrainians that the nationalist partisans found. Regional cultural differences played an important role in this case. Although ethnic Ukrainians constituted more than half of the Soviet partisans, they came predominantly from Eastern Ukraine. (Armstrong, 1990, p. 110; Subtelny, 1988, pp. 473-476.)

Ukrainians from Western Ukraine and Eastern Ukraine were often on the opposite sides of the war. Several military units composed mainly of Western Ukrainians, most notably the SS volunteer Galicia Division, fought as part of the German Army against the Soviet Army, which included more than five million Eastern Ukrainians. (Mukovskyi and Lysenko, 1997). The Ukrainian Insurgent Army also clashed with Soviet Army units and the Soviet partisans. Ukrainian nationalists in Western Ukraine continued their armed resistance to the Soviet state and its representatives, who included many Eastern Ukrainians, after World War II until the Soviet state suppressed it by military force and mass expulsions of its supporters. (See Burds, 1997.)

The World War II experience was used by the Communist leadership as a basis for legitimizing Soviet rule; it played a prominent role in Soviet propaganda, education, and popular culture in both Ukraine and Moldova. Pro-Communist and pro-Russian parties and politicians in Ukraine and Moldova also often invoked the war experience.

Class-based factors contributed to the development of a more pro-Communist political culture in the Eastern regions of Ukraine and Moldova in the first half of the twentieth century. The working class was strongest in Eastern Ukraine, particularly in industrial centers of Donbas and Kharkiv, and in the Transdniestria region of Moldova. Donbas became a major industrial region, with a large working class, in the Russian Empire. In contrast, Ukrainian regions of the Austro-Hungarian Monarchy were less industrialized. The national income per capita in Western Ukrainian regions of the Austro-Hungarian Monarchy was lower than in Ukrainian regions of the Russian Empire before World War I. (See Koropeckyj, 1990, pp. 72-92.) On the eve of the Bolshevik Revolution in 1917, the Communists had a much stronger influence in Donbas than in other regions of Ukraine (Krawchenko, 1985, p. 99). Communists in Eastern Ukraine, aided by Bolshevik troops, proclaimed the existence of the Soviet Republic in Kharkiv in 1918. Soviet industrialization policy in the 1930s intensified the growth of the working class in Eastern Ukraine, most notably in Donbas. The Transdniestria region in Moldova also grew into a major industrial center with a strong working class during the Soviet period. (King, 2000, pp. 183-184.)

The evolution of economic culture differed to a lesser extent among regions of Ukraine and Moldova during the inter-war period than did the evolution of political culture. Ukrainians, Moldovans, and the Gagauz overwhelmingly remained poor peasants (King, 2000; Krawchenko, 1985; Polonsky, 1972, p. 37). Land was confiscated from the large landowners and divided among peasants in Eastern Ukraine and Transdniestria following the Bolshevik Revolution, but its sale was prohibited. At the end of the 1920s, Stalin abandoned the NEP (New Economic Policy) introduced by the Bolsheviks in the beginning of the 1920s after their failed attempt to establish Communism, and instead instituted a policy of mass collectivization (Boettke, 1990). The land, capital, and labor of peasants became state property. By the early 1930s, rich peasants in the Soviet Ukraine and Transdniestria had been deprived of their property and sent to Siberia into exile, where many of them perished. The proportion of Ukrainians employed in industry and trade occupations significantly increased in the 1920s and 1930s. However, these economic sectors, with the partial exception of the NEP period, became non-market-oriented after the nationalization of private property and the introduction of state economic planning.

In the Western regions of Ukraine and Moldova, Ukrainian, Moldovan, and Gagauz peasants remained overwhelmingly poor, but their involvement in market activity at the end of the 1930s was relatively higher than in Soviet Ukraine and Soviet Moldova. Cooperatives and credit unions became widespread among Ukrainian peasants, especially in Galicia and Volhynia in Poland. However, regional differences in market activity involvement were not as strong as differences in the realm of political involvement. (King, 2000, p. 41; Subtelny, 1988, pp. 432-433, 437-438, 448-449.)

4.3   Post-war Soviet legacy in Ukrainian and Moldovan regions

As a result of World War II, Western Ukraine and the Bessarabian region of Moldova were incorporated, like the Baltic States and Western Belarus, into the Soviet Union. According to the Soviet-Nazi Pact of 1939, the Soviet Union occupied Galicia and Volhynia provinces following Nazi Germany's invasion of Poland in 1939, and took over Bukovyna and Bessarabia (including right-bank Moldova and the Southern part of the Odesa region) from Romania in

1940. Transcarpathia was transferred from Czechoslovakia to Soviet Ukraine in 1945. (Magocsi, 1993a, pp. 160-162; Subtelny, 1988.)

Crimea, which became part of Soviet Ukraine in 1954, had a distinctive historical experience. The region was transferred from Russia by a decision of Nikita Khrushchev, who succeeded Stalin as the Soviet Communist Party leader. The Soviet authorities promoted the decision, which was linked to the three-hundredth anniversary of a union treaty between Cossack leaders in Eastern Ukraine and the Russian Tsar, as a symbol of close ties between Ukrainians and Russians. (Solchanyk, 1995, pp. 4-5.) The political culture in Crimea was strongly affected by the population movement. Large-scale Russian and Ukrainian settlement in the region, which had begun in the nineteenth century, intensified during the aftermath of World War II, when the Soviet authorities deported Crimean Tatars, as well as Germans, Armenians, Bulgarians, and several other smaller ethnic groups. These population changes fostered the pro-Russian political culture in Crimea. After the war, Russians became the largest ethnic group in the region. They constituted the absolute majority of the population. (Lieven, 1999, pp. 105-111; Yevtoukh, 1995.)

World War II and the mass expulsion of Crimean Tatars by Stalin, which affected lives of almost every Crimean Tatar, had reinforced their cultural differentiation from Russians and Ukrainians. During the war, about 10 percent of the Crimean Tatars, a large proportion of them voluntarily, joined German military and police units and fought against Soviet partisans. Although comparable proportions of Crimean Tatars served in the Soviet Army and belonged to Soviet partisans in Crimea, the proportion of Tatars collaborating with the Nazis was much higher than proportions of collaborators among Russians and Ukrainians. (Zinchenko, 1998.)

Available data indicate that about 13 to 15 percent of Russians and Ukrainians in Crimea perished as a result of the Nazi genocidal policy, which included mass executions, deprivation of elementary medical care, and deliberate starvation of civilians and POWs. Approximately 5 to 7 percent of Russians and Ukrainians in Crimea, who served in the Soviet Army, were killed fighting Nazi Germany and its allies. About 8 to 10 percent of Russians and Ukrainians in Crimea were sent by the Nazi wartime administration into forced labor.[65] The Nazis, who regarded not only Russians and Ukrainians but also Crimean Tatars as racially inferior, planned to colonize Crimea and extermi- nate or expel most of the local population to Siberia. (See Aly and Heim, 2002; Kosyk, 1993.)

At the end of the war, Stalin collectively punished the Crimean Tatars because a fraction of them had collaborated with the Nazis. All Crimean Tatars were deported, along with other ethnic minorities, by force from Cri- mea to Central Asia in 1944, and the autonomous status of the Crimean Tatar Republic was eliminated. A significant proportion of Crimean Tatars, esti- mated at more than 20 percent, perished during the deportation and its after- math, primarily, as a result of infectious diseases and poor nutrition. (See Bekirova, 2004; Pohl, 1999.) Like the experience of Russians and Ukrainians during the war in Crimea, the experience of Crimean Tatars during their mass deportation and life in exile had a profound effect on the evolution of their po- litical culture.

Both the ethnic cleansing of Crimean Tatars and the historical ex- perience of Russians and Ukrainians during World War II – and the subse- quent mythologization of these events on both sides – fueled political tensions between Crimean Tatars and Russians, as well as pro-Russian Ukrainians. The experience of deportation and exile, which lasted until the end of the Soviet Union, led to the emergence of the Crimean Tatar national movement. This movement, which initially focused on the demand for their re- turn to Crimea, received strong support among Crimean Tatars by the time of the Soviet Union's collapse. (See Bekirova, 2004.) Similarly, pro-Communist and pro-Russian parties and politicians in Crimea often invoked the historical experience during World War II to justify their political demands, in particular their stance towards Crimean Tatars.

Experience of the Gagauz in the Soviet Union differed from the ex- perience of Crimean Tatars. The Gagauz were one of the least educated and most impoverished groups in Moldova during Romanian rule during the peri- ods of 1918 to 1940 and 1941 to 1944. After Moldova came under Soviet rule

---

[65]   These numbers are estimated from the data on the ethnic composition of the popula- tion before the war, civilian and POW losses in Crimea, and the overall Soviet civil- ian, POW, and military losses in Ukraine during World War II. (See Kosyk, 1993, pp. 625-627; *Nazi Crimes in Ukraine: 1941-1945*, 1987, p. 363.)

as a result of World War II, a significant number of the Gagauz benefited from the Soviet policy of mass education and economic development in the region. This experience helped to foster pro-Communist and pro-Russian political values among the Gagauz.

Many Gagauz died during a post-war famine when Bessarabian Moldova again came under Soviet rule. However, like the artificial famine (the *Holodomor*) in Eastern Ukraine in the 1930s, the famine in Moldova failed to transform the political culture of the Gagauz into an anti-Russian and anti-Soviet culture. Because the totalitarian Soviet state, which controlled all institutions with the exception of family, maintained strict censorship and actively spread propaganda that prevented the dissemination of information about this event, many Gagauz remained unaware of the extent of the famine beyond their own personal experience or the experience of their families. In contrast to many Crimean Tatars in exile in Central Asia, who attributed the extremely high death rate from infectious diseases and lack of food to Soviet policy towards them, the Gagauz attributed the famine to natural causes and to the destruction of agriculture and industry by World War II, and they did not associate the famine with Soviet policy towards them.

During World War II and its aftermath, there were significant changes to the population structure in the territories of Ukraine and Moldova. As noted, the majority of the Jewish population in Ukraine and Moldova perished as the result of the Nazi-organized Holocaust, in which the governments of Romania and Hungary participated. Many inhabitants of Moldova moved to Romania before the Soviet troops occupied the region in 1940.[66] Most of the Germans from Western Ukraine and Bessarabia (including right-bank Moldova) were transferred to Germany in accordance with the 1939 Soviet-Nazi agreement. Other Germans evacuated along with the retreating German troops. Many were later captured by the Soviet authorities and, along with the Germans remaining in the area, were exiled to Siberia and Central Asia.[67] Most of the Poles, Czechs, and Slovaks in Western Ukraine (more than a million people)

---

[66] For example, Emil Constantinescu, who was President of Romania from 1995 to 2000, was born in the Bessarabian region of Moldova.

[67] During World War I, Germans in Volhynia were moved by the Russian authorities to other regions not affected by the war. A large proportion of these Germans immigrated to the United States after the war rather than returning to the region.

were forced to move to Poland and Czechoslovakia, and most of the Ukrainians in Poland and Czechoslovakia (about half a million people) were forcibly resettled in Western Ukraine. This ethnic cleansing was the result of governmental policies of the Soviet Union, Poland, and Czechoslovakia, which were approved by the US and British governments, and of violent actions of Ukrainian and Polish radical nationalists (See Magocsi, 1993a, pp. 164-168; Snyder, 1999; Ther and Siljak, 2001.)

The Holocaust of the Jews and the forcible transfers of other groups of people made the historical regions of Ukraine and Moldova much more ethnically homogeneous during the post-war period. The Soviet policy of residence permits prevented large scale inter-regional migration in Ukraine and Moldova, except for certain categories of specialists and army personnel, which were mostly assigned from Russia, Eastern Ukraine, and Transdniestria to Western regions of Ukraine and Moldova. These factors helped to conserve cultural differences between Ukrainians and Moldovans living in different historical regions during the Soviet period.

Western regions of Ukraine and Moldova experienced the Soviet terror after they came under Soviet rule. Many members of the intelligentsia in Western Ukraine and Moldova were arrested and perished or exiled to Siberia as a result of the Stalin terror, which continued from the end of the 1930s to the beginning of the 1950s. Estimates of the number of people arrested or deported to Siberia from Western Ukraine and Moldova range from a hundred thousand to more than a million. In addition to Ukrainian and Moldovan intelligentsia, rich peasants, members of nationalist organizations, most members of the Polish, Romanian, and Jewish upper classes, government officials, army officers, and party leaders were also arrested, executed, or deported.

The Russian Communist leadership played a significant role in both Soviet Republics during that time. For example, Leonid Brezhnev was the head of a regional party committee in Eastern Ukraine at the end of the 1940s and occupied the highest post in the Communist Party of Moldova at the beginning of the 1950s. Konstantin Chernenko, another future Soviet leader, served as party propaganda chief in Moldova from 1948 until 1956.[68] (King,

---

[68] Although Konstantin Chernenko had a Ukrainian last name, he was born in Siberia and regarded himself as a Russian.

2000, p. 98.) Nikita Khrushchev headed the Communist party of Ukraine from the end of the 1930s until the end of the 1940s.

The policy of Communist modernization, implemented from the late 1920s in Eastern Ukraine and Transdniestria, was conducted in Western Ukraine and Western Moldova from 1939 to 1941 and after the war.[69] This policy included the nationalization of private property, mass collectivization, the arrest and exile of rich peasants, and industrialization. (See King, 2000, p. 96; Marples, 1992, pp. 24-41.) Soviet policy aimed to accelerate the integration of Western regions into the Soviet system and to level economic differences among historical regions. For example, Western Ukrainian regions had faster rates of economic growth, urbanization, and educational development than Eastern Ukraine. (Bilinsky, 1975.) By the end of the 1980s, inter-regional and inter-ethnic differences in the urbanization rate, education level, and occupation structure had significantly declined in Ukraine and Moldova.

Beginning in 1939, Soviet education policy in both groups of historical regions in Ukraine and Moldova was based on standard education programs, courses, and textbooks. The curriculum, heavily influenced by Soviet ideology, was uniform in all regions during the Soviet period. The only major difference was that the Ukrainian language was more widely used in education in Western Ukraine than in Eastern Ukraine. Unlike Eastern Ukrainians, who increasingly switched to the Russian language, Western Ukrainians became urbanized without adopting the Russian language. (Szporluk, 1979.)

As noted, differences in economic culture or social capital were not as significant as political differences among historical regions of Ukraine and Moldova. However, family, which remained outside of direct Soviet control, helped to sustain different political cultures in the Western regions of Ukraine and Moldova during Soviet times. Extended family members, including parents and grandparents, who had been born before Western Ukraine and Moldova came under Soviet rule, influenced the political socialization of the generations born during Soviet rule.[70]

---

[69]   Almond (1983, 1990) argues that one can view Communist modernization as a test of political culture theory.

[70]   Coleman (1988) argues that family plays a major role in the transmission of social capital from one generation to the next.

Despite their economic convergence and uniform education policy, Western and Eastern Ukraine showed some signs of political differences during Soviet rule. Western Ukraine, when compared with Eastern Ukraine, played a disproportionate role in the anti-Soviet dissident movements. (Kuzio and Wilson, 1994.) More than half of the ethnic Ukrainian dissidents were born in Western Ukraine; this is several times more than the region's share of Ukraine's population (Bilocerkowycz, 1988, p. 112). Ukrainian remained the primary language of inter-personal communication in Western Ukraine even during Soviet times, in contrast to Eastern Ukraine, where Russian was the main language.

The Communist Party of the Soviet Union (CPSU) possessed the monopoly of power in Ukraine and Moldova, which had the status of Union republics in the Soviet Union. The Communist Party of Soviet Ukraine and the Communist Party of Soviet Moldova were integral parts of the CPSU. However, there were regional differences even in Communist party leadership. Prior to the start of *perestroika*, the top Communist leaders in Ukraine and Moldova came either from Eastern regions of these Republics or from Russia. (King, 2000, p. 100.) Communists from the Western regions rose to upper leadership positions only at the end of the 1990s; many of them, including future presidents Luchinski and Snegur in Moldova and Kravchuk in Ukraine, became supporters of independence from the Soviet Union.

As soon as the monopoly of the Soviet Communist Party was lifted and the prosecution of non-Communist organizations was suspended during Gorbachev's reforms at the end of the 1980s, opposition organizations emerged in Western Ukraine and right-bank Moldova. Western Ukraine showed a higher level of political participation and stronger support for anti-Communist opposition than did Eastern Ukraine during Gorbachev's *perestroika*. (See Kuzio and Wilson, 1994.) Western regions led other regions of Ukraine in the development of civil society, including political, cultural, and religious organizations (Subtelny, 1995). During the 1990 elections to the Soviet Ukraine and Moldova republican parliaments – the first elections in more than

70 years to allow the participation of opposition politicians — the nationalist candidates received the strongest support in the Western regions.[71] Candidates from the oppositional Democratic Bloc, dominated by nationalists in Western Ukraine, won the absolute majority of seats in the former Galicia (93 percent) and two-thirds of the seats in the Volyn region. In contrast, the Democratic Bloc won less than one-fifth (18 percent) of the seats in the Eastern regions. (Birch, 1995; Potichnyj, 1992).

The city of Kyiv was the only region in Eastern Ukraine where the opposition won the majority (82 percent) of parliamentary seats. A concentration of Ukrainian cultural intelligentsia, students, and migrants from Western Ukraine provided support for the development of nationalist parties and organizations in Kyiv city during Gorbachev's reforms. For example, Ukrainian writers in Kyiv played a major role in founding *Rukh*, which became the leading nationalist organization in Ukraine.

In the elections to the republican parliament of Moldova in 1990, about one-third of the elected deputies were adherents of the nationalist Popular Front (Crowther, 1997a, p. 293). Most of them won their seats in the Western part of Moldova. Support for Moldovan nationalist candidates was much weaker in the Transdniestria region. A majority of the deputies elected in the Transdniestria were adherents of the United Council of Workers' Collectives and strike committees (Babilunga and Bomeshko, 1998, p. 25). These organizations, led by directors of large state enterprises in Transdniestria, opposed the language law that made Romanian the official language in Moldova, and favored the preservation of the Soviet Union and many elements of the Communist political and economic system (see Dima, 1999; King, 1994b).

---

[71]   The 1990 elections to the republican parliaments of Ukraine and Moldova were the first elections that allowed multiple candidates to participate. However, nationalist candidates ran as independents or even as members of the Communist Party because other parties were not allowed to officially nominate their candidates. (See Potichnyj, 1992.)

4.4   Religion and historical legacies in Ukraine and Moldova

Religious divisions coincide with historical regional divisions in Ukraine to some extent, but they are not equivalent as is sometimes assumed. For example, Huntington (1993, pp. 158-159, 165) and Miller et al. (1998, p. 71) state that the division between Western Ukraine and Eastern Ukraine corresponds to the cultural division between the Greek Catholic and Orthodox religions. However, among historical regions of Western Ukraine, the Greek Catholic (Uniate) religion is influential in the former Galicia and to a lesser degree in Carpatho-Ukraine, while in Volhynia and Bukovyna it has almost no influence. In these regions, as in Eastern Ukraine, the Orthodox religion is prevalent. The 1996 World Values Survey shows that half (51 percent) of the respondents in Galicia are Catholic, compared with 31 percent in Carpatho-Ukraine, 4 percent in Bukovyna, and 0 to 1 percent in other regions of Ukraine. In all historic regions other than Galicia, the Orthodox constitute the majority of the population.[72] (See Table 4.1.)

The religious division in Ukraine dates back to the end of the sixteenth century, when a group of Orthodox bishops from Western Ukraine accepted the Pope's authority but preserved their Orthodox rite. The Greek Catholic Church, or Uniate Church as it was called, became the leading church in Galicia during the eighteenth century, when its union with the Vatican was implemented and it received backing from the Habsburg Monarchy. (Himka, 1999.) The Greek Catholic Church lost its position in Volhynia after the Russian government launched a campaign to reconvert the Church members to Orthodox Christianity in the 1830s (Subtelny, 1988, p. 211).

---

[72] Another study shows similar regional patterns of the religious composition of the population of Ukraine. (See Table A.1.)

Table 4.1 Religious affiliation in historical regions of Ukraine and Moldova (%). (1996 World Values Survey)

	Crimea	Eastern Ukraine excl. Crimea	Galicia	Bukovyna	Carpatho-Ukraine	Volhynia	Gagauzia	Moldova excl. Transdniestria
Orthodox	49	58	40	80	55	95	98	83
Catholic	0	1	51	4	31	0	0	0
Other	5	1	7	3	7	3	0	2
None	46	40	2	13	7	2	3	16
Total (%)	100	100	100	100	100	100	100	100
N	127	2035	260	46	58	164	40	943

Note: Survey question: "Do you belong to a religious denomination. If 'Yes,' which one?"

The influence of the Greek-Catholic and Orthodox Churches on the development of national identity was greatly enhanced by the fact that most Ukrainians and Moldovans were illiterate prior to World War I. Uniate clergy played a major role in the development of a Ukrainian national identity in Galicia (see Himka, 1999; Isaievych, 1994). In contrast to Roman Catholic Poles, Ukrainians in Austrian Galicia were mostly Greek Catholics. This made their Polonization more difficult than the Russification of Ukrainians in the Russian Empire. The Soviet authorities liquidated the Ukrainian Greek Catholic Church in 1946, and forced its members either to join the Russian Orthodox Church or to give up their religious beliefs. However, some of the Greek Catholic priests and church members continued their religious activity underground despite prosecution. Motyl (1993, p. 8) summarized the role of the Greek Catholic Church in developing Ukrainian national identity as follows:

> For most of the last two centuries, Uniate Catholicism has served as the main prop for Ukrainian national identity in Western Ukraine: in its retention of Orthodox rites, Greek Catholicism distinguished Ukrainians from the Poles, and in its subordination to the Pope, it distinguished them from the Orthodox Russians.

Eastern Ukrainians and Russians shared the same religion, Orthodox Christianity. The Orthodox Church in Ukraine came under the authority of the Moscow patriarch at the end of the seventeenth century (Kohut, 1988, p. 68). Greenfeld (1992, pp. 238-239) notes that a significant number of the first cohorts of university students in Moscow and St. Petersburg in the second half of the eighteenth century, who became the earlier promoters of Russian nationalism, came from the Kyiv Academy, which was the largest seminary in the Russian Empire. Ukrainians occupied a disproportionately large number of leadership positions in the Russian Orthodox Church (Wilson, 2000, pp. 74-75).

The development of a separate national identity was slowed somewhat in Bukovyna because Ukrainians and Romanians were members of the same Orthodox Church. In Volhynia, the role of the Orthodoxy was more mixed. The Orthodox Church hindered the development of the Ukrainian identity during the Russian and Soviet rule. However, many Orthodox priests started to use Ukrainian after the Church in the region became part of an independent (Autocephalous) church in inter-war Poland. (Subtelny, 1988, pp. 440-441.)

Both Moldovans and Russians belonged to the Orthodox Church, which was a factor encouraging Russification in both historical regions of Moldova during the Russian, and then Soviet, rule. The Orthodox Church in right-bank (Bessarabian) Moldova became part of the Moscow patriarchate at the beginning of the nineteenth century, and the Russian language was instituted in many of its establishments (King, 2000, p. 25). However, during the inter-war period, the Orthodox Church in right-bank Moldova underwent a process of Romanization.

During the inter-war period, the Soviet Communist Party promoted atheism in Eastern Ukraine and Transdniestria and prosecuted a significant proportion of the Orthodox clergy. For example, the Ukrainian Autocephalous Orthodox Church, which was created to undermine the influence of the Russian Orthodox Church, was dissolved in 1930 because of its connection with the show trial of the Union for the Liberation of Ukraine, an organization invented by the Soviet Communist leadership and security organs. A significant proportion of the convicted members of the non-existent organization were associated with the Church. In the 1930s, most of the Church's leaders were arrested, as were ordinary priests (Magocsi, 1996, p. 565).

The Soviet policy of atheism continued after World War II, when Western regions of Ukraine and Moldova were incorporated into the Soviet Union. However, beginning during the war, when the Russian Orthodox Church was used to help mobilize the Soviet population in the war against Nazi Germany, the Soviet authorities adopted a more lenient position towards the Church.

These policy differences contributed to the stronger position of the Orthodox Church in the Western Ukraine regions outside of Galicia compared with Eastern Ukraine. It is estimated that 60 percent of all Orthodox parishes in Soviet Ukraine were located in those Western regions; however, these figures significantly overestimate the strength of the Orthodox Church in Western Ukraine because they include many former Greek Catholic parishes that were forcibly incorporated by the Russian Orthodox Church (Bilocerkowycz, 1988, pp. 86-91). Residents of Western Ukraine are more religious than their

Eastern counterparts. The proportion of non-believers is significantly higher in Crimea and other regions of Eastern Ukraine (40 to 46 percent) than in Western Ukrainian regions (2 to 13 percent). (See Table 4.1.) The density of religious communities is also significantly higher in Western regions (Iurash, 2000).

During the post-Communist period, the division between different Orthodox churches followed the historical division to a considerable extent. The newly established Ukrainian Orthodox Church (Kyiv Patriarchate) and the Ukrainian Autocephalous Church, which declared their independence from the Russian Orthodox Church and were associated with nationalist politicians, gained their strongest support in Western regions, while the Ukrainian Orthodox Church (Moscow Patriarchate) and the Russian Orthodox Church maintained their strongest positions in Eastern regions. (See Martyniuk, 1994.)

A similar regional division occurred in the Orthodox Church of Moldova after the collapse of Communism. The absolute majority of Moldovans remained Orthodox Christians. However, the newly formed Bessarabian Metropolitan Church became strongest in the Bessarabian region of Moldova, while Transdniestria and Gagauzia remained strongholds of the Russian Orthodox Church. (See Table 4.1.)

The role of religion was closely interlinked with historical legacy in the emergence and evolution of political culture among the Gagauz. Compared with other regions of Moldova, the Gagauz region had a distinct history. Before their arrival, at the end of the eighteenth century and beginning of the nineteenth century, in Southern Moldova and the neighboring area in the Odesa region of Ukraine, the Gagauz had populated the Dobrudja area, which is now part of Romania and Bulgaria (King, 2000, pp. 210-211). The reason for their resettlement in the region was due to their adherence to Orthodox Christianity. Because of their religion, the Gagauz in the Ottoman Empire suffered discrimination and persecution, especially at the time of the Russian-Turkish wars. The Russian Tsars proclaimed themselves defenders of the Orthodox people in the Balkans; they were involved, including militarily, in Balkan politics and provided lands to the Gagauz in Bessarabia.[73] This fa-

---

[73]   In addition to the Gagauz, thousands of Bulgarians, Serbs, Albanians, and Greeks resettled from the Balkans to Southern Moldova and Southern Ukraine.

vored treatment led to the Gagauz's pro-Russian views, which lasted through Soviet times (Chinn and Roper, 1998, p. 89; Katchanovski, 2005).

Similarly, religion and historical legacy were closely interlinked in the emergence of the political culture of Bulgarians, who, like the Gagauz, had migrated from the Ottoman Empire to Southern Moldova and the Odesa region of Ukraine because of their adherence to Orthodox Christianity. This experience was crucial to the emergence of pro-Russian values among Bulgarians in Moldova.

As noted in chapter 2, some scholars, such as Huntington (1996), attribute regional political cleavages in Ukraine to religious differences and conflicts between the Greek Catholics and the Orthodox Christians. Analysis of the 1996 World Values Survey data shows that the Greek Catholics are much more likely to support nationalist parties than are the Orthodox Christians (79 and 35 percent, respectively), who are in turn much more likely to favor Communist parties than Catholics (28 and 2 percent, respectively).

However, historical legacy outweighs the effect of religion. The difference between Catholics and Orthodox Christians in their political orientations in Western Ukraine is smaller than the difference in political orientations of Orthodox Christians in historically Western and Eastern regions. Eighty-one percent of the Catholic respondents and 58 percent of the Orthodox respondents in Western Ukraine support nationalist parties, compared with 28 percent of the Orthodox respondents in Eastern Ukraine. The same pattern characterizes support for Communist parties among Western Ukrainian Catholics and Orthodox Christians (2 and 12 percent, respectively), compared with Eastern Ukrainian Orthodox Christians (34 percent).[74]

Among other religious groups, Muslims are concentrated in Crimea, where the absolute majority of them are Crimean Tatars. The emergence of differences in political culture between Crimean Tatars and Ukrainians, as well as Russians, goes back to the period when the Crimean khanate controlled Crimea and neighboring regions in Southern Ukraine and Southern Russia. The Crimean khanate was a remnant of the Mongol Tatar Empire and its successor states, which ruled much of Eurasia in the first half of the previ-

---

[74]   The number of the Greek Catholic respondents in Eastern Ukraine is too small to include in this analysis.

ous millennium. The khanate became a vassal state of the Ottoman Empire at the end of the fifteenth century.

Differences in historical experience between Crimean Tatars, Ukrainians, and Russians were linked to religion. The main line of division in the Crimean khanate, as in other parts of the Ottoman Empire, ran between Muslims and Christians. Crimean Tatars were Muslims, while Ukrainians and Russians were Orthodox Christians. Slavery and the slave trade were important institutions in the Crimean khanate. Because Islam prohibited the enslavement of fellow Muslims, Ukrainians and Russians were the targets of frequent raids by Crimean Tatars. A significant number of them, estimated at tens of thousands each year, were captured and sold as slaves in Crimea. Such practices lasted several centuries. (See Khodarkovsky, 2002; Kryms'kyi, 1924/1996; Hellie, 1982; Inalcik, 1979; Lieven, 2001; Pohl, 1999; Williams, 2001.)

Scholars who describe the religious tolerance of the Ottoman Empire overlook the massive slave trade of the Crimean khanate, an Ottoman vassal state and a major source of slaves sold in the Empire. The subject of slavery in the Crimean khanate receives extremely limited coverage in Western scholarly literature despite its massive scale and its continuing effect on ethnic tensions in Crimea. Soviet historians also downplayed the role of slavery in the Crimean khanate because it did not fit the Marxist view of historical development as the movement from a slave-owning society in ancient times towards feudalism in medieval times, and then into capitalism and Communism in modern times.

While the religious law of Islam recognized Orthodox Christians as "People of the Book" and granted them a protected but second-class status, informal institutions and practices in the Ottoman Empire did not always follow this formal interpretation of the law, as evidenced by the enslaving of Orthodox Christian children in the Balkans for the military and government service, the genocide of Christian Armenians during World War I, and the persecution of the Orthodox Gagauz and Bulgarians.

According to available estimates, the scale of Ottoman slavery in Eastern Europe was comparable to that on the other side of the Atlantic. (See Hellie, 1982, pp. 21-22, 679-680; Khodarkovsky, 2002, p. 22.) Ukraine, Southern Russia, and the Caucasus were the major sources of slaves. In

Ukraine alone, at least 2 to 2.5 million people were forced into slavery or killed during raids by Crimean Tatar troops (*Istoriia Ukrainy*, 1995, p. 131). Agricultural slavery was not as widespread in the Ottoman Empire as it was in the United States, but it existed along with military, household, and maritime forms of slavery. While Ottoman slavery differed in its forms from American slavery, the experience of the minority of slaves who – like the Ukrainian wife of Sultan Suleiman the Magnificent – rose to the top of the Ottoman ranks was not representative of the experience of most slaves from Ukraine and Russia. (See Inalcik, 1979; Khodarkovsky, 2002; Kryms'kyi, 1924/1996; Lieven, 2001; Williams, 2001.)

This historical experience played a major role in the formation and cultural transmission among Ukrainians and Russians of a popular image that associated Crimean Tatars with slavery. The role of Ukrainian and Russian Cossacks as defenders against the slave and military raids of Crimean Tatars became mythologized in popular memory, even though the Crimean khans and Ukrainian Cossack leaders were allies in a number of battles. The very name "Ukraine," from which the name of Ukrainians derives, began to take hold during this period. As noted, it means "the borderland" or "on the edge." The Polish Kingdom, which controlled large parts of Ukraine, and the Russian Empire tried to use Ukrainian peasants, many of whom had settled in areas close to the Ottoman Empire to escape from serfdom, as guards against the incursions of the Crimean Tatars. It is noteworthy that these frontier warriors became known as Cossacks, a term derived from a Turkic word for "adventurer" or "free man" (see Magocsi, 1996; Subtelny, 1981).

The Russian conquest of Crimea at the end of the eighteenth century brought a major change in the historical experience of Crimean Tatars: they became subject to discrimination as Muslims and therefore became potential allies of the Ottoman Empire in its wars with the Russian Empire. As a result, a large proportion of the Crimean Tatar population migrated to the Ottoman Empire. (See Lieven , 2001, p. 153; Quataert, 2000, p. 115.)

Picture 5 Ukrainian Cossacks writing a defiant letter to the Sultan of the Ottoman Empire. Painting by Ilya Repin. Reproduced from Visipix.com

As noted, World War II and the mass expulsion of Crimean Tatars by Stalin reinforced their cultural differentiation from Ukrainians and Russians. Respondents of a December 2001 nationwide survey, conducted in Ukraine by the Kyiv International Institute of Sociology, viewed Crimean Tatars as the second most distant group living in Ukraine after the Gypsies. Crimean Tatars had a score of 5.11 on the Bogardus index of social distance, compared with a score of 2.43 for Russians, 3.30 for Belarusians, 4.45 for Poles, 4.54 for Jews, 4.62 for Moldovans, and 5.75 for Gypsies. This index ranges from 1, when all respondents would agree to have representatives of a given group as their family members, to 7, when all respondents would not permit the group members into the country. The score of 2 means that members of a group are accepted as close friends; the score of 3 means that members of a group are accepted as neighbors; the score of 4 means that members of a group are accepted as co-workers; the score of 5 means that members of a group are accepted as residents of Ukraine; and the score of 6 means that members of a group are accepted as visitors to Ukraine. (KIIS, 2002.)

Jews continue to live mostly in urban centers in Ukraine and Moldova. In the 1996 World Values Survey, when asked about their religious denomination, less than 1 percent of respondents in different historical regions of Ukraine and Moldova said that they were Jewish. According to the 1989 Soviet Census, Jews constituted about 2 percent of the population in Moldova and 1 percent in Ukraine. Since the collapse of Communism, emigration to Israel, the United States, and other Western countries has further reduced the number of Jews in Ukraine and Moldova. The 2001 census in Ukraine recorded 104 thousand Jews, or 0.2 percent of the total population. In comparison, the Jewish population in 1897 was 12 percent in Bessarabia and 9 percent in the Ukrainian regions of the Russian Empire and in Transdniestria. In Austrian Galicia, 11 percent of the population was Jewish in 1910. (Derzhavnyi, 2002; Magocsi, 1996, pp. 331, 424.)

This dramatic decline of the Jewish population was the result of the Nazi-organized Holocaust during World War II, when most of the Jews in Ukraine and Moldova were killed. Political and economic emigration during the first half of and the late twentieth century also contributed to the decline. (Gitelman, 1999; Magocsi, 1996, p. 633; Weiner, 1999.) Soviet policy, particularly since the end of the 1940s, when Stalin initiated the campaign against "cosmopolitanism" and the Soviet Union took and anti-Israel position in the Middle East conflict, led to discrimination against Jews in higher education and many occupations and promoted their assimilation. The Soviet authorities treated Jews as an ethnic group and restricted or prosecuted the expression of their religious identity. Many Jews in Ukraine and Moldova became Russified and secularized. For example, Yevgenii Primakov and Grigory Yavlinsky, who were born in Soviet Ukraine, became leading Russian politicians. Iukhym Zviahilskii , who served as Ukraine's acting prime minister from 1993 to 1994, headed a regional anti-Zionist committee in Eastern Ukraine during the Soviet regime. According to the 2001 national census, only 3 percent of the Jews in Ukraine considered Yiddish to be their native language, compared with 83 percent who specified Russian and 13 percent who specified Ukrainian. Similarly, the overwhelming majority of Jews in Moldova claimed Russian as their native language. (*Belarus and Moldova*, 1995, p. 122; Derzhavnyi, 2002.)

Jews developed a much more market-oriented economic culture than did Ukrainians and Moldovans. In both groups of historical regions prior to World War II, Jews were predominantly urban and were employed primarily in trades, crafts, professions, and industry. (Gitelman, 1999, p. 21; Magocsi, 1996, p. 338; Polonsky, 1972, pp. 42-44; Slezkine, 2004.) At the same time, Jewish intelligentsia and workers were disproportionately represented in different Socialist and Communist parties that were active in the territory of Ukraine and Moldova[75] (see Brym, 1978; King, 2000, p. 99; Slezkine, 2004). Jewish intellectuals were also disproportionately represented among Soviet dissidents and activists of the liberal democratic parties in Ukraine.

The religious, economic, and ethnic differences among Ukrainians, Russians, Moldovans, and Jews contributed to anti-Jewish pogroms, which occurred mainly in Eastern Ukraine and Moldova in the pre-World War I period and during the civil war after the Communist revolution. Tens of thousands of Ukrainians, mostly from Western regions, were employed by the Nazis in local police and military units, and a part of them were involved in the Holocaust. Troops and police in Romania, where many Moldovans served, were also involved in the Holocaust in Romanian-controlled right-bank

---

[75] For example, Communist and Socialist leaders of Jewish descent such as Lev (Leon) Trotsky, Lazar Kaganovich, and Pavel Axelrod, were born in Ukraine.

Moldova, Transdniestria, Bukovyna, and the Odesa region. (See Magocsi, 1996, pp. 626-633; Subtelny, 1988, pp. 471-472; Weiner, 1999.)

However, the rise of militant nationalism and violent anti-Semitism was limited to a small fraction of Ukrainians and Moldovans (Prizel, 1997, pp. 361-362). Opinion polls show that anti-Semitism in post-Communist Ukraine and Moldova does not have a mass base. According to the 1996 World Values Survey, only 1 percent of ethnic Ukrainians in both groups of historical regions selected Jews as the least-liked group.[76] The numbers in Moldova are similar: 0 percent of the Gagauz and 1 percent Moldovans felt this way about the Jews.

The Pulse of Europe poll conducted in 1991 showed that 69 percent of respondents in Ukraine had favorable opinions of Jews. In comparison, this number was 40 percent in Poland, 43 percent in Slovakia, 52 percent in the Czech Republic and Germany, 58 percent in European Russia, 63 percent in Bulgaria, 68 percent in Hungary, 72 percent in France, and 81 percent in Lithuania. Twenty-two percent of the respondents in Ukraine, compared with 9 percent in Bulgaria, 10 percent in Lithuania, 11 percent in Hungary, 14 percent in France and the Czech Republic, 24 percent in Germany, 26 percent in European Russia, 33 percent in Slovakia, and 34 percent in Poland, expressed unfavorable opinions of Jews.[77] (*Pulse of Europe*, 2001.)

Jews score in the middle compared with other groups on the Bogardus index of social distance, as is shown by the December 2001 survey of the Ukrainian population. The respondents regarded Jews (4.54) as more distant than Russians (2.43), Belarusians (3.30), and Poles (4.45), but as closer than Americans (4.56), Moldovans (4.62), Germans (4.74), Romanians (4.91), Georgians (4.92), Crimean Tatars (5.11), and Gypsies (5.75). The December 2001 score of the social distance of Jews was the highest it had been since this question was first asked in 1994. However, the fact that the principal change (from 3.92 to 4.54) occurred during 2001 indicates the negative influ-

---

[76]   Because the WVS does not include a separate category for the Gagauz, respondents from Gagauzia who identified themselves as national minorities are classified as the Gagauz.

[77]   In the US, 89 percent had favorable opinions towards Jews. Six percent of Americans expressed unfavorable opinions of Jews. (*Pulse of Europe*, 2001.)

ence of Israeli policy towards Palestinians rather than the significant rise of anti-Semitism. (See KIIS, 2002; Paniotto, 1999.)

It is noteworthy that the perception of distance between the Ukrainian population and Jews was similar in the period 1998 to 2001 to the perceived social distance between residents of Ukraine and Ukrainians who live in other countries. For example, the January 2001 poll showed that the social distance score for Ukrainians who lived in other countries was 4.11. In the same poll, 11 percent of respondents said they would consent to having Jews as family members, compared with 6 percent who would not permit them into Ukraine. (*Ukrains'ke suspil'stvo*, 2002.)

Since Ukraine became independent, Jewish politicians have been in office in Ukraine, including as prime minister, government ministers, speaker of the Crimean parliament, and mayor of Odesa (Odessa). About 15 deputies of Jewish descent, more than 10 times higher than the proportion of Jews in the population of Ukraine, were elected to the 450 seat national parliament in 2002.

Jewish politicians played prominent roles in parliamentary factions and political parties of different orientation. For example, Iukhym Zviahilskii, a member of parliament and the former acting prime minister of Ukraine, Viktor Pinchuk, an influential deputy in the Ukrainian parliament, and Hryhorii Surkis, a member of parliament and one of the leaders of the Social Democratic Party of Ukraine (United), supported the candidacy of Viktor Yanukovych during the 2004 presidential elections. Other prominent Jewish politicians, such as Yevhen Chervonenko, a minister in the Tymoshenko government, and Eduard Hurvits, the mayor of Odesa, were supporters of Viktor Yushchenko and members of the parliamentary faction of the "Our Ukraine" Bloc.

Similarly, Jews were overrepresented among wealthy businessmen, including oligarchs. For example, Viktor Pinchuk acquired ownership of many large state enterprises and private companies, attaining a combined worth of billions of dollars in heavy industry, television, and print media. Hryhorii Surkis became an owner of regional electricity distributing companies and the leading soccer club in Ukraine. The political and economic culture that emerged as result of the distinct historical experience and religious ethic of Jews has been a major factor in the rapid upward mobility of many members of this minority compared with other religious and ethnic minorities.

Aside from criminals, Stalinists are the least-liked group by ethnic Ukrainians in Western Ukraine (31 percent) compared with 7 percent among Eastern Ukrainians. Western Ukrainians and Eastern Ukrainians share a similar dislike of neo-Nazis (13 and 16 percent respectively). Nine percent of West Moldovans and 44 percent of the Gagauz selected neo-Nazis as the least-liked group. Attitudes towards Stalinists show the opposite regional pattern: 12 percent of West Moldovans chose Stalinists as least-liked and zero percent of the Gagauz did so.

There is a lack of detailed studies of the precise mechanisms that transmit distinct regional historical experiences from one generation to another. However, the data available make it possible to outline a general mechanism of such transmission. Socialization through family, educational institutions, and religion play crucial roles in the cultural transmission of historical experiences. Family was a key institution that was not directly controlled by the Soviet state and the Communist Party. Each consecutive generation was brought up hearing the personal, folk, and historical stories told by their parents and grandparents. As a result, the contemporary populations in different historical regions of Ukraine and Moldova retained their distinct historical memory – or a modern interpretation of past historical experiences that were to a certain extent simplified, distorted, and mythologized in the process of their intergenerational transmission.

The uniform education system in the Soviet Union promoted the convergence of the political cultures of different regions and ethnic groups. However, in the case of Crimean Tatars, this mechanism of socialization reinforced their differences with Russians, Ukrainians, and the Gagauz. Soviet historical textbooks and literary texts emphasized the military conflicts between Crimean Tatars and Ukrainian and Russian Cossacks, the slave raids of Crimean Tatars, and the military help provided by the Russian government to the Gagauz, Bulgarians, and other Orthodox Christian people of the Ottoman Empire. The history of World War II presented in Soviet textbooks showed Crimean Tatars as Nazi collaborators and ignored the ethnic cleansing of Crimean Tatars by the Soviet government. Soviet mass media and popular culture promoted similar historical images of Crimean Tatars and the Gagauz.

The organized Greek Catholic, Orthodox, and Muslim religions helped to transfer distinct political cultures from one generation to another in the Ottoman Empire, the Russian Empire, and to some extent in the Soviet Union. The role of religion was especially important in this aspect in the Ottoman Empire and the Russian Empire, because the absolute majority of their populations were illiterate. Even though religion was persecuted in the Soviet Union, a significant proportion of the population preserved their religious beliefs.

The comparative analysis of regional historical development in this chapter shows that people in Western Ukraine and Western Moldova had a different historical experience in the Austro-Hungarian Monarchy and Eastern and Central European states than did people in Eastern Ukraine, Transdniestria, and Gagauzia. With the exception of World War II, when they were occupied by Nazi Germany and its ally Romania, Eastern Ukrainian regions and Transdniestria were part of the Russian Empire and then of the Soviet Union.

The territorial changes in the lands populated mostly by ethnic Ukrainians and ethnic Moldovans occurred largely as the result of wars and diplomatic agreements among the monarchs of the Russian, Austro-Hungarian, and Ottoman Empires; Polish, Romanian, Czech, Ukrainian, and Moldovan leaders; and totalitarian rulers of the Soviet Union and Nazi Germany. However, these changes had an unintended consequence. Different historical experiences contributed to the development of different political cultures among ethnic Ukrainians and Moldovans in the regions under different rule. Ukrainian national identity became much more developed in Western Ukraine than in Eastern Ukraine. However, differences within regions of Western Ukraine also emerged. Historical circumstances in the former Austrian province of Galicia were the most favorable for the spread of Ukrainian nationalism and the development of a national identity. These circumstances included the relatively more liberal political system, the supportive policy of the Austrian government, and the existence of the Greek Catholic Church. Although to a lesser extent than in Galicia, historical conditions were also more favorable for the development of a national identity in the Bessarabian region of Moldova than in the Transdniestria region. In contrast, more pro-Russian and pro-Communist political cultures evolved in Eastern Ukrainian regions and in Transdniestria and Gagauzia regions in Moldova.

5   Culture, ethnicity, economy, and political leadership

5.1   Ethnicity and language

Most scholars attribute the regional political cleavages and conflicts in Ukraine and Moldova to factors of ethnicity, economy, and political leadership. Regional divisions in these two countries are often considered to be a reflection of ethnic cleavages and conflicts. Many researchers argue that significant political divisions exist between ethnic Ukrainians and Russians in Ukraine, and Moldovans and Russians in Moldova. In addition, they point to conflicts between the Gagauz and Moldovans in Gagauzia, and between the Crimean Tatars and Russians in Crimea.

There is a significant Russian minority population, which is concentrated predominantly in Eastern parts of Ukraine and Moldova. However, data from the most recent census, conducted in 2001, shows that ethnic Russians form the majority of the population (60 percent) in only one region, Crimea. Ethnic Russians make up between a quarter and a half of the population in the other three regions of Eastern Ukraine. In contrast, in all seven regions of Western Ukraine, the proportion of ethnic Russians is less than 5 percent. (Derzhavnyi, 2002.)

The 1989 Soviet census data indicates that ethnic Russians constituted about one quarter (23 percent) of the Transdniestrian population. It is noteworthy that the proportion of ethnic Ukrainians in the region (26 percent) is as large as the proportion of Russians (O'Loughlin, Kolossov, and Tchepalyga, 1998, p. 339). In the rest of Moldova, the proportion of ethnic Russians is 14 percent. In fact, more than twice as many ethnic Russians live in Western regions of Moldova than in the Transdniestria region. In Gagauzia, ethnic Russians make up about 5 percent of the population. (UNDP-Moldova, 2001, p. 20.)

Among other ethnic minorities in Ukraine, only Crimean Tatars, Romanians, and Hungarians live in significant regional concentrations. The 2001 Ukrainian census recorded that 10 percent of the population in Crimea, including Sevastopol, are Crimean Tatars, compared with only 2 percent of the population in 1989. This significant increase is a result of the return migration of Crimean Tatars from Central Asian republics, where they had been exiled by Stalin at the end of World War II. (Yevtoukh, 1995.) Romanians account for 13 percent of the population in the Chernivtsi region (the former Bukovyna), while Moldovans make up 7 percent of the population in the same region. Hungarians constitute about 12 percent of the population in the Transcarpathia region (the former Carpatho-Ukraine). (Derzhavnyi, 2002.)

It is noteworthy that there is a high concentration of ethnic minorities in the Southern part of the Odesa region. This territory, along with Western Moldova, was part of Romania during the inter-war period, in contrast to the rest of the Odesa region, which belonged to the Soviet Union at the time. As discussed in chapter 3, the effect of historical division is not visible in the aggregate voting patterns of the Odesa region, in contrast to other historic regions of Ukraine and Moldova. This can be attributed in part to the distinct ethnic composition of the population in this region. The average unweighted proportion of ethnic Bulgarians in the population of Southern districts of the Odesa region is 26 percent, while ethnic Russians and Moldovans each make up 18 percent and the Gagauz make up 5 percent of the population. Bulgarians, Russians, and the Gagauz, as noted in the case of Moldova, are likely to support pro-Communist and pro-Russian candidates and parties for cultural and ethnic reasons. Support for nationalist and pro-Ukraine parties and candidates is low in these districts, in which ethnic Ukrainians constitute only 32 percent of the population. (Nadolishnii, 1998, p. 135.)

Even though election, aggregate, and survey data on these districts are available to a much lesser extent than for other regions of Ukraine, the available data are consistent with the political culture explanation. For example, 80 percent of the voters in the Bolgrad district in the Odesa region, which is populated predominantly by Bulgarians (61 percent) and the Gagauz (17 percent), supported Leonid Kravchuk, who ran against nationalist candidates in the December 1991 presidential elections in Ukraine. (Nadolishnii, 1998, p. 134.) This level of support was higher than in any other of the 26 regions of Ukraine. A survey conducted in the Odesa region in 1995 found that a third (35 percent) of the Gagauz still consider themselves to be citizens of the Soviet Union, while 22 percent consider themselves to be representatives of the

Gagauz people; only 12 percent consider themselves to be citizens of independent Ukraine.[78] (Guboglo and Yakubovski, 1997, p. 180.)

Ethnic Gagauz account for 79 percent of the population of the Gagauz autonomy in Moldova (*European*, 1997). As noted, this Turkic people migrated to Bessarabia in the eighteenth and nineteenth centuries from the present territory of Bulgaria and Romania to avoid religious persecution in the Ottoman Empire. Bulgarians, who make up about 2 percent of the population of Western Moldova, including 40 percent of the population in the Taraclia district, moved to Moldova for the same reason.[79]

Ethnic Ukrainians form the absolute majority of the population in all regions of Ukraine except Crimea. Ethnic Moldovans account for 70 percent of the population in the Western regions of Moldova; they remain the largest ethnic group in Transdniestria. Moldovans made up 38 percent of the Transdniestria population in 1989 and 33 percent in 1996 (O'Loughlin, Kolossov, and Tchepalyga, 1998, p. 339). In the Gagauz autonomy, ethnic Moldovans constitute about 4 percent of the population. (UNDP-Moldova, 2001, p. 20.)

In comparison with the pre-war period, the proportion of Russians in the population of Ukraine and Moldova considerably increased, while the proportion of Romanians in Bukovyna declined, as a result of the Soviet takeover in 1940. Crimean Tatars, who accounted for a quarter (26 percent) of all Crimean residents in 1921, were forcibly resettled because a fraction of them had collaborated with the Nazis when Crimea was occupied by German troops. The populations of Poles, Jews, and Germans declined significantly during and after World War II in both Ukraine and Moldova. These groups formed a significant part of the population in several historical regions, mainly in Western Ukraine, before World War II. In 1931, ethnic Poles constituted about one quarter of the population in Galicia and one sixth (16 percent) in Volhynia. Jews made up about 14 percent of the population in Carpatho-Ukraine, 11 percent in Bukovyna, and 10 percent in both Galicia and Vol-

---

[78]   Seventeen percent of the Gagauz replied that this identity did not matter to them, and 14 percent were not sure which they would select.

[79]   Bulgarians resisted an attempt to merge the Taraclia district with neighboring districts when a new administrative-territorial system was introduced in Moldova in 1999. Instead, they succeeded in transforming the Taraclia district into a separate county.

hynia. In Eastern regions of Ukraine in 1926, the proportion of Jews in the population was 5 percent. Germans constituted 9 percent of the population in Bukovyna in 1930. In Volhynia, the proportion of Germans in the population decreased several times until it reached 2 percent in 1931 due to forced re-settlement during World War I and emigration. In Bessarabia, which included Western regions of Moldova, Germans made up 3 percent of the population in 1930. The absolute majority of Germans in Western Ukraine and Western Moldova were resettled in both Germany and occupied Poland after these re-gions became part of the Soviet Union as the result of the 1939 Soviet-Nazi pact. The remaining Germans in Ukraine and Moldova were forcibly resettled to other parts of the Soviet Union at the beginning and the end of World War II because some of them had supported the Nazis. The populations of Poles, Jews, and Germans do not now exceed 5 percent in any of Ukrainian and Moldovan regions. (See Derzhavnyi, 2002; *Encyclopedia*, 1984, p. 317, 1993, p. 634; Gitelman, 1999; Piotrowski, 1998, p. 353; von Meurs, 1994, pp. 395-397; Yevtoukh, 1995.)

Significant changes in the ethnic composition of the populations of Ukraine and Moldova are often used as illustrations of the ethnic nature of cleavages and conflicts. Many scholars view the *Holodomor* in Eastern Ukraine, the Holocaust, and the expulsion of Poles, Romanians, Crimean Tatars, and Germans as the results of exclusively ethnic factors. Such con-clusions are frequently extrapolated to whole populations based on the na-tionality of political leaders and the ethnic composition of the military forma-tions involved in conflicts and wars. However, the political orientations and actions of leaders and military forces might not be fully representative of mass attitudes and behaviors. In addition, this approach neglects the role of other factors, such as ideology and political leadership, as well as other types of cleavages, such as class.

For instance, the artificial famine (the *Holodomor*) in Soviet Ukraine in the 1930s had not only anti-Ukrainian but also anti-peasant intent. The famine followed the mass collectivization campaign initiated by Stalin and was di-rected against the "rich" and many middle class peasants. A version of Com-munist ideology, advocated by Communist leaders in the Soviet Union at that time, declared the need for a "dictatorship of proletariat" and viewed peas-ants, especially their well-to-do strata (*kulaks*), as class enemies to be liquidated or exploited for the purposes of industrialization. A similar version of Marxist ideology was behind the policy of War Communism, which included requisitions of grain from peasants and the abolition of private property, money, and trade. (See Boettke, 1990.) The famine also affected a significant proportion of non-Ukrainian peasants in grain-producing areas, yet did not affect Ukrainian workers in urban areas (see Conquest, 1986, Kulchytskyi, 1995).

Similarly, the arrest and expulsion of Poles and Romanians, carried out by the Soviet authorities after Western regions were incorporated in the Soviet Union, reflected class structure, as it was defined by the Soviet version of Marxism, and the pattern of the Stalinist terror. Most members of the upper class, government officials, and military officers in Ukrainian and Moldovan regions, which were parts of Poland and Romania during the inter-war period, were Poles and Romanians. Significant proportions of those Ukrainians, Moldovans, and Jews, who were classified as class enemies and "bourgeois nationalists," were also arrested and expelled by the Soviet authorities.

The Holocaust of the Jewish and Gypsy populations of Ukraine and Moldova, and non-combat deaths of several million Ukrainians, as well as millions of Poles and Russians, during World War II, reflected to a significant extent the Nazi racist ideology advocated by Hitler, who viewed Jews, Gypsies, and Slavs as racially inferior. (See Rummell, 1992.) It is noteworthy, that the Nazi-led terror did not extend in similar proportions to Moldovans or Karaims, a Jewish sect of Turkic origin in Ukraine.

As noted in chapter 4, forced resettlements, of Poles from Western Ukraine to Poland, Ukrainians from Poland to Ukraine, and Crimean Tatars from Crimea to Central Asia, were carried out under Stalin's orders. Ethnic cleavages between Ukrainians and Poles played a role in the war, in which tens of thousands people, predominantly Poles and many Ukrainians from mixed families, were killed between 1943 and 1947. However, Ukrainian nationalist partisans also killed those ethnic Ukrainians who did not share their ideology. (See Snyder, 1999.)

An analysis of inter-marriage patterns in Ukraine and Moldova allows us to examine the role of ethnic divisions in social behavior.[80] This is particularly useful for periods when attitudinal data is absent, as in the case of the pre-World War II years and the Soviet times. Inter-marriage is an important indicator of relationships between people from different groups (Merton, 1941/1976) – *ceteris paribus*, the higher the inter-marriage rate, the less salient the ethnic cleavages.

It is a little-noted fact that, in the Ukrainian part of Galicia in Poland, one in six (16 percent) of marriages in 1927 was between a Ukrainian and a Pole, even though the region was a center of political tension, with subsequent violent conflict and ethnic cleansing during and after World War II (see Piotrowski, 1998, p. 187; Ther and Siljak, 2001).[81] Similarly, in 1927 in Donbas in Soviet Ukraine, one in five marriages (22 percent) was mixed (Pirie, 1996, p. 1086). In 1936, the rate of mixed marriages for Jewish men in Eastern (Soviet) Ukraine reached 15 percent compared to 4 percent in 1924. (See Slezkine, 2004, p. 179.)

The 1989 Soviet census data indicated that the proportion of ethnically mixed families in Ukraine was much higher in Eastern than in Western regions. For example, in Donbas more than 40 percent of families were mixed. Similarly, in Crimea, where separatism received the strongest support, the proportion of mixed families was more than a third (36 percent). In contrast, in the Ivano-Frankivsk region, part of the former Galicia, about one in ten families was mixed. (See Pirie, 1996, p. 1086.)

Data on inter-marriage in Moldova, derived from the 1998 Laitin/Hough survey, shows a similar pattern. In the Transdniestrian Republic, about half (48 percent) of the respondents are in mixed marriages compared with a third (32 percent) in the Western part of the country. The inter-marriage involves not only Russians and Ukrainians, but also Moldovans, although at a lower level. A third of Moldovans (35 percent) are in mixed marriages in the Transdniestrian Republic: 17 percent with Russian spouses and 18 percent with spouses of another minority, mostly Ukrainian. In Western Moldova, a

---

[80]   A lack of data complicates a comparison of inter-marriage rates in many ethnically-divided countries.

[81]   Piotrowski (1998) ignores this fact and tends to identify all Ukrainians with radical nationalists.

quarter (25 percent) of ethnic Moldovans have spouses of a different nationality (9 percent Russian and 16 percent another minority). More than half of the ethnic Russians in Transdniestria (60 percent) and Western Moldova (56 percent) are in mixed marriages. In Transdniestria, a fifth (21 percent) of Russians have Moldovan spouses, and 39 percent have spouses of another minority, though mostly Ukrainian, compared with 26 and 30 percent respectively in the Western part of the country.

Lower inter-marriage rates in Western Ukraine and Moldova than in Eastern regions reflect not only a much lower proportion of ethnic minorities, and consequently less opportunity to marry someone from another ethnic group, but also cultural differences. As noted, the population in Western regions is much less ethnically mixed than in Eastern regions. For example, in Donbas (Donetsk and Luhansk regions), half (48 to 49 percent) of the population classify themselves as Russian or other minorities, compared with 5 percent in the Ivano-Frankivsk region of the former Galicia. It is noteworthy that the inter-marriage rate is positively associated with the size of the ethnic group. For example, 18 percent of Ukrainians, 59 percent of Russians, and 75 percent of Jews in Ukraine married outside of their ethnic group in 1994 (Rapawy, 1998). However, Western Ukrainians express lower levels of tolerance towards Russians than do Ukrainians from Eastern regions (Pirie, 1996).

The 1998 Laitin/Hough survey demonstrates that Gagauz attitudes towards inter-marriage are similar to the attitudes of the Transdniestrians and more tolerant than the attitudes of other Bessarabians. About two-thirds of the Gagauz and Transdniestrian respondents say that the marriage of their son or daughter to a person of a different nationality makes no difference to them, while only 1 and 2 percent of these respondents consider inter-marriage completely undesirable. Forty-six percent of non-Gagauz respondents in Bessarabia are indifferent, and 6 percent are totally opposed to inter-marriage for their children.

A 1995 survey of the Gagauz living in the Odesa region of Ukraine shows that 37 percent of the respondents are willing to accept ethnic Moldovans as spouses of their close relatives. It is noteworthy that the Gagauz are much more likely to approve of inter-marriage with Slavs than with members of other Turkic ethnic groups. Two-thirds (67 percent) of the respondents are willing to accept the marriages of their close relatives to Russians, 61 percent to Bulgarians, and 60 percent to Ukrainians, compared with 43 percent to Turks and 28 percent to Azeris. (Guboglo and Yakubovski, 1997, pp. 179-206.)

From a comparative perspective, ethnic inter-marriage rates in Ukraine and Moldova are high, taking into account both the heterogeneity of the population and measurement differences. For example, the 1998 Laitin/Hough survey indicates that 57 percent of ethnic Russians, who compose 23 percent of the survey respondents in Moldova, have spouses of different nationality. As noted, figures for inter-marriage (59 percent) and the proportion of Russians in the population (22 percent) are similar in Ukraine. In comparison, in the United States, which is often described as a model melting pot, the 1980 census data showed that the inter-marriage rates of English and German American-born women in their first marriages were 44 and 51 percent respectively. English-Americans and German-Americans each constituted 25 percent of married men. (Lieberson and Waters, 1988.) This proportion is similar to the proportions of Russians in Ukraine and Moldova in the aforementioned inter-marriage statistics. In Canada, the 1971 census data show that 33 percent of English-Canadian and 14 percent of French-Canadian married men had spouses from different ethnic groups. Each of these ethnic groups constituted 29 percent of the population in Canada at that time (Richard, 1991, pp. 44, 110).

Yugoslavia, as it was before its break-up and its violent conflicts, is sometimes used as an example of a country with a relatively high inter-marriage rate. Nine percent of Yugoslavian families were mixed, according to the 1981 census, compared with 25 percent in Ukraine according to the 1989 census, even though Yugoslavia was much more ethnically heterogeneous. A third (30 percent) of marriages were ethnically exogamous in Ukraine in 1979, compared with 13 percent in Yugoslavia between 1980 and 1982 and 15 percent in the Soviet Union as a whole. Similar large differences exist between regions with significant ethnic minorities in Ukraine and the former Yugoslavia, even taking into account the varying degrees of heterogeneity in the populations. For example, in the 1970s, 55 percent of the marriages in Donbas in Eastern Ukraine, 39 percent in Southern Ukraine, and 36 percent in the North East (Kharkiv) involved spouses from different nationalities. In contrast, the inter-marriage rate in the 1980s was 6 percent in Kosovo, 8 percent in Macedonia, 12 percent in Bosnia, 13 percent in Montenegro, and 17 percent in Croatia. Ukrainians constituted half (51 percent) of the population in Donbas, 25 to 76 percent in the Southern regions, and 63 percent in the Kharkiv region according to the 1989 Soviet census. In comparison, in 1981, the dominant ethnic groups accounted for 40 percent of the population in Bosnia, 67 percent in Macedonia, 69 percent in Montenegro, 75 percent in Croatia, and 77 percent in Kosovo. (See Botev, 1994, pp. 466-469; Pirie, 1996, p. 1086; Rapawy, 1998.) It is noteworthy that Voevodina, which had the highest inter-marriage rate in the former Yugoslavia, is the only region that has not had a violent conflict or significant separatist movement since 1990. Twenty-eight percent of 1980s marriages in Voevodina, in which Serbs accounted for 55 percent and Hungarians accounted for 19 percent of the population, were mixed (Botev, 1994, pp. 466-469).

Many top political leaders, who represented different political camps in Ukraine and Moldova, either had spouses from a different ethnic group or came from ethnically-mixed families. For example, Leonid Kuchma, the president of Ukraine from 1994 to 2004 had a Russian wife.[82] Viktor Yanukovych, the leader of the pro-Russian Party of Regions and a presidential candidate in the 2004 elections, had a Belarusian father and a Russian mother.

Yurii Yekhanurov, who was the second prime minister in the Yushchenko administration, had a Buryat father and a Ukrainian mother; he was born in Russia. Borys Tarasyuk, the foreign minister in Kuchma's and Yushchenko's governments and the leader of the nationalist People's Movement of Ukraine, had a Russian mother and a Ukrainian father. Yulia Tymoshenko, the prime minister of Ukraine in 2005 and one of the leaders of the "Orange Revolution," said that her father was of Latvian descent and her mother was Ukrainian. When Yevhen Chervonenko, a prominent member of the People's Union "Our Ukraine" Party and the president of the Eurasian Jewish Congress, claimed publicly that Yulia Tymoshenko's mother was Jewish, her ethnicity was of little interest to Ukrainians and did not become an issue in Ukrainian politics.

---

[82]   The second wife of President Viktor Yushchenko was an American of Ukrainian descent.

Presidents of Moldova and the president of the separatist Transdniestrian Republic had ethnically mixed families. Mircea Snegur, the first president of independent Moldova, had a Russian wife. Vladimir Voronin, whose father was Russian, had a Ukrainian wife. Igor Smirnov, president of the Transdniestrian Republic, was Russian and was married to a Ukrainian.

Table 5.1 shows that ethnic Ukrainians differ in their political orientation from other ethnic groups. As one would expect, support for nationalist parties is higher among ethnic Ukrainians than among ethnic minorities, which mostly include Russians. However, with the exception of members of centrist and other parties, differences between Western and Eastern Ukrainians outweigh inter-ethnic differences. The proportion of ethnic Ukrainians who support nationalist parties in Western historical regions (67 percent) is more than twice as high as the proportion in Eastern regions (32 percent). Statistics on those who intend to vote for Communist parties show the reverse regional pattern: almost a third (30 percent) of ethnic Ukrainians in the Eastern part of the country support Communist parties, compared with 8 percent in Western Ukraine. (Table 5.1.)

Table 5.1 Support for political parties by historical region and ethnicity in Ukraine (%). (1996 World Values Survey)

	Western Ukraine		Eastern Ukraine	
	Ukrainian	Other	Ukrainian	Other
Nationalist	67	40	32	23
Centrist/ Other	25	40	37	44
Communist	8	19	30	33
Total (%)	100	100	100	100
N	391	52	918	712

Although significant ethnic differences show when measured by the pro-Soviet and pro-Russian scale in Moldova, the variation by historical region is also very high. Ethnic Moldovans score much lower on this region scale than ethnic Russians and other minorities (mostly Ukrainians). However, almost half (47 percent) of Moldovans in the Transdniestrian Republic express pro-Soviet and pro-Russian attitudes, compared with 17 percent in Western regions. Conversely, 44 percent of Moldovans in the Western part of the country and 15 percent in the Eastern regions, share anti-Soviet and anti-Russian attitudes. (Table 5.2.)

Table 5.2 Pro-Soviet and pro-Russian scale by historical region and ethnicity in Moldova (%). (1998 Laitin/Hough survey)

	Western Moldova			Transdniestria		
	Moldovan	Russian	Other	Moldovan	Russian	Other
Pro-Soviet/ pro-Russian	17	43	43	47	66	63
Neutral	39	41	34	38	24	29
Anti-Soviet/ anti-Russian	44	16	24	15	10	8
Total (%)	100	100	100	100	100	100
N	503	217	410	126	148	133

It is noteworthy that regional differences extend to ethnic Russians and Ukrainians. Two thirds, or 66 percent of Russian respondents and 63 percent of respondents from other ethnic groups (mostly Ukrainians) in Transdniestria, express pro-Soviet and pro-Russian attitudes, compared with 43 percent in Western Moldova. Ten percent of Russians and 8 percent of other minorities reveal anti-Soviet and anti-Russian attitudes in the Transdniestrian Republic, compared with 16 and 24 percent respectively in Western regions (Table 5.2).

There are significant differences between ethnic groups in attitudes towards language in Moldova. However, the 1998 Laitin/Hough survey shows that differences between ethnic Moldovans in historical regions outweigh the differences shown by other ethnic groups on these issues. For example, 98 percent of ethnic Moldovans in Transdniestria, compared with 69 percent in Bessarabia, supported the Russian language as a required subject in all schools, while 1 and 26 percent respectively opposed this idea. Ninety-seven percent of the Gagauz and 91 percent of other ethnic minorities in Moldova favored Russian as a mandatory subject, while 3 and 6 percent respectively were against such a measure.

Ethnic Moldovans in different historical regions view even their own language differently. Thirty-seven percent of Moldovans in Bessarabia, as opposed to 13 percent in Transdniestria, consider the Moldovan and Romanian languages to be the same language. Only 13 percent of ethnic Moldovans in Bessarabia, compared with 33 percent in the Transdniestrian Republic, regard Moldovan and Romanian as extremely or completely different languages. Those remaining either think that these languages differ only somewhat or do not express a definite opinion.

Ethnic minorities in Ukraine show a regional pattern of political orientation similar to that in Moldova, although the low number of Russian respondents in Western Ukraine makes it impossible to separate them from this category of respondents. Support for Communist parties is higher among ethnic minorities in Eastern Ukraine than in Western Ukraine (33 and 19 percent respectively). The regional pattern of support for nationalist parties is reversed (23 percent in the East and 40 percent in the West of the country). (Table 5.1.)

Analysis of a 1996 survey, commissioned by the United States Information Agency (USIA) and conducted by SOCIS-Gallup, shows that differences in political attitudes between ethnic Russians and Ukrainians in Crimea are not as strong as their differences with Crimean Tatars. For example, 91 percent of Russians and 80 percent of Ukrainians in the region, compared with 62 percent of Crimean Tatars, favor a confederation of Ukraine with Russia and other former Soviet Republics. Twenty-six percent of Tatars, 13 percent of Ukrainians, and 4 percent of Russians support the independence of Ukraine. It is noteworthy that not only ethnic Russians but also ethnic Ukrainians in Crimea are much more supportive of the confederation option and less supportive of the independence of Ukraine than are the respondents in Ukraine as a whole. Fifty-nine percent of the respondents in the nationwide sample favor confederation and 31 percent favor independence. As noted in chapter 4, the Ukrainian national identity was historically least developed in Crimea, which before its transfer to the Soviet Ukraine in 1954, was part of the Russian Federation in the Soviet Union.

Regarding the status of Crimea, more than half of Crimean Tatars (54 percent), compared with 29 percent of Ukrainians and 13 percent of Russians, say that the region should be part of Ukraine. A much lower proportion of Crimean Tatars (8 percent) than Russians (59 percent) and Ukrainians (41 percent) favors Crimea becoming part of Russia. However, Crimean independence receives stronger backing among Tatars (27 percent) than among Russians and Ukrainians in the region (15 and 17 percent respectively). (USIA, 1996.)

Table 5.3 Support for political parties by historical regions and language in Ukraine (%). (1996 World Values Survey)

	Western Ukraine		Eastern Ukraine	
	Ukrainian	Other	Ukrainian	Other
Nationalist	65	40	33	25
Centrist/Other	26	44	34	45
Communist	9	16	33	30
Total (%)	100	100	100	100
N	417	25	899	712

The substitution of ethnic identification for language in Ukraine and Moldova does not significantly change the results. A considerable proportion of ethnic Ukrainians and Moldovans, primarily in the Eastern parts of these countries, are Russian speakers (see Arel, 1995, 1996; King, 2000). However, Tables 5.3 and 5.4 show that historical cleavages between Western and Eastern regions outweigh linguistic cleavages in the case of support for Nationalist and Communist parties in Ukraine and the pro-Soviet/pro-Russian attitude scale in Moldova.

Table 5.4 Pro-Soviet and pro-Russian scale by historical regions and language in Moldova (%). (1998 Laitin/Hough survey)

	Western Moldova			Transdniestrian Republic		
	Moldovan	Russian	Other	Moldovan	Russian	Other
Pro-Soviet/ pro-Russian	17	44	35	44	64	63
Neutral	43	41	30	40	27	29
Anti-Soviet/ anti-Russian	40	15	35	16	9	8
Total (%)	100	100	100	100	100	100
N	392	324	414	100	245	62

5.2   Economic factors

As noted in chapter 2, regional political divisions are often attributed to economic factors, such as urban-rural and class cleavages, levels of economic development, and income. The Eastern regions of Ukraine and Moldova are more urbanized than Western regions, with few exceptions. Gross Domestic Product (GDP) per capita and average personal income have similar regional patterns. (Figure 5.1 and Table A.1, Appendix.) The Eastern regions of Ukraine and Moldova are more developed than Western regions.

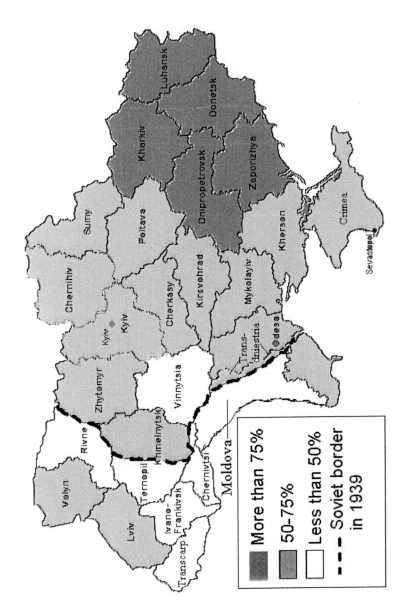

Figure 5.1 The rate of urbanization in regions of Ukraine and Moldova in 2001

However, as discussed in chapter 3, support for Communist and pro-Russian parties and politicians is weakest and the pro-nationalist/pro-Western vote is strongest in both the city of Kyiv, the most developed region and the largest urban center in Ukraine, and in less developed and less urbanized regions of Western Ukraine. It is noteworthy that public support for the "Orange Revolution" was most pronounced in both Kyiv city, where GDP per capita was several times higher than GDP levels in other Eastern Ukrainian regions, and in Western Ukrainian regions, where GDP per capita lagged behind the national average (see Aslund, 2005, p. 333). The pro-Communist and pro-Russian vote in the city of Chishinau, the main urban center of Moldova, has been comparable to that in Western Moldova as a whole, with the exception of the 1994 parliamentary elections. However, in Western Moldova, support for pro-Communist/pro-Russian candidates is strongest in the Gagauz autonomy, which is one of the least developed and urbanized regions in Moldova.[83] These exceptions indicate that urban/rural cleavages, the GDP level, and income level cannot adequately account for regional political cleavages and conflicts in Ukraine and Moldova.

The effect of class-related cleavages, as measured by the World Values Survey and the Laitin/Hough survey, is most pronounced in the pro-Communist and pro-Russian party vote. Not surprisingly, the lower and working classes show higher support for these parties than do the upper and upper-middle classes. Although variation among occupational levels and the pro-Soviet/pro-Russian attitude scale in Moldova is in the expected negative direction, the effect is not very strong. As in the case of ethnic factors, historical cleavages between Western and Eastern regions outweigh class-related cleavages in support for Nationalist and Communist parties in Ukraine and in the pro-Soviet/pro-Russian attitude scale in Moldova. (Table 5.5 and 5.6.)

---

[83]   For the level of economic development in Gagauzia compared to other regions of Moldova, see UNDP-Moldova (2001).

Table 5.5 Support for political parties by historical regions and class in Ukraine (%). (1996 World Values Survey)

	Western Ukraine				Eastern Ukraine			
	Upper and up-per middle	Lower middle	Working	Lower	Upper and upper middle	Lower middle	Working	Lower
Nationalist	44	62	68	60	28	31	29	22
Centrist/Other	56	29	23	22	52	39	42	34
Communist	0	9	9	18	20	30	29	44
Total (%)	100	100	100	100	100	100	100	100
N	16	217	151	45	54	708	542	253

Table 5.6 Pro-Soviet and pro-Russian scale by historical regions and occupational level in Moldova (%). (1998 Laitin/Hough survey)

	Western Moldova				Transdniestrian Republic			
	Managerial	Specialist	Clerical	Labor	Managerial	Specialist	Clerical	Labor
Pro-Soviet/ pro-Russian	32	32	39	34	64	60	64	68
Neutral	37	33	42	41	28	31	31	30
Anti-Soviet/ anti-Russian	31	35	19	25	8	10	5	2
Total (%)	100	100	100	100	100	100	100	100
N	116	320	105	409	36	94	42	128

5.3   Political leadership factors

Some scholars attribute regional political cleavages and conflicts in Ukraine and Moldova to political leadership factors. Leaders played a greater role in Ukrainian and Moldovan politics than did parties after the collapse of Communism. Many leading politicians preferred to either run as independent candidates or form their own parties. As a result, there were several parties that advocated pro-Communist and pro-Russian views in each polity: Ukraine, the Transdniestrian Republic, and Western Moldova. The same applies to the pro-nationalist and pro-Western parties in Ukraine and Moldova, with the exception of the Transdniestrian Republic, where they were de facto banned.

Top state officials in Ukraine and Moldova used their influence and government resources to create pro-presidential parties. However, these parties, called "parties of power," tended to lose their influence after changes in the leadership of the country. For example, the People's Democratic Party of Ukraine, led by the prime minister of Ukraine, the head of the administration of President Kuchma, the former speaker of the parliament, and several regional governors, had the second largest faction in the Ukrainian parliament after the 1998 elections. However, by the end of 2000, the size of its faction had decreased from 19 percent – the second highest after the Communist Party of Ukraine faction, which held 27 percent seats – to 4 percent, or an eighth in size. This steep decline followed the appointment of the new prime minister and the new head of the presidential administration, as well as a split in the party leadership. Similarly, the Agrarian Democratic Party of Moldova went from being the majority party in the parliament after the 1994 elections to being a party with no parliamentary seats in the 1998 elections; this took place after the party lost the support of Mircea Snegur, the president of Moldova, and Petru Lucinschi, the head of parliament, before the 1996 presidential elections. (King, 2000, pp. 158-162.)

As noted in chapter 3, the regional pattern of support for both presidents of Ukraine, Leonid Kravchuk and Leonid Kuchma, was reversed in the second round of elections. Both Kravchuk and Kuchma received significantly higher proportions of the vote in Eastern Ukraine than in Western Ukraine when they were first elected to office. Similarly, the pattern of the regional vote reversed during the 1999 presidential elections. However, both candidates had shifted their platforms from relatively pro-Russian to pro-Ukrainian.

Such radical shifts in political orientation can be viewed as motivated by personal interest rather than ideology. For example, Leonid Kravchuk, the chief of ideology in the Communist Party of Ukraine during Soviet rule, became a supporter of Ukrainian independence after the collapse of Communism and advocated a pro-nationalist program in the 1994 elections. Eventually, he associated himself with the Social Democratic Party (United), which represented the interest of a number of oligarchs during the 1998 parliamentary elections.[84]

Leonid Kuchma, who was a director of a major missile plant and a member of the Central Committee of the Communist Party of the Soviet Union, became close to some liberal and centrist organizations after the collapse of Communism. He advocated a pro-Russian program in the 1994 elections. However, Kuchma adopted a more pro-Ukrainian political orientation during the 1999 presidential elections, when he faced a challenge from a Communist candidate. In the first two rounds of the 2004 presidential elections, Leonid Kuchma backed a pro-Russian candidate. However, he largely abandoned Viktor Yanukovych in the repeat second round of the presidential elections.

Yevhen Marchuk, another leading politician in Ukraine, showed a similar reversal in political orientation. He was a high-ranking official of the Ukrainian KGB during Soviet rule, headed the Security Service of Ukraine after independence, and served as a prime minister under Kuchma in the mid-1990s. Marchuk became one of the leaders of the Social Democratic Party (United) during the 1998 parliamentary elections, but turned to radical nationalist organizations for support in the first round of the 1999 presidential elections. However, he then became Kuchma's supporter after the president appointed him head of the National Security and Defense Council of Ukraine in exchange for Marchuk's backing in the second round of the elections. After he was fired from the position of minister of defense before the 2004 presidential elections, Yevhen Marchuk abandoned his public support of Kuchma.

---

[84] It is noteworthy that this party received its highest proportion of votes in the Transcarpathia region (former Carpatho-Ukraine) in Western Ukraine.

Top politicians in Moldova have also switched their political orientations. Mircea Snegur, who was the agriculture secretary of the Communist Party of Soviet Moldova during Soviet rule, became a nationalist during *perestroika* and was elected president of Moldova. Petru Lucinschi, the leader of the Communist Party of Moldova during *perestroika*, ran as an independent in 1996 with a platform that was relatively more pro-Russian than Snegur's, but he did not implement it after becoming the president. As noted in chapter 3, a number of the former Communist party officials in the Gagauzia region became leaders of both the Gagauzia autonomy and the separatist movement after start of *perestroika*.[85]

Such shifts in political orientation are most consistent with rent-seeking motivations. Support for Ukrainian, Moldovan, and Transdniestrian independence was a result, not of ideological beliefs, but of personal self-interest that linked the pursuit of economic interests with the office of the president and other high positions. Numerous Western, Ukrainian, and Moldovan media reports contained allegations of corruption, referring to top Ukrainian and Moldovan leaders or their close family members, including Leonid Kravchuk, Leonid Kuchma, Oleksandr Tkachenko (the leader of the pro-Communist Peasant Party of Ukraine), Mircea Snegur, and the leaders of the Transdniestrian Republic, Gagauzia, and Crimea.

For example, recordings of conversations from Ukrainian President Leonid Kuchma's office contained evidence of rent-seeking and the large-scale corruption of top officials, including the president. These recordings, partly authenticated by the United States government, were secretly made by a former member of the presidential guard and were publicized in the parliament, the media, and on the Internet. (See Melnychenko Tapes Project, 2001; Tyler, 2001.)

---

[85]   In another example, Vladimir Solonari, a Bessarabian-born ethnic Ukrainian scholar of British history, was transformed from a leader of the pro-Communist and pro-Russian *Edinstvo* (Unity) movement in Soviet Moldova, a prominent deputy of the Socialist Unity bloc (1990-1997), and a lecturer in Russian and Ukrainian history at a Transdniestrian university to an ideological and parliamentary leader of the pro-presidential centrist bloc "For a Democratic and Prosperous Moldova" (1998-2001). After his party was defeated in the 2001 parliamentary elections, he became a NED Reagan-Fascell Fellow, a Rosenzweig Fellow at the US Holocaust Memorial Museum, and professor specializing in Jewish, Moldovan, Romanian, and Russian history at the University of Central Florida in the United States.

As noted in chapter 3, a number of measures implemented by Leonid Kuchma, such as the referendum to significantly increase the power of the president and diminish the power of parliament, as well as restrictions imposed on mass media, indicated his movement towards authoritarianism. Kuchma was accused of using his position to manipulate votes in the April 2000 referendum. As noted, the vote in favor of the president's proposals in the referendum was anomalous in both its regional pattern and the level of its support.

Creation of political parties for business purposes or personal enrichment is another example of rent-seeking in Ukraine. Such businessmen and businesswomen turned politicians, or oligarchs, as they are called, became very influential in Ukrainian politics despite weak popular support in the elections (See Table 5.7.) The source of oligarch support in parliament came from the recruiting deputies from other factions, often with the help of pecuniary rewards or bribes, and from elections in the majoritarian districts.

For example, the Revival of Regions became the third largest faction in the Ukrainian parliament in the end of 2000, even though its main party, the Democratic Union, had been created only a year earlier. The faction and the party were organized by Oleksandr Volkov, who became one of the richest people in Ukraine as result of his support for Kuchma in the 1994 elections. Even though Volkov was accused of having ties to organized crime, and a criminal case against him was pursued in Belgium, he helped to finance and organize both Kuchma's reelection in 1999 and the 2000 referendum.

Similarly, Viktor Medvedchuk and Hryhoriy Surkis were able to substantially increase their wealth after they gained control over the Social Democratic Party (United) and became supporters of Leonid Kuchma. A large number of businessmen and businesswomen joined other leading parties, including the Motherland, the Party of Regions, the Socialist Party, and the People's Union "Our Ukraine," for reasons of self-interest, such as to take advantage of the immunity from prosecution that was provided to members of parliament and local councils. Businessmen dominated even the parliamentary faction of the Green Party, whose campaign they financed during the elections in Ukraine. Similarly, many deputies from the "Renewal" movement, which won the parliamentary elections in the Transdniestrian Republic in December 2005, were businessmen.

Table 5.7 Composition of the Ukrainian parliament, 1998 and 2000

	Post 1998 elections		December 2000
Communist	*167*	*Communist*	*127*
Communist Party	120	Communist Party	111
Left Center (Socialist & Peasant Parties)	33	Socialist Party	16
Progressive Socialists	14		
Centrist and mixed	*86*	*Centrist and mixed*	*72*
People's Democratic Party	86	People's Democratic Party	20
		Reforms-Congress	15
		Solidarity	23
		Apple	14
Nationalist	*47*	*Nationalist*	*40*
People's Movement of Ukraine (*Rukh*)	47	People's Movement of Ukraine	19
		Ukrainian People's Movement	21
Oligarchic	*94*	*Oligarchic*	*166*
Hromada	45	Motherland	31
Social Democratic Party (United)	25	Social Democratic Party (United)	33
Green Party	24	Green Party	17
		Working Ukraine	48
		Revival of Regions	37
Independent and unaffiliated	*56*	*Independent and unaffiliated*	*44*
Total	450	Total	449

Sources: D'Anieri, Kravchuk and Kuzio (1999, p. 158), and Parliament (2000).

The 2002 parliamentary elections produced a similar pattern. Two main pro-presidential parties, the For United Ukraine bloc and the Social Democratic Party (United), together received 18 percent of the vote in the multi-mandate constituency. However, they managed to form the parliamentary majority because of their domination in single-mandate districts and their recruitment of independent deputies as well as deputies from the opposition factions. But this parliamentary majority disintegrated after its presidential candidate lost elections in December 2004. Many deputies and even factions in the Ukrainian parliament abandoned the former majority, and they began to support President Viktor Yushchenko. Such changes indicate motivations that are based not on ideology but on self-interest. Many deputies joined the pro-Kuchma majority as result of rational choice because of positive and negative incentives offered by the administration of Leonid Kuchma. These deputies became supporters of President Viktor Yushchenko and Prime Minister Yulia Tymoshenko for similar reasons.

While many journalists and academic experts in the West and in Ukraine described the victory of Viktor Yushchenko as a revolution similar to the Velvet Revolution in Czechoslovakia in 1989, interpretative analysis shows that the changes in the leadership of Ukraine as a result of the "Orange Revolution" were significant but not revolutionary. An analysis of the behavior of the leaders of the "Orange Revolution" is more revealing than the text of their revolutionary political speeches and slogans of *Maidan*.

Many key representatives of the Yushchenko-led oppositional coalition that formed the new government were once supporters of the former President Kuchma or members of the Soviet elite. Yulia Tymoshenko was an example of a wealth- and power-seeking political entrepreneur, who frequently changed her business and political allies and political orientation. She made a fortune, which according to some estimates was worth at least several billion dollars, by exploiting her personal ties among the regional elite in the Dnipropetrovsk region. Her business partners included her husband's father, who was a member of the regional government in the Soviet times, Oleksandr Turchynov, a regional leader of Soviet *Komsomol*, Viktor Pinchuk, who became President Kuchma's son-in-law, and Pavlo Lazarenko, who headed the administration of the Dnipropetrovsk region and became prime minister of Ukraine. Yulia Tymoshenko started her political career by joining a pro-Kuchma faction in the parliament of Ukraine. She soon became a leader of the pro-Lazarenko party, which had the most support in the Dnipropetrovsk region. Tymoshenko turned to the anti-Kuchma opposition as a result of her personal conflict with the former president and his inner circle over economic revenues from controlling natural gas delivery. After she was briefly imprisoned on corruption charges, she became one of the leaders of the anti-Kuchma opposition movement, and her popularity shifted to Western Ukraine.

Before the 2004 presidential elections, Yulia Tymoshenko had agreed, in a written secret agreement with Viktor Yushchenko, to support his bid for the presidency in return for the position of prime minister of Ukraine. She used her brief term as prime minister to increase her popularity by adopting populist economic policies, such as the introduction of government price caps on meat and gasoline, and by publicizing her fight against corruption, while, as Viktor Yushchenko alleged following her dismissal, she secretly interfered with the reprivatization of a highly profitable plant on behalf of an oligarch from the Dnipropetrovsk region and arranged for the dismissal of the large debt of a gas-trading company that she had run in the past. Tymoshenko de facto joined the anti-Yushchenko opposition after her dismissal.

Similarly, Petro Poroshenko, a wealthy businessmen who became the head of the National Security and Defense Council after the "Orange Revolution," started his political carrier by organizing a small pro-Kuchma faction in parliament. He used his significant wealth to support Viktor Yushchenko in the 2004 presidential elections. After Poroshenko lost the struggle for the position of prime minister to Yulia Tymoshenko, he endeavored to increase his political influence by significantly expanding the powers of the National Security and Defense Council. Accusations that Petro Poroshenko used his office for personal enrichment, which were levied against Poroshenko by Oleksandr Zinchenko, head of the presidential administration, provide another indication of the rent-seeking motivations of Poroshenko.

Oleksandr Zinchenko himself was a top *Komsomol* leader in the Soviet Union. He returned to Ukraine after its independence and became one of the leaders of the Social Democratic Party of Ukraine (United), an oligarchic political organization that supported Leonid Kuchma. Zinchenko abandoned this party and became one of the organizers of the presidential campaign of Viktor Yushchenko. He resigned from his position as head of the presidential administration in September 2005. Zinchenko became a leader of a small party that contested the 2006 parliamentary elections.

Picture 6 Viktor Yushchenko, whose face was disfigured by dioxin poison, speaks at a rally during the "Orange Revolution." Photo by K. Potrokhova. Reproduced with permission from "The Orange Revolution" CD (Kyiv, 2005), Oleksandr Sparinsky ©.

Viktor Yushchenko himself headed the National Bank and was prime minister during the presidency of Leonid Kuchma, and he supported Kuchma during "the tapegate scandal." He became a leader of anti-Kuchma opposition only after his government was dismissed in 2001. However, Yushchenko's behavior, including his decision to continue the presidential campaign even after he was poisoned, demonstrated his commitment to his ideas even when he faced significant threats to his life. Allegations of corruption levied against Viktor Yushchenko were less serious and direct than corruption allegations involving Leonid Kuchma and many other political leaders. Neither Ukrainian and Western media reports nor the Melnychenko tapes revealed evidence that Viktor Yushchenko had used his political power for purposes of personal enrichment.[86]

The role of oligarchs in politics and rent-seeking among the political leadership is not as large in Western Moldova (the former Bessarabia) as it is in Ukraine. An analysis of case studies, a search of media reports in the Lexus-Nexus database, and interviews with Moldovan experts did not reveal the existence of politically powerful oligarchs or cases of rent-seeking and corruption that would be comparable with the situation in Ukraine. This might be partially attributed to the much smaller size of Moldova, which limits the scale and visibility of rent-seeking and corruption. However, the composition of the Moldovan parliament after the 1998 elections did not show the rise of oligarchic factions as was the case in the Ukrainian parliament.

The orientation and behavior of deputies from centrist and mixed factions in the Moldovan parliament was similar to those of their counterparts in Ukraine. These factions were not motivated by ideology, but by patronage and rent-seeking. Centrist and mixed factions were used mainly to provide support to the president or to different business interests. For example, the Bloc for Democratic and Prosperous Moldova was created by supporters of Lucinschi after he won the presidential elections. As in Ukraine, the nationalist faction in the Moldovan parliament suffered internal splits and the defections of significant numbers of its members. However, the faction of the Party of Moldovan Communists remained the largest faction in parliament. (Table 5.8.)

The leadership of the Transdniestrian Republic was often described as being motivated not by ideology, but by rent-seeking. For example, General Lebed characterized the Transdniestrian leaders as "thieves and protectors of thieves." Another commander of the 14th Russian Army in this region gave a similar characterization of Igor Smirnov, the president of the Transdniestrian Republic. (See Lieven, 1998 p. 248.)

In contrast to Ukraine, direct evidence that linked the Transdniestrian leaders with large-scale smuggling, corruption, and other illegal activity in the region is not publicly available. However, indirect evidence suggests such

---

[86]   However, the Ukrainian media did uncover evidence that one of Yushchenko's sons had used Viktor Yushchenko's status as president to enrich himself.

rent-seeking motivations. For example, one of the sons of President Smirnov heads the Customs Committee of the unrecognized Republic. Many media reports in the West and in Moldova have characterized the Transdniestria region as a hotbed of smuggling and illegal weapons trade. Because the region's situation provides means for the enrichment of the family of the Transdniestrian president, he has a powerful self-interest in preserving its de facto independence. This self-interest was one of the factors that prevented a peaceful resolution of the Transdniestrian conflict, particularly after the leader of the Party of Moldovan Communists became president of Moldova.

Table 5.8 Composition of the Moldovan parliament, 1998 and 2000

	Post 1998 elections		December 2000
Communist	*40*	*Communist*	*40*
Party of Moldovan Communists	40	Party of Moldovan Communists	40
Centrist and mixed	*35*	*Centrist and mixed*	*28*
Bloc for Democratic and Prosperous Moldova	24	Bloc for Democratic and Prosperous Moldova	19
Party of Democratic Forces	11	Party of Democratic Forces	9
Nationalist	*26*	*Nationalist*	*21*
Democratic Convention of Moldova	26	Democratic Convention of Moldova	14
		Christian Democratic People's Party	7
Independent and unaffiliated	*0*	*Independent and unaffiliated*	*12*
Total	101	Total	101

Sources: King (2000, p. 158); Parliament (2001).

Political leaders played a much more significant role than parties did in the Transdniestrian Republic. For example, the United Council of Workers'

Collectives, the main separatist organization in the early 1990s, had lost its influence by the end of the decade. However, most of its former leaders, including the president of Transdniestria and the head of parliament, remained in top positions in the Transdniestrian Republic during this whole period. Directors of state industrial and agricultural enterprises increased their political influence despite the demise of the party, in which many of them, including Igor Smirnov, had played a significant role. The faction of the Union of the Industrialists, Agrarians, and Entrepreneurs, which represented economic interests of the business elite in the region, became the largest faction in parliament after the December 2000 elections. The Union won 40 percent of the seats, compared with 23 percent won by the left, which in previous elections had received the absolute majority of the vote.

Many scholars attribute the strength of the pro-Russian and pro-Communist vote in Transdniestria to the undemocratic leadership of the self-declared state. The statistical analysis of election results supports this conclusion to a certain extent. However, the higher level of pro-Communist and pro-Russian support in the Transdniestrian region than in the rest of Moldova was evident before the establishment of the authoritarian regime led by Igor Smirnov. The opinion poll data and case studies showed that the Transdniestrian leadership had a certain degree of popular legitimacy. (See King, 2000, p. 197; Kolsto, et al., 1993.)

The actions of Moldovan and Transdniestrian leaders, who received support from some politicians in Romania and Russia, contributed to the escalation of regional political cleavages into violent conflict in the beginning of the 1990s. For example, Moldovan government leaders facilitated escalation of the regional cleavages into the violent conflict in Transdniestria by sending government militia and troops into the secessionist region. Two commanders of the Russian Fourteenth Army, which remained in Transdniestria after the break-up of the Soviet Union, defected to the Transdniestrian separatists and became heads of the armed forces and the defense ministry of the Transdniestrian Republic in the beginning of 1992. The army took the side of the Transdniestrian separatists in violent clashes with the Moldovan forces in the spring and summer of 1992. Although the Fourteenth Army was nominally subordinate to the Russian government, it was, most likely, the Army commander who made the decision to militarily back the Transdniestrian forces.

Similarly, Alexander Lebed, a Russian Army general sent by the Russian leadership to replace the commander responsible for these decisions, acted with a great degree of independence in Transdniestria. Lebed, under whose leadership the Fourteenth Army was nominally a neutral and peace-keeping force, helped to secure the de facto independence of the Transdniestrian region. (See Dunlop, 1997; King, 2000.) However, the actions and charisma of General Lebed also helped to prevent the escalation of violence in the region.

The Russian leadership, under both Boris Yeltsin and Vladimir Putin, did not openly support the Transdniestrian separatists. For example, Russia did not recognize the Transdniestrian Republic. Both presidents of Russia, as well as Soviet President Mikhail Gorbachev, declared a peaceful solution of the conflict to be their goal. It is noteworthy that the Transdniestrian leaders received much stronger support from the Communist and nationalist opposition leaders in Russia. In turn, the Transdniestrian separatists supported the aborted anti-Gorbachev coup attempted by the anti-reformist Soviet leaders in 1991 and backed the anti-Yeltsin opposition in the confrontation that followed the dissolution of the Russian parliament in 1993.

However, the actions of some Russian leaders, in particular President Vladimir Putin, revealed their tacit support for the Transdniestrian separatists. For example, the agreement to withdraw the Fourteenth Army from Transdniestria was not fulfilled by the Russian government. A plan proposed by Dmitrii Kozak, the deputy head of Putin's administration, was more supportive of the Transdniestrian leadership stance on the settlement of the conflict. The plan envisioned significant autonomy, including a de factor power of veto, for the Transdniestria Region and Gagauz Yeri in federal Moldova.

Even the Communist government in Moldova, which came within hours of signing the Kozak plan, reversed its approval of the Russian proposal, in part because of strong opposition in Bessarabia to federalization of the country. (See Protsyk, 2005.) Furthermore, the popular opposition and fear of the "Orange style revolution" forced the Voronin administration to shift its political orientation from Russia and the CIS to a more pro-Western orientation. (Quinlan, 2004; "Moldova Contemplates a European Future," 2005).

Picture 7 Pro-Yushchenko demonstrators face special militia units guarding the Administration of the President of Ukraine during the "Orange Revolution," Kyiv city, 2004. Photo by H. Kysil. Reproduced with permission from "The Orange Revolution" CD (Kyiv, 2005) produced by Oleksandr Sparinsky ©.

The central government of Moldova initially opposed the creation of the Gagauz Republic and declared martial law in the region. Gagauz separatist leaders lacked the military support that the Fourteenth Army provided to Transdniestrian separatist leaders. An agreement on the autonomy of the Gagauz region, which was approved by the Moldovan parliament in 1994, reduced tensions. The Gagauz autonomy obtained the right to decide its own status if Moldova reunites with Romania.

In contrast to the actions of the Moldovan government leaders and separatist leaders in Transdniestria, the most influential government and the opposition leaders in Ukraine chose a peaceful solution to the political crisis at the end of 2004. Media reports indicate that a number of government leaders, including Prime Minister Viktor Yanukovych, lobbied for the use of force against opposition protesters in Kyiv city. Militarized units of the Ministry of Internal Affairs received such an order along with ammunition at the end of November 2004. (See Chivers, 2005; Leonov, 2005; "Oleksandr Turchynov," 2005; Wagstyl, Freeland, and Warner, 2004.)

Similarly, some leaders of the Orange opposition contemplated the use of force in order to seize power after the second round of the elections. Yulia Tymoshenko called for the seizure of the presidential administration headquarters and other government buildings during a mass rally in Kyiv. Viktor Yushchenko and a number of his advisors, with the assistance of some military commanders, planned to use tanks from a military unit stationed in the Chernihiv region to confront the internal troops and special police units, which were guarding the presidential headquarters, and seize that building along with the main government building and the National Television building in Kyiv city. (Lykhovii, 2005.)

However, the order to internal troops to disband opposition protesters in Kyiv city was reversed, and violent conflict was avoided in Ukraine. Although details about the actions of key participants in the political conflict in Ukraine at the end of 2004 are not yet available, most data indicate that leadership factors helped to prevent a violent conflict. Some reports state that a number of top leaders of the Security Service of Ukraine and the Ukrainian Army helped to rescind the order by threatening that their units would confront the troops of the Ministry of Internal Affairs. Other reports state that President Leonid Kuchma reversed his own order to use force, and that he largely abandoned his support for Viktor Yanukovych during the repeat second round of the presidential elections because of threats of economic, political, and legal sanctions made by a number of top politicians from the United States, Poland, and some other Western countries. Because Leonid Kuchma, Viktor Yanukovych, and many other pro-Russian leaders in Ukraine, for example leaders of the Party of Regions and other oligarchic parties, were motivated primarily by self-interest and not by ideology, these threats helped to change their political behavior. The fact that Viktor Yushchenko, in contrast to Yulia Tymoshenko and some other leaders of the Ukrainian opposition, was against the use of violence by his supporters was another major factor allowing the political crisis, which reflected to some extent traditional regional divisions in Ukraine, to remain peaceful. (See Bosacki, Wojciechowski, and Kramski, 2005; Chivers, 2005; Lykhovii, 2005; McLaughlin, 2005; "Oleksandr Turchynov," 2005; Wagstyl, Freeland, and Warner, 2004.)

The main pro-Russian party during the "Orange Revolution" was an oligarchic organization, and was more interested in compromise than in violent conflict. The Party of Regions was primarily motivated not by ideology but by the business and personal interests of its leaders, including Viktor Yanukovych and businessmen who represented this party in the Ukrainian parliament and regional governments, and oligarchs, such as Renat Akhmetov, who backed the party financially. For example, Viktor Yanukovych signed a memorandum with the party's former main rival President Viktor Yushchenko in 2005. The Party of Regions agreed to vote for Yushchenko's candidate for prime minister in exchange for de facto immunity from criminal prosecution for its leaders and backers.

In contrast to Transdniestria, pro-Russian separatists in Eastern Ukraine lacked significant support from sections of the Russian military and government leaders. The Russian troops, which were still stationed in Ukraine at the beginning of 1992, and the Black Sea Fleet, which remained stationed in Crimea, did not militarily back pro-Communist or pro-Russian forces in Ukraine. Press reports notwithstanding, there is no reliable evidence that elite units of Russian troops were sent to Ukraine to provide military support to President Leonid Kuchma and pro-Russian presidential candidate Viktor Yanukovych during the political crisis in November and December 2004. The mayor of Moscow and some other Russian political leaders gave strong backing to a congress of local leaders and deputies from Southern and Eastern Ukraine in November 2004 and separatist leaders in Crimea. However, President Yeltsin and President Putin did not provide military support for pro-Russian separatist leaders in Ukraine. Although Vladimir Putin supported Viktor Yanukovych during the 2004 presidential election, the Russian president ultimately recognized the victory of Viktor Yushchenko and visited Ukraine soon after the Ukrainian president's visit to Moscow at the beginning of 2005.

Information about many aspects of the conflict in Transdniestria, in particular the degree of control over the situation by Transdniestrian and Moldovan leaders, is too limited to draw definite conclusions about their role in starting the conflict. However, a comparison of Transdniestria with Gagauzia and regions of Eastern Ukraine shows that significant regional political cleavages do not necessarily lead to violent conflicts. Separatist leaders in all of these regions had similar political orientations, but violent conflicts did not occur in Gagauzia or in Eastern Ukraine, in particular in Crimea, whereas they did occur in Transdniestria.

Family and personal networks played more important roles in historically Eastern regions of Ukraine and Moldova than did voluntary associations and other forms of civil society. The importance of family and personal networks was also reflected in politics. For example, the Working Ukraine, which became one of the largest factions in the Ukrainian parliament, was led by Viktor Pinchuk, son-in law of Leonid Kuchma. Andrii Derkach was able to create a swift-moving political and business career because he was the godson of Kuchma and the son of the former head of the Security Service of Ukraine (SBU). Using their family ties and personal connections, Pinchuk and Derkach, like leaders of the Social Democratic Party of Ukraine (United) and the Revival of Regions faction, amassed control over many large and profitable enterprises, TV networks, and newspapers. (See Aslund, 1999; "Schemes and Scandals in Ukraine," 2001; Tsentr, 2000.) The importance of close family connections is demonstrated by the fact that Anatolii Franchuk, who served as prime minister of Crimea under Leonid Kuchma, lost much of his political influence after Kuchma's daughter divorced him.

It is noteworthy that a disproportionately large number of top government and parliamentary leaders in Ukraine came from the Dnipropetrovsk region in Eastern Ukraine. For example, Leonid Kuchma, the former prime minister and president of Ukraine, Pavlo Lazarenko and Valerii Pustovoitenko, prime ministers of Ukraine during Kuchma's first presidency, and Yulia Tymoshenko, prime minister of Ukraine during Yushchenko's presidency, all started their careers in the Dnipropetrovsk region.[87] Such influential politicians as Serhii Tyhipko, the former leader of the Working Ukraine faction and the head of the National Bank of Ukraine during Kuchma's second presidency, Leonid Derkach, the former head of SBU, Olekasandr Turchynov, one of the

---

[87]   *Hromada*, a party led by Lazarenko and Tymoshenko and later transformed into the Motherland Party, received most of its votes during the 1998 elections in the Dnipropetrovsk region.

leaders of the Motherland faction and the head of SBU in the Tymoshenko government, also started their rapid rise to positions of power in this region. (See *Dnipropetrovska*, 1996; *Who's Who*, 1997.) The rise to power of so many individuals from the Dnipropetrovsk region can be attributed to a network of personal connections.[88] For example, Ukrainian media reports show that Yulia Tymoshenko used her personal and business connections in Dnipropetrovsk region with Pavlo Lazarenko, Viktor Pinchuk, Serhii Tyhipko, and other politicians and officials in the region to amass political influence and a large fortune in the initial stage of her career.

Viktor Yushchenko also relied to a significant extent on his family and personal networks during his presidency and electoral campaigns. For example, Petro Poroshenko, Oleksii Ivchenko, and Oksana Bilozir were all godparents of his children. Petro Poroshenko, a deputy in the "Our Ukraine" faction led by Yushchenko, was an important financier of Yushchenko's presidential campaign; after the "Orange Revolution," Yushchenko appointed him as the head of the National Security and Defense Council. Oleksii Ivchenko, leader of the Congress of Ukrainian Nationalists, was a member of the "Our Ukraine" faction; after the "Orange Revolution," he became the head of Naftohaz Ukrainy, the state gas monopoly, and the chief negotiator in natural gas talks with Russia. Oksana Bilozir, a popular singer, was a member of the "Our Ukraine" faction in parliament; she was appointed minister of culture in the Tymoshenko cabinet.

During the 2006 parliamentary election campaign, the Yushchenko Bloc "Our Ukraine" used in its designation the last name not of Viktor Yushchenko but of his brother in order to both capitalize on popular recognition of the president's name and comply with the campaign law that prohibited use of the names of people who were not running for parliament. Petro Yushchenko was a deputy of the "Our Ukraine" faction and a leading member of the People's Union "Our Ukraine," whose honorary chairman was President Yushchenko. A young nephew of Viktor Yushchenko became a deputy head

---

[88]   When Leonid Brezhnev was the secretary general of the CPSU, a disproportionately large number of the top leaders of the Soviet Union and Soviet Ukraine were also associated by their party career, work, education, or birth with the Dnipropetrovsk region, where Brezhnev started his party career. (See *Dnipropetrovska*, 1996.)

of the administration of the Kharkiv region after his uncle's victory in the 2004 presidential elections.

The involvement of family and personal networks in politics is associated with corruption. For example, Pavlo Lazarenko was arrested and charged, first in Switzerland and then in the United States, for large-scale money-laundering and other illegal financial dealings. He was accused of granting illegal privileges to a gas trading company headed by Yulia Tymoshenko and receiving large pay-offs from her. The combined charges leveled against Lazarenko and Tymoshenko exceed two billion dollars. In comparison, the annual official export from Ukraine to countries outside of the former Soviet Union was estimated at six to seven billion dollars for the period 1994 to 1996 (EBRD, 1997, p. 238). The recordings of meetings in Kuchma's presidential cabinet made by his bodyguard contained evidence of illegal financial transactions in the amount of hundreds of millions of dollars by several other businessmen and government officials who were personally and politically connected to the president of Ukraine.

These leading businessmen-politicians were not part of the Communist leadership during Soviet times; this undermines the argument that the Communist elite in Ukraine forced the break-up of the Soviet Union in order to gain economic benefits. After the collapse of the Soviet Union, the Communist parties in Ukraine and Moldova were headed not by the top leaders of the Republican branches of the CPSU, but by lower ranked functionaries. For example, Petro Symonenko, the head of the Communist Party of Ukraine, was a party functionary in the Donetsk region during Soviet times. Similarly, Oleksandr Moroz, the head of the Socialist Party of Ukraine, was a party official in the Kyiv region until he became the leader of the Communist faction in the Soviet Ukraine parliament in 1990. Oleksandr Tkachenko, a leader of the Peasant Party of Ukraine and the former chairman of parliament, was the minister of agriculture in Soviet Ukraine. (See *Who's Who*, 1997.) Vladimir Voronin, the leader of the Party of Moldovan Communists, served as the minister of internal afairs in Soviet Moldova. The top leadership of the Transdniestrian Republic included former district-level officials of the Communist Party of the Soviet Union.

It is noteworthy that all of these Communist leaders were born in Eastern regions of Ukraine and Moldova. Igor Smirnov, a leader of the separatist movement and the president of the Transdniestrian Republic, was born in Russia and worked as a manager in factories in both Eastern Ukraine and Transdniestria during Soviet times. In contrast, many of the nationalist leaders, including those who abandoned the Communist Party, were born in the Western regions: Leonid Kravchuk was born in the Rivne region, part of the historical Volhynia region in Western Ukraine; Mircea Snegur was born in the Western part of Moldova, or the former Bessarabia, which was part of Romania during the inter-war period. (See King, 2000, pp. 134-135.) Although Viktor Yushchenko, president of Ukraine and the leader of the "Our Ukraine" bloc, was born in Eastern Ukraine, he studied and worked in the former Galicia region in Western Ukraine, which affected his political socialization.[89]

Many of the former dissidents became actively involved in politics and were elected to the parliaments of Ukraine and Moldova. However, the highest positions that they attained after the independence were confined to the leadership of nationalist parties and to ministerial and regional positions. For example, Viacheslav Chornovil, who was arrested and sentenced for dissident activity in Soviet Ukraine, became a leader of *Rukh*, the main nationalist party in post-Communist Ukraine.[90] (See Browne, 1971.)

Despite the frequent shifts in political orientation of top leaders, which are often motivated by rent-seeking, regional voting behaviors and attitudes remained consistent in both Ukraine and Moldova as long as elections were democratic. As noted, Western regions gave the strongest support to pro-nationalist and pro-Western candidates, while Eastern regions supported more pro-Communist and pro-Russian candidates, even if it meant reversing votes from one election to another. For example, the recordings of Kuchma's conversations revealed that, during the 1999 presidential campaign, he ordered the use of pressure, including threats of criminal prosecution, against local officials only in Eastern regions, while specifically requesting that Western regions be excluded from such methods for vote-gathering. (See Melnychenko Tapes, 2001.) Analysis of the data from the World Values Survey in

---

[89]   Anatolii Kinakh, the former prime minister of Ukraine and an ally of Viktor Yushchenko during the "Orange Revolution," was born in the Bessarabia region of Moldova.

[90]   Chornovil died as a result of a mysterious traffic incident before the 1999 presidential elections. Some of his allies argued that it was a political assassination.

Ukraine and the Laitin/Hough survey in Moldova shows a similar regional variation in the political preferences of the respondents.

It is noteworthy that differences in political developments in Ukraine and Moldova were largely consistent with historical divisions in Eastern Europe among countries that had been part of the Russian Empire, the Austro-Hungarian Monarchy, Germany, or the Ottoman Empire. Ukrainian politics became dominated by the elite and voters from the Eastern regions, which had experienced long Russian and then Soviet rule. With notable exceptions of the successful pro-independence movement and the "Orange Revolution," the influence of historically Western regions on national politics was less significant, because of the lack of influential oligarchic groups and the much smaller population.

Weak political parties, wide-spread corruption, rent-seeking among the political elites, the emergence of oligarchs, and the influence of informal networks made Ukraine before the "Orange Revolution" much more similar to Russia than to Poland, Czech Republic, Hungary, and post-Meciar Slovakia, which were historically parts of the Austro-Hungarian Monarchy and Germany. The presidency of Kuchma paralleled the Russian presidency in many of these aspects. The authoritarian measures adopted by Leonid Kuchma after his reelection in 1999 corresponded to developments in Russia during Putin's presidency. These decisions included the expansion of presidential power, of control over parliament and regional governments, and of the influence of domestic security ministries and police, as well as the persecution of independent and opposition mass media and selected oligarchs. (Way, 2005.) Results of numerous elections and surveys show that, were it not for the Western regions of Ukraine, this post-Soviet country would most likely have continued to follow Russia's authoritarian path, and pursue a pro-Russian orientation as did the Transdniestrian Republic and Belarus.

Political developments in Moldova differed between Western regions, which were part of Romania during the inter-war period, and historically Eastern regions, where the Transdniestrian Republic emerged. The behavior of political elites in post-Communist Moldova was more similar to that in Romania than in Russia. However, Moldova's political system and development path remained volatile. Political development in the Transdniestrian Republic was most closely related to the authoritarian path of Belarus, which was politically dominated by Eastern regions, whose historical development was similar to that of Transdniestria and Eastern Ukraine.

5.4   Comparison of regional culture with other factors

Statistical analysis allows us to summarize the results of various elections and referendums and compare culture to other factors of regional political divisions in post-Communist Ukraine and Moldova. Regional results of national elections and referendums between 1991 and 2005 are used.

Statistical analysis of election and referendum results between 1991 and 2004 in 26 Ukrainian regions shows a remarkable persistence of regional cleavages. Votes for nationalist/pro-Western candidates and parties in seven presidential and parliamentary elections are highly intercorrelated. The correlations range from 0.51 to 0.95. The vote for the Communist and pro-Russian parties and candidates in Ukrainian regions also shows a highly consistent pattern. The correlations are from 0.47 to 0.94. The vote for the preservation of the Soviet Union in the March 1991 referendum is strongly associated with support for the pro-Communist/pro-Russian parties and candidates. Correlations range from 0.63 to 0.94. (See Table A.2 in the Appendix.)

The results of the referendum on the independence of Ukraine in December 1991 are correlated more moderately with the results of the other elections and the March 1991 referendum. However, all correlation coefficients are in the expected direction. Correlations between the vote for independence and the nationalist/pro-Western vote range from 0.33 to 0.71. Principal factor component analysis of the vote for Communist and pro-Russian presidential candidates and parties and the vote for the preservation of the Soviet Union in Ukrainian regions produces a single factor solution. The same result is obtained from the factor analysis of nationalist and pro-Western votes. (See Tables A.2, A.3, and A.4 in the Appendix.)

Two separate scales, which range from 0 to 100, have been created on the basis of the factor analysis. The scales include the results of all analyzed elections and referendums, since they are highly inter-correlated and have high factor scores. The first scale measures regional support for the Communist and pro-Russian parties and candidates and the March 1991 vote for the preservation of the Soviet Union (Table 5.9). The second scale measures regional support for the nationalist and pro-Western parties and candidates and the vote for the independence of Ukraine in the December 1991 referendum. Both scales have very high reliability coefficients (0.96.) The very high negative correlation between these scales (-0.97) lends support to the view that a strong ideological cleavage exists between Ukrainian nationalist/pro-Western and Communist/pro-Russian electorates.

The pro-Communist and pro-Russian vote scale in Ukraine is based on the proportion of the vote in 26 regions for: preservation of the Soviet Union in the March 1991 referendum; Leonid Kravchuk in the 1991 presidential elections; candidates from the Communist, Socialist, Peasant and Unity parties in the 1994 parliamentary elections; Leonid Kuchma in the second round of the 1994 presidential elections; the Communist Party, the Socialist, and Peasant parties Bloc, and the Progressive Socialist Party in the 1998 parliamentary elections; Petro Symonenko in the second round of the 1999 presidential elections; the Communist Party, the Communist Party of Workers and Peasants, the Communist Party (Renewed), the Socialist Party, the Progressive Socialist Party, and *ZUBR* (For the Union of Ukraine, Belarus, and Russia) in the 2002 parliamentary elections; and Viktor Yanukovych in the repeat second round of the 2004 presidential elections.[91]

The small number of regions makes it impossible to replicate the same kind of correlation and factor analysis in Moldova. Data on elections and referendums between 1991 and 2005 are not always available at the district level. Several of these votes were boycotted in some regions, for example, in Gagauzia. In addition, changes in the structure and territorial composition in both Moldova's districts and the Gagauz region make it impossible to extend the same kind of statistical analysis to the district level.

---

[91]   See Craumer and Clem, 1999; CVK, 2000, 2002, 2004; Kuzio and Wilson 1994; Wilson, 1997. Even though the Socialist Party supported Viktor Yushchenko in the final rounds of the 2004 presidential elections and joined the government coalition after the "Orange Revolution," this party backed Communist presidential candidates in the second rounds of the previous elections, including the 1999 elections. The inclusion or the exclusion of the vote for the Socialist Party in the 2002 parliamentary elections does not alter main results of the statistical analysis.

Table 5.9 Regional variation of the Communist/pro-Russian and Nationalist/pro-Western vote indexes

Region	Communist/pro-Russian vote index	Nationalist/pro-Western vote index
Western Ukraine		
Ternopil	7	82
Lviv	7	79
Ivano-Frankivsk	9	82
Rivne	23	69
Volyn	23	62
Transcarpathia	25	50
Chernivtsi	28	56
Eastern Ukraine		
Kyiv city	29	49
Kyiv region	38	50
Khmelnytsky	43	46
Vinnytsia	45	42
Zhytomyr	46	40
Cherkassy	46	42
Dnipropetrovsk	50	30
Sumy	51	38
Kirovohrad	52	36
Poltava	52	37
Chernihiv	53	35
Odesa	53	28
Kharkiv	54	27
Mykolayiv	55	31
Kherson	56	31
Zaporizhzhia	58	27
Crimea	59	18
Donetsk	61	23
Luhansk	67	20
Bessarabia	36	
Transdniestrian Republic	70	

However, a comparative analysis of the regional electoral results, case studies, and survey data demonstrates the existence of strong and persistent cleavages between Moldovan nationalists and Communist/pro-Russian forces. In Moldova, like Ukraine, these cleavages coincide with regional political divisions. The index of the pro-Communist and pro-Russian vote in the two main regions of Moldova has been created by averaging the vote for pro-Communist and pro-Russian parties and candidates in the elections held from 1991 to 2005, and the support for the preservation of the Soviet Union in the March 1991 referendum. The index in Western regions of Moldova is the unweighted average of the vote for the preservation of the Soviet Union in the 1990 opinion poll; the Socialist Unity Bloc in the 1994 parliamentary elections; the Party of Communists and the Socialist Unity Bloc in the 1995 local elections; Petru Lucinschi in the second round of the 1996 elections; the Party of Moldovan Communists in the 1998 parliamentary elections; the Party of Moldovan Communists and *Edinstvo* bloc in the 2001 parliamentary elections; the Party of Moldovan Communists, bloc "*Patria-Rodina*," and the movement "*Ravnopravie*" in the 2005 parliamentary elections; and against Mircea Snegur in the 1991 presidential elections.[92] The index in Transdniestria includes a proportion of the vote for the following: preservation of the Soviet Union in the March 1991 referendum; the Union of Patriotic Forces in the 1995 local elections; pro-Communist parties in the 2001 parliamentary elections; and Igor Smirnov in the 1991, 1996, and 2001 presidential elections.[93]

The pro-nationalist/pro-Western scale is based on the proportion of the vote in 26 regions of Ukraine received by or in favor of the independence of Ukraine in the December 1991 referendum; nationalist candidates in the 1991 presidential elections; nationalist parties in the 1994 parliamentary elections; Leonid Kravchuk in the second round of the 1994 presidential elections; nationalist parties in the 1998 parliamentary elections; Leonid Kuchma in the second round of the 1999 presidential elections; "Our Ukraine" bloc in the

[92]   Because this referendum was not held in Western regions of Moldova, this study uses the results of a survey that asked a similar question. (See *Obshchestvennoe*, 1990.)

[93]   See IFES, 1994, 1995, 1996, 1998, 1999, 2001a; King, 2000; *Obshchestvennoe*, 1990; "Preliminary Results," 2005; and various media sources.

2002 parliamentary elections; and Viktor Yushchenko in the repeat second round of the 2004 presidential elections.

Table 5.9 shows that support for pro-Communist and pro-Russian candidates and parties and for the preservation of the Soviet Union is much higher in regions of Ukraine and Moldova, which are located within the August 1939 borders of the Soviet Union, than in the Western regions, which became part of the Soviet Union as a result of the Molotov-Ribbentrop Pact of 1939 and World War II. All regions but the city of Kyiv (29 percent) in Eastern Ukraine score 38 to 67 percent on the pro-Communist and pro-Russian vote scale, while the score is 28 percent or less in all regions in Western Ukraine. It is noteworthy that support for pro-Communist and pro-Russian candidates and parties is strongest in Luhansk and Donetsk regions and Crimea (59 to 67 percent) and weakest in the three regions of the former Austro-Hungarian province of Galicia (7 to 9 percent on the 100-point scale.) Similarly, electoral support for pro-Communist and pro-Russian candidates and parties and for the preservation of the Soviet Union is much higher in the Transdniestrian Republic (70 percent) than in Western part of Moldova (36 percent).

The pro-nationalist and pro-Western vote scale shows the reverse pattern (Table 5.9). It is equal or higher than 50 percent in all regions of Western Ukraine, compared with 18 to 50 percent in Eastern regions. Support for nationalist and pro-Western candidates and parties and the independence of Ukraine is highest in three regions of the former Galicia province (79 to 82 percent) and lowest in Crimea, which was transferred from the Russian Republic in the Soviet Union to the Ukrainian Soviet Republic by Khrushchev in 1954, and in Luhansk and Donetsk regions (18 to 23 percent).

Communist/pro-Russian and nationalist/pro-Western votes and preferences are the dependent variables in regression analysis. These variables are based on election and referendum results and public opinion data. The 1996 World Values Survey (WVS) in Ukraine and the 1998 Laitin/Hough Surveys in Western Moldova and the self-declared Transdniestrian Republic provide individual level data. The survey data help to ensure that the results of the analysis are not sensitive to either the ecological inference problem, which stems from the reliance on aggregate data, or a likely bias created by less democratic elections and referendums in Transdniestria. (See King, 1997.)

The independent variables are derived from the regional historical legacy and aggregate data on the religious, ethnic, and linguistic composition of the population; the levels of economic development in 26 regions of Ukraine and two main regions of Moldova; and individual level data on ethnicity, language, religion, income, education, class, age, and gender. (See Table A.1 in the Appendix.) Historical legacy is measured by the number of years between 1793 and 1944 that a region was not under Russian/Soviet control. Since culture evolves slowly, short periods of non-Russian and non-Soviet rule during World War I, the Civil War, and World War II are not included in the total. In some regions, such as Chernivtsi and Odesa, which include areas with different historical legacies, this measure is weighted according to the proportion of registered voters living in these areas. The year 1793 is chosen as the approximate date by which the present territory of Ukraine was divided between the Russian Empire and the Austro-Hungarian Monarchy and the Transdniestria region of Moldova was incorporated by Russia.

The regression analysis shows that several variables affect significantly pro-Communist and pro-Russian vote in regions of Ukraine and Moldova (Figure 5.2). The historical experience variable, expressed as the number of years of non-Russian/non-Soviet rule, has the strongest effect on the regional pro-Communist and pro-Russian vote index. The historical legacy variable has a stronger effect than the other factors – such as ethnicity or the urbanization rate – because this variable has the largest standardized (Beta) coefficient, which shows the relative influence of different factors.

Keeping other variables constant, 100 years of non-Russian/non-Soviet rule decrease the pro-Communist/pro-Russian vote by more than 20 percent (Figure 5.2). The historical legacy variable is statistically significant at the 0.001 level, which means that the probability of an error in determining the relationship between this factor and the pro-Communist/pro-Russian vote is very small, not exceeding 1 in 1000.

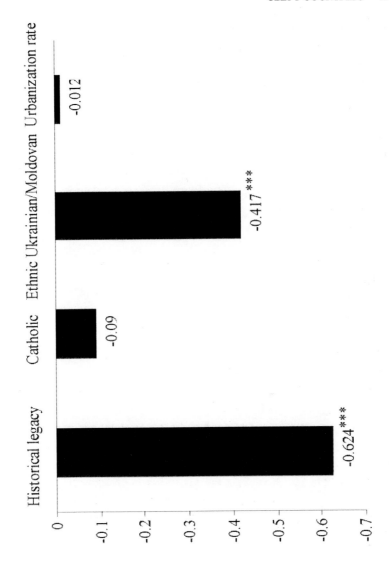

Figure 5.2 Determinants of regional pro-Communist/pro-Russian vote in Ukraine and Moldova, 1991-2005

Note: The figure shows standardized regression coefficients. *** denotes significance at 0.001, ** denotes significance at 0.01, * denotes significance at 0.05.

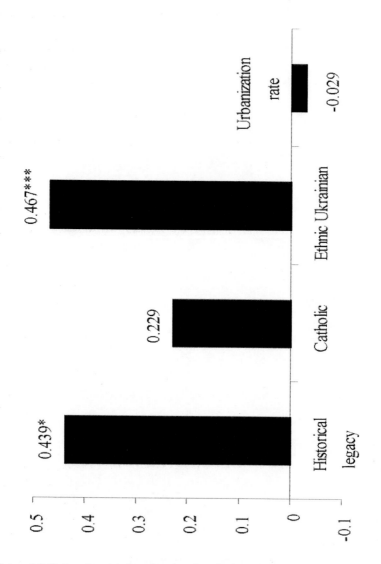

Figure 5.3 Determinants of regional nationalist/pro-Western vote in Ukraine in 1991-2005

Note: The figure shows standardized regression coefficients. *** denotes significance at 0.001, ** denotes significance at 0.01, * denotes significance at 0.05.

The ethnic variable, defined as the proportion of ethnic Ukrainians or Moldovans in the regional population, has the second largest negative effect on the pro-Communist and pro-Russian vote. This variable is statistically significant at 0.001 level. The proportion of Catholics in the population and the urbanization rate have no statistically significant effects on the pro-Communist and pro-Russian vote in Ukraine and Moldova.[94]

The regression results do not depend on the inclusion of Transdniestria and the rest of Moldova. The historical experience variable has the largest standardized coefficient and is statistically significant at 0.01 level in the regression confined to Ukrainian regions. These and other regression results are not sensitive to choices of different base years for historical legacy, inclusion of years of non-Russian and non-Soviet rule during World War I, Civil War, and World War II, inclusion of the results of the December 2005 parliamentary elections in the Transdniestrian Republic, or the use of GDP per capita in 1995 as a measure of the regional level of economic development produces similar results to those produced by the urbanization rate.

Multivariate regression with the nationalist/pro-Western vote index as the dependent variable shows a similar pattern. The non-Russian/non-Soviet historical experience variable has the second largest and most highly significant effect on the pro-nationalist and pro-Western vote in Ukraine. This variable is statistically significant at 0.05 level, and its standardized (Beta) coefficient is slightly lower than the standardized coefficient of the ethnicity. (See Figure 5.3.) Keeping other variables constant, 100 years of non-Russian/non-Soviet rule increases the pro-nationalist/pro-Western vote by almost 15 percent.

The ethnic Ukrainian variable has a positive and statistically significant effect on the pro-nationalist/pro-Western vote. When the ethnicity variable is substituted for the language variable in the regression, Beta coefficients of the historical legacy and language variables become similar. Statistical analysis shows that language is strongly associated with ethnicity. The

---

[94]   A high correlation between the Catholic and historical experience variables (0.79) indicates a multicollinearity problem. Each of these variables becomes statistically significant at the 0.001 level at separate regressions, but the historical experience produces larger standardized coefficients and R squared.

correlation coefficient between the proportion of Ukrainian speakers and the proportion of ethnic Ukrainians in the population in 1989 is 0.99. The World Values Survey data also show a high correlation between Ukrainian language and ethnicity (0.48). The Laitin/Hough survey data demonstrate an even stronger relationship between Romanian language and Moldovan ethnicity: 0.83.

Regression analysis shows that the use of a Western historical regions dummy variable instead of years of non-Russian/non-Soviet rule produces similar results. The Western historical regions variable is the strongest predictor of pro-Communist/pro-Russian vote and nationalist/pro-Western vote. This measure of regional political culture is statistically significant at the 0.001 level. When other factors are kept constant, the average Western region scores 25 percent lower than the average historical Eastern region on the pro-Communist/pro-Russian vote scale in Ukraine and Moldova. The regional difference in the level of the nationalist/pro-Western vote in Ukraine that is attributed to historical legacy equals 23 percent.

Several other regional variables, suggested by previous studies as measures of political culture, are statistically significant predictors of the pro-Communist/pro-Russian vote scale and the nationalist/pro-Western vote scale in Ukraine. However, these dummy variables have significantly less predictive power and consistency compared with the Western historical region variable and years of non-Russian/non-Soviet rule as determinants of regional voting patterns in individual elections and referendums in Ukraine. The Western geographical dummy, which splits Ukraine along the Dnieper River, has a statistically significant effect on pro-Communist/pro-Russian vote and the nationalist/pro-Western vote in one-third of 16 regressions. Center and South regional dummies in the four-region model are statistically significant predictors in about one-third of the regressions.[95]

These three geographically based dummy variables perform especially poorly in parliamentary elections. The vote for pro-Communist/pro-Russian political parties and nationalist/pro-Western parties offers a more refined measure of regional political cultures than does support for presidential candidates, because the vote in the final round of presidential elections is af-

---

[95]   East is the omitted dummy variable.

fected by the personality of politicians and this support includes considerable proportions of voters who backed different candidates in the first round. Regression analysis shows that the South regional dummy is not statistically significant in any cases of parliamentary elections. Center is a statistically significant predictor only in the 2002 parliamentary elections. The geographic West variable is statistically significant only in cases of support for pro-Communist and pro-Russian parties in the 1998 parliamentary elections and the 2002 parliamentary elections in Ukraine.

In comparison, the Western historical region variable is statistically significant in four-fifths of the regressions, including all cases of parliamentary elections. The years of non-Russian/non-Soviet rule variable has a statistically significant effect in about three-fifths of the cases, including one-half of the parliamentary elections. The 2004 presidential elections is the only case in which neither of these two versions of measuring regional historical legacy is a statistically significant predictor of the regional vote.

This result can be explained by the fact that Viktor Yushchenko widened his regional appeal by assembling a broad electoral coalition, which included not only some nationalist parties and leaders but also a number of liberal, centrist, and oligarchic parties and leaders; emphasizing his successful economic record as former prime minister of Ukraine; and using his charisma. For example, Yushchenko was supported by the Motherland Party, led by the former oligarch Yulia Tymoshenko, and by the Socialist Party, which had supported a Communist Party candidate in the second round of the 1999 presidential elections but decided to support Yushchenko in the second round of the 2004 elections. The orange color and many other campaign attributes used by Viktor Yushchenko during the elections were never employed by nationalist leaders and organizations.

Yushchenko's popular appeal was based not only on ideology, which combined populist, liberal, and nationalist ideas, but also on his personal charisma. For example, two national polls conducted by "the Ukrainian barometer" at the end of February 2005 and again at the beginning of April 2005 showed that support for the bloc "Our Ukraine" dropped by more than one-third (from 32 percent to 21 percent) after the name of Viktor Yushchenko, who became a honorary chairman of the party, was replaced by the name of another leader of this party. Two other polls, conducted by the Razumkov

Center during the same time period, revealed that changes in support for this political organization (30 and 27 percent) remained within the margin of statistical error despite the modification of its name, leadership, and composition when Viktor Yushchenko was identified as its leader.

Personal observations show that young women and secondary school students, who are traditionally least active in Ukrainian politics, constituted a significant proportion of pro-Yushchenko demonstrators. The participation of these groups in anti-Soviet demonstrations at the end of the 1980s and the beginning of the 1990s, and in anti-Kuchma demonstrations in 2000 and 2001, was far less significant. In contrast, Viktor Yanukovych lacked charisma. His past criminal convictions for robbery and assault lessened the popular appeal of the main pro-Russian candidate in spite of overwhelmingly positive coverage on most TV channels.

While historical legacy was the main determinant of regional support for the bloc "Our Ukraine" that was led by Viktor Yushchenko in the 2002 parliamentary elections, ethnicity became the main predictor of the vote in the 2004 presidential elections. The proportion of ethnic Ukrainians in the regional population had a positive and statistically significant effect on the regional vote for Viktor Yushchenko, and it had a negative effect on regional support for Viktor Yanukovych.

The 1996 World Values Survey and the 1998 Laitin/Hough survey allow us to analyze individual level attitudes in different regions of Ukraine and Moldova. The 1995 to 1997 wave of World Values Surveys was conducted in 1996 in both Ukraine and Moldova. As noted before, the survey conducted in Moldova did not include the Transdniestria region. However, the 1998 Laitin/Hough survey was conducted in Transdniestria and the rest of Moldova. Measures of support for Communist and nationalist parties in Ukraine, as well as the index of pro-Soviet/pro-Russian attitudes in Moldova, are derived from these surveys.

Figure 5.4 shows that the historical legacy variable has the strongest effect on support for nationalist parties in Ukraine. This variable has the largest standardized coefficient and is significant at the 0.001 level. Keeping other variables constant, 100 years of non-Russian/non-Soviet historical legacy increases support for the nationalist parties among the respondents by 18 percent. The average Catholic is 18 percent more likely than the average non-Catholic to say that he or she would vote for nationalist parties. The religion variable is statistically significant at the 0.001 level. This variable measures the effects of both a religious element of political culture and of present-day religious affiliation.

Ethnicity also strongly affects the vote for nationalist parties in Ukraine. Not surprisingly, support for nationalist parties is much weaker among ethnic Russians and other ethnic minorities than among ethnic Ukrainians. The ethnic variables are statistically significant at the 0.001 level. Other variables – such as class, education, income, and age – are not significant, with the exception of gender. The average male respondent is 6 percent less likely to support nationalist parties than the average female respondent. (Figure 5.4.)

The historical legacy variable strongly affects the pro-Communist vote in Ukraine. One hundred years of non-Russian/non-Soviet rule in a region decreases support for the Communist parties by 12 percent. However, age also has a highly significant effect on the support of pro-Communist parties in Ukraine. An expressed desire to vote for Communist parties is much stronger among older respondents. Both historical legacy and age variables are statistically significant at the 0.001 level, but the former has a smaller standardized coefficient than the latter. The average Catholic is 10 percent less likely to support the Communist parties than the average non-Catholic. This variable is significant at the 0.05 level. (Figure 5.5.)

Education and income are negatively associated with the pro-Communist vote in Ukraine. The higher the respondent's education level or income, the lower his or her support for Communist parties. The first variable is statistically significant at the 0.001 level, and the second variable is significant at the 0.05 level. The effect of ethnic variables on the Communist vote is not as strong as the effect on the support for the nationalist parties.

The effect of historical legacy on party preference in Moldova cannot be statistically evaluated by means of the World Values Survey, because the survey does not include Transdniestria. The survey includes Gagauzia, but the number of respondents in the region is small (40). Less than half of them claimed to be a national minority. The ethnicity of the rest of the respondents is given as "don't know."

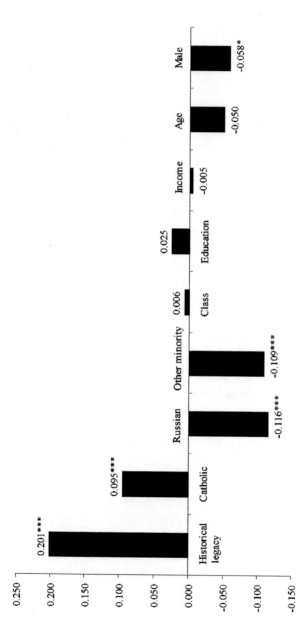

Figure 5.4 Determinants of support for nationalist parties in Ukraine (1996 World Values Survey)

Note: The figure shows standardized regression coefficients. The survey question is "If there were a national election tomorrow, for which party on this list would you vote?" Parties coded as nationalist are as follows: the All Ukrainian Political Alliance "State Independence of Ukraine," the Congress of Ukrainian Nationalists, the People's Movement of Ukraine (*Rukh*), the Democratic Party, the Ukrainian Conservative Republican Party, the Ukrainian National Assembly, the Ukrainian National Conservative Party, the Ukrainian Republican Party, and the Ukrainian Peasant Democratic Party. *** denotes significance at 0.001, ** denotes significance at 0.01, * denotes significance at 0.05.

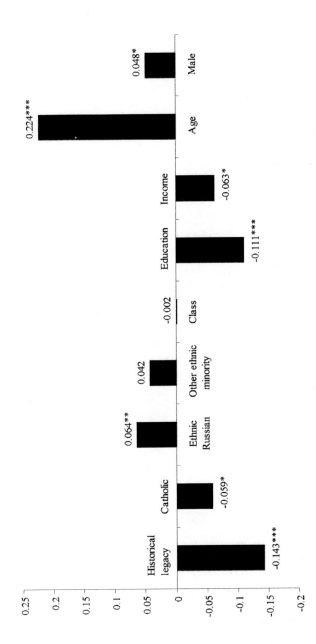

Figure 5.5 Determinants of support for Communist parties in Ukraine (1996 World Values Survey)

Note: The figure shows standardized regression coefficients. The pro-Communist parties include the Communist Party, the Socialist Party, and the Peasant Party. *** denotes significance at 0.001, ** denotes significance at 0.01, * denotes significance at 0.05.

The index of pro-Soviet/pro-Russian attitudes in Moldova derived from the 1998 Laitin/Hough survey is used instead. (See Table A.5 in the Appendix.) The index is based on the following questions: "How do you assess the passing of the Soviet Union?"; "To what degree do you consider yourself a citizen of the former USSR?"; and "What future state structure would you prefer to see in Moldova?" These questions were asked in surveys conducted in both Transdniestria and in the rest of Moldova. The scale reliability coefficient is 0.60.

Regression results show that both historical legacy and ethnicity have a strong effect on the index of pro-Soviet/pro-Russian attitudes in Moldova. The historical legacy variable is significant at the 0.001 level. One hundred years of non-Russian/non-Soviet historical experience in a region increases a respondent's score on the pro-Soviet and pro-Russian attitude scale (which ranges from 0 to 4) by 1.4 units. The effect of this cultural factor is the largest. Keeping other factors constant, the Gagauz respondents score much higher on the pro-Soviet and pro-Russian attitude scale than do other ethnic groups. (Figure 5.6.)

The standardized coefficients and significance levels (0.001) of the ethnic Russian variable, the Gagauz variable, and the other ethnic minority variable are similar to those of the historical legacy variable. As noted, ethnic Ukrainians form the predominant portion of the non-Russian minority population in Moldova. Age is positively and strongly associated with pro-Soviet/pro-Russian attitudes in Moldova. The occupation rank variable, which puts managerial occupations at the top, negatively affects pro-Soviet and pro-Russian attitudes. (Figure 5.6.)

One should note limitations of the statistical analysis. The regressions explain a relatively small fraction of the variation in stated support for both nationalist and Communist parties in Ukraine (12 and 14 percent). In addition to the aforementioned problems associated with the ecological inference[96] and randomness of sample, some factors are difficult to quantify. Regression analysis, which uses election results and expressed party prefer-

---

[96] The ecological inference method developed by Gary King (1997) shows that regression results are not affected by the ecological inference problem. This statistical method indicates that ethnic Moldovans and Ukrainians vote differently in different historical regions.

ence, cannot explain why regional political divisions turned into violent conflict in Moldova but not in Ukraine. The role of political leaders in regional political divisions in Ukraine and Moldova cannot be readily quantified.

However, even taking the limitations of statistical approaches into account, multivariate analysis of the regional voting data, ecological inference methods, and regression analysis of the survey data consistently show that cultural factors – mainly linked to different historical legacies – strongly affect voting results and party preferences in post-Communist Ukraine and Moldova. Although their effects are less significant and consistent, ethnic and economic variables are also important.

Statistical analysis shows that historical legacy in the regions of Ukraine and Moldova has a significant effect on support for privatization. The number of years under non-Russian and non-Soviet rule is positively associated with support for increased private ownership in Ukraine, even when other factors, such as income, age, and ethnicity, are held constant. The effect of the historical legacy is stronger than the effect of other factors, such as income and age. This relationship is statistically significant at the 0.001 level. (Figure 5.7.)

Similarly, the number of years under non-Russian and non-Soviet rule has a positive effect on the support for a transition to a market economy in Moldova. The average respondent from Gagauzia is less likely to support privatization than is the average respondent in other regions of Western Moldova (Bessarabia). The Gagauzia and Transdniestria variables are statistically significant at the 0.01 and 0.05 levels in the regression based on the World Values Survey data. However, the ethnic Gagauz variable has no statistically significant effect on support for a transition to a market economy in Moldova in the 1998 Laitin/Hough survey. (See Figures 5.8 and 5.9.)

Age, gender, education, and class positively and significantly affect support for privatization in Ukraine. Religion and ethnicity have no significant effect on support for an increase in private ownership. Age has the strongest effect on support for a transition to a market economy in Moldova. (See Figures 5.7, 5.8, and 5.9.)

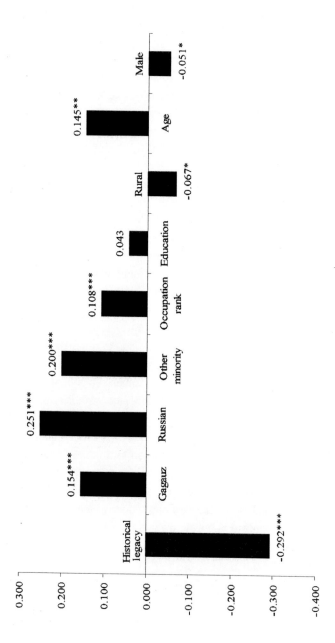

Figure 5.6 Determinants of the index of pro-Soviet/pro-Russian attitudes in Moldova (1998 Laitin/Hough survey)

Note: The figure shows standardized regression coefficients. *** denotes significance at 0.001, ** denotes significance at 0.01, * denotes significance at 0.05.

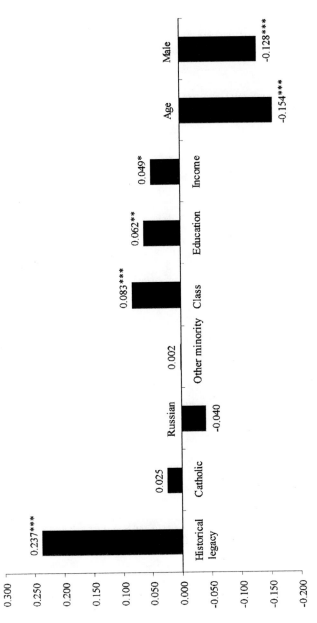

Figure 5.7 Determinants of support for privatization in Ukraine (1996 World Values Survey)

Note: The figure shows standardized regression coefficients. *** denotes significance at 0.001, ** denotes significance at 0.01, * denotes significance at 0.05.

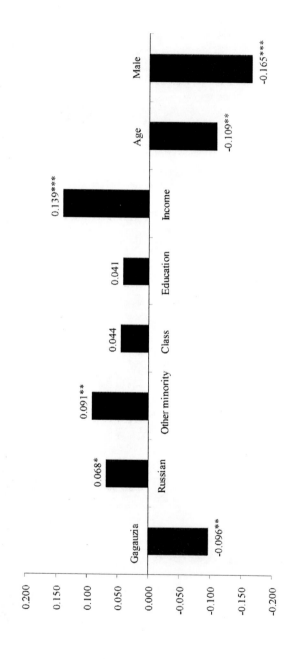

Figure 5.8 Determinants of support for privatization in Moldova (1996 World Values Survey)

Note: The figure shows standardized regression coefficients. The survey question is "Private ownership of business and industry should be increased, government ownership of business and industry should be increased." *** denotes significance at 0.001, ** denotes significance at 0.01, * denotes significance at 0.05.

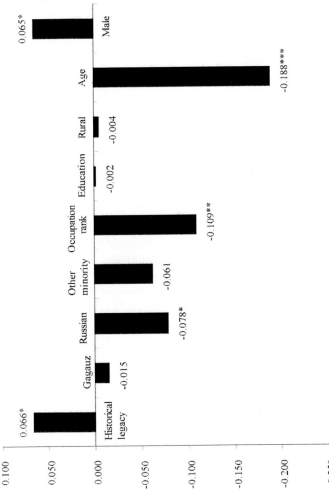

Figure 5.9 Determinants of the support for transition to market economy in Moldova (1998 Laitin/Hough survey)

Note: The figure shows standardized regression coefficients. The survey question is "What do you think of the transition to a market economy in Moldova/Transdniestria?" *** denotes significance at 0.001, ** denotes significance at 0.01, * denotes significance at 0.05.

Gender, ethnicity, and economic factors also have strong effects on attitudes towards the transition to a market economy in Moldova and support for privatization in Bessarabia. The average female expresses much stronger approval of private ownership in Ukraine and Western Moldova than does the average male. However, the gender variable has the reverse effect on support for a market economy in Moldova. The average ethnic Russian is less likely to favor a transition to a market economy in Moldova than the average Moldovan and other ethnic minority. However, in the regression limited to the Bessarabian part of Moldova, ethnic Russians show an opposite pattern on the issue of support for an increase in private ownership. (See Figures 5.7, 5.8, and 5.9.)

6   Conclusion

Ukraine and Moldova, like many other post-Communist, developed, and developing countries, have experienced significant regional political divisions. Strong regional political cleavages were observed through the results of parliamentary and presidential elections, referendums, and opinion surveys in Ukraine and Moldova since 1990. Western regions of Ukraine consistently supported the independence of Ukraine and voted for nationalist and pro-Western parties and politicians. In contrast, Eastern regions of Ukraine favored pro-Communist and pro-Russian parties and politicians. Meanwhile, a separatist pro-Russian movement emerged in Crimea and some other regions of Eastern Ukraine.

Similarly, support for national independence and nationalist pro-Western movements and politicians was strongest in the Western parts of Moldova. Eastern regions opposed Moldova's independence, backed a pro-Russian and pro-Communist orientation, and declared the existence of the independent Transdniestrian Republic. In the Gagauzia region of Moldova, a separatist movement emerged, but it remained largely non-violent in contrast to Transdniestria's.

The analysis carried out in this book has provided a way to test cultural theories of regional division. Most theories of regional political cleavages and conflicts focus on factors of ethnicity, economics, and political leadership. Political culture theories, in contrast, emphasize the role of values and historical legacies. However, culture is often neglected in studies of regional cleavages and conflicts, because it is difficult to quantify political values.

Quasi-experimental conditions in Ukraine and Moldova, the large number of regions in both countries, and the availability of both aggregate and survey data, has enabled us to quantify the role of culture relative to the role of ethnic, economic, religious, and political leadership factors in regional divisions. These two post-Communist countries contain regions that once belonged to different states for significant historical periods and became subject to the same Soviet policy after their unification as a result of World War II.

The main conclusion of this study is that historically based cultural differences explain a significant part of the variation in support for nationalist/pro-Western and Communist/pro-Russian parties and politicians in regions of Ukraine and Moldova. This book identifies the pre-World War I and pre-World War II divisions as critical junctures in the formation and evolution of regional political cultures in Ukraine and Moldova. These historical time periods were crucial to regional political culture because they coincided with the birth of national identity and mass education of the population.

Prior to World War I, most regions of Western Ukraine were part of the Galicia province of the Austro-Hungarian Monarchy. During the inter-war period, Western Ukrainian regions belonged to Poland, Czechoslovakia, and Romania. Moldova's Western region, called Bessarabia, was part of Romania during this period. In contrast, Eastern Ukraine and Transdniestria had been part of the Russian Empire since the seventeenth and eighteenth centuries, and part of the Soviet Union from the time of its establishment.

The analysis of comparative historical development shows that distinct historical legacies contributed to the development of different regional political cultures. Ukrainian national identity became much stronger in Western Ukraine than in Eastern regions because of different historical circumstances. The relatively more democratic political institutions in the Austro-Hungarian Monarchy and inter-war Czechoslovakia, Poland, and Romania gave Ukrainian intellectuals and nationalist organizations more opportunity to spread their ideas and cultivate national identity. Language, education, and religious policies in Western Ukrainian regions, particularly in the Austro-Hungarian province of Galicia, were also more supportive of the formation of Ukrainian national identity than policies of the Russian Empire.

Historical conditions were more favorable for the development of national identity in Western Moldova (Bessarabia) than in the Transdniestria region. The differences in political systems and policies were most notable in the inter-war period, when Bessarabia was unified with Romania, and the Autonomous Moldovan Republic, which included all of Transdniestria, was part of Soviet Ukraine. The different historical experiences of Crimean Tatars and the Gagauz were linked to Islam and Orthodox Christianity respectively, which helped to transmit their political cultures from one generation to another before the advent of mass literacy.

Religion is interlinked with historical legacy in both Ukraine and Moldova. Different historical experiences of Crimean Tatars and the Gagauz were linked to Islam and Orthodox Christianity respectively, which helped to transmit their political culture from one generation to another before the advent of the era of mass literacy. The critical juncture in the evolution of the political culture of the Gagauz, a unique group that combines Turkic ethnic roots with the Orthodox Christian religion, was their experience in the nineteenth century. At that time, the Russian government helped the Gagauz escape persecution as Orthodox Christians in the Ottoman Empire and settle in the South of Moldova. This experience, along with the legacy of Soviet rule, fostered pro-Russian and pro-Communist orientation in the Gagauzia region.

Religious tradition was a major factor in the differentiation of political values among Crimean Tatars, Ukrainians, and Russians. Ukrainians and Russians often associated the Ottoman rule in Crimea with slavery, because Islam prohibited enslavement of Muslim Crimean Tatars and the institution of slavery was therefore disproportionately applied to Orthodox Christians in Ukraine. During the Russian rule and Soviet rule, Crimean Tatars, like many other Muslim ethnic groups, suffered from discrimination and were exiled to Central Asia. The Ukrainian Greek Catholic Church in Galicia played a significant role in the development of the Ukrainian national identity.

Statistical analysis of voting results from different elections and referendumsreferendums on independence held between 1991 and 2005 shows that cultural factors, linked to different historical experiences before Soviet unification, strongly affect voting behavior and political attitudes in post-Communist Ukraine and Moldova. The effect of culture is consistent and its influence, with few exceptions, is stronger than the influence of economic, ethnic, and political leadership factors.

Multivariate analysis of the 1996 World Values Survey and the 1998 Laitin/Hough survey data produces analogous results. Keeping other factors such as ethnicity and age constant, the long history of Russian, and then Soviet, rule is a major factor that affects the pro-Communist and pro-Russian vote and political attitudes. In contrast, the history of Austro-Hungarian, Polish, Romanian, and Czechoslovak rule is strongly associated with support for nationalist and pro-Western parties and candidates. The statistical analysis shows that the distinct pre-World War II experience in Western regions of

Ukraine and Moldova positively affects support for an increase of private ownership and a transition to a market economy,

Religion is a major factor of regional political cleavages in Ukraine, which has Greek Catholic and Muslim minorities, but not in Moldova, which is religiously homogeneous. Ethnic and economic factors affect regional voting behaviors and attitudes in Ukraine and Moldova, but the effect is less significant and consistent. As one would expect, support for nationalist parties and politicians and the independence of Ukraine and Moldova is much stronger among ethnic Ukrainians and Moldovans than among Russians and other ethnic minorities, who are, in turn, more likely to have pro-Communist and pro-Russian orientations.

The role of linguistic cleavages, between Russian speakers and Ukrainian speakers in Ukraine and Russian and Romanian speakers in Moldova, parallels the role of ethnic cleavages in these countries. However, this study shows that ethnic and linguistic factors cannot, by themselves, account for the existing patterns of regional cleavage and conflict.

The effect of economic factors on regional political divisions is less consistent than the effect of cultural and ethnic factors. Western Ukraine and Moldovan Bessarabia are less urbanized and less economically developed than Eastern Ukraine and Transdniestria. However, the analysis shows that the relationship between economic factors and regional political orientation is not straightforward. Kyiv city, the capital of Ukraine, has the highest level of pro-nationalist and pro-Western support among Eastern regions. This pattern was also demonstrated by mass actions during the "Orange Revolution." Similarly, Gagauzia is less urbanized and developed than other regions of Moldova, but it consistently has one of the highest levels of pro-Communist and pro-Russian political support.

Age is positively associated with support for pro-Communist parties in Ukraine and both pro-Soviet and pro-Russian attitudes in Moldova. However, the effect of age on the support for nationalist parties in Ukraine is not significant. The results of the multivariate analysis show that regional political divisions in Ukraine and Moldova cannot be primarily attributed to generational factors. However, these findings imply that, although regional cultural differences will not disappear in a post-Communist generation, common experience in independent Ukraine has worked to diminish these differences.

Analysis of the behavior and attitudes of top political leaders in post-Communist Ukraine and Moldova suggests that many were motivated not by ideology, but by rent-seeking, or the use of their power for personal gain. Radical shifts in political orientation over short periods of time, authoritarian tendencies, and allegations of corruption characterized the post-Communist presidents of Ukraine and Moldova, as well as the separatist leaders of the Transdniestrian Republic and the Gagauz autonomy. For example, the secret recordings in the office of the former Ukrainian president Leonid Kuchma contained evidence of his involvement in the persecution of opposition journalists and politicians, as well as in large-scale corruption. An analysis of voting results shows that the regional pattern of support for the same candidates changed consistently with changes in the voters' political orientation, as long as elections or referendums were democratic. This demonstrates that reversals in regional support for the same candidates over relatively short periods of time are consistent with cultural values.

The comparison of Ukraine and Moldova shows that significant regional political cleavages do not necessarily lead to violent conflicts and the break-up of countries. Separatist leaders in Transdniestria, Gagauzia, and Eastern Ukraine had similar pro-Russian political orientations, but significant violent conflicts did not occur in Gagauzia and Eastern Ukraine, unlike in Transdniestria; however, Ukraine did come close to a violent conflict and even a possible break-up during the "Orange Revolution" at the end of 2004. Leadership factors played the main role in the non-violent resolution of the conflicts in Ukraine and Gagauz Yeri.

Leadership factors contributed to the violent conflict in the Transdniestria. Commanders of the Fourteenth Army, which was stationed in the region, provided military support to the Transdniestrian separatists and even joined the ranks of their leaders. Such behavior contrasted with the behavior of the former Soviet military commanders in Ukraine – most notably in Crimea – and the Gagauzia region of Moldova.

This study shows that culture is not fixed in the distant past. It constantly evolves as a result of different historical experiences. For example, the political culture in Galicia reflects the legacy of Austrian rule before World War I, of Polish rule during the interwar period, of German rule in World War II, and of Soviet rule between 1939 and 1941 and after World War II. In contrast, political culture in Volhynia was not influenced by Austrian rule because this historic region, like Western Moldova, belonged to the Russian Empire before World War I. As a result, nationalist and pro-independence values became more common in Galicia than in Volhynia and Western Moldova. Similarly, political culture in Eastern Ukraine and Transdniestria became more pro-Communist and pro-Russian compared with historically Western regions, because they were affected by a much longer period of Soviet rule.

What does this analysis tells us about the future of Ukraine and Moldova? Because culture changes slowly over the span of generations, regional cleavages are likely to persist for a long period of time. However, their strength and forms might change, depending on political institutions and policies, over the long run. In addition, the emergence of new cleavages, and the increasing salience of old functional cleavages that cut across historic regions, diminish the significance of regional divisions. The emergence of generational and class differences are prime examples of this. The possibility of violent regional conflicts in Ukraine and Gagauzia and the likelihood of a peaceful settlement of the conflict in the Transdniestria region of Moldova depend to a significant extent on the behaviors and interests of national and regional political leaders in these countries and in key foreign countries.

The conclusions of this study have implications beyond Ukraine and Moldova and are helpful in understanding regional political and policy divisions in other countries, such as the newly independent states in the former Soviet Union and the former Yugoslavia. This book suggests that historical legacy has a significant effect on regional political cleavages and conflicts. The analysis of the regional divisions in Ukraine and Moldova shows that historical legacies shape the evolution of regional political cultures and have an enduring influence on political attitudes and behavior.

Appendices

Table A.1 Cultural, economic, and ethnic characteristics of regions of Ukraine and Moldova

Region	Years of non-Russian/ non-Soviet historical experience 1793-1944	Proportion of urban population (%)[1]	Proportion of ethnic Ukrainians/ Moldovans (%)[1]	GDP per capita 1995 ($)	Proportion of Catholics, 1994 (%)
Western Ukraine					
Chernivtsi	114	42	97	1749	4
Ivano-Frankivsk	151	59	93	2177	52
Lviv	151	39	80	1856	50
Ternopil	134	42	98	2135	87
Rivne	26	41	73	2335	3
Volyn	26	46	95	1961	0
Transcarpathia	151	50	96	1198	17
Eastern Ukraine					
Crimea[2]	0	66	59	1950	0
Cherkassy	0	54	92	2953	0
Chernihiv	0	56	93	2254	0
Kyiv region	0	69	25	2829	0
Kirovohrad	0	83	76	2176	3
Khmelnytsky	0	90	54	3190	2

Poltava	0	79	67	3842	0
Sumy	0	61	79	2928	0
Vinnytsia	0	49	92	2408	1
Zhytomyr	0	80	84	2184	0
Donetsk	0	79	83	3659	0
Kharkiv	0	58	90	2463	0
Zaporizhzhia	0	86	55	3532	2
Luhansk	0	66	79	2829	1
Kherson	0	58	90	1706	0
Mykolayiv	0	64	88	2770	2
Odesa	9	45	94	2608	1
Dnipropetrovsk	0	76	67	3153	1
Kyiv city	0	55	88		0
Bessarabia	48	43	70	2122	0
Transdniestrian Republic	0	64	38	3056	0

Sources: *Kharakteristika* (1993); Martyniuk (1994); *Naselennia* (1993); UNDP (1996, 1999).

Notes:
[1]   The average of the 2001 Ukrainian census and the 1989 Soviet census.
[2]   Includes Sevastopol city.

Table A.2 Correlation matrix of the vote in national elections and referendums in regions of Ukraine

	Yush-chen-ko 2004	Our Uk-raine 2002	Kuch-ma 1999	Natio-nalist 1998	Krav-chuk 1994	Natio-nalist 1994	Natio-nalist 1991	Refe-rendum Dec. 1991	Refe-rendum March 1991	Yanu-kovych 2004	Com-munist 2002	Symo-nenko 1999	Com-munist 1998	Com-munist 1994	Kuch-ma 1994	Krav-chuk 1991
Yushchen-ko 2004	1.00															
"Our Ukra-ine" 2002	0.83	1.00														
Kuchma 1999	0.51	0.82	1.00													
Nationa-list 1998	0.66	0.93	0.86	1.00												
Kravchuk 1994	0.82	0.92	0.82	0.87	1.00											
Nationa-list 1994	0.64	0.85	0.77	0.92	0.82	1.00										
Nationa-list 1991	0.66	0.90	0.88	0.95	0.86	0.86	1.00									
Referen-dum Dec. 1991	0.71	0.53	0.33	0.43	0.65	0.43	0.48	1.00								

Referendum March 1991	-0.64	-0.88	-0.90	-0.94	-0.85	-0.85	-0.97	-0.44	1.00							
Yanukovych 2004	-1.00	-0.81	-0.49	-0.64	-0.82	-0.62	-0.64	-0.72	0.63	1.00						
Communist 2002	-0.71	-0.92	-0.93	-0.86	-0.90	-0.79	-0.87	-0.44	0.89	0.70	1.00					
Symonenko 1999	-0.53	-0.82	-1.00	-0.84	-0.82	-0.77	-0.87	-0.35	0.90	0.52	0.94	1.00				
Communist 1998	-0.49	-0.80	-0.95	-0.84	-0.82	-0.73	-0.84	-0.30	0.88	0.47	0.90	0.95	1.00			
Communist 1994	-0.62	-0.71	-0.70	-0.65	-0.76	-0.58	-0.66	-0.28	0.67	0.62	0.77	0.71	0.78	1.00		
Kuchma 1994	-0.83	-0.92	-0.81	-0.86	-0.80	-0.80	-0.85	-0.66	0.85	0.82	0.90	0.81	0.82	0.76	1.00	
Kravchuk 1991	-0.50	-0.83	-0.87	-0.91	-0.74	-0.81	-0.95	-0.20	0.94	0.48	0.82	0.85	0.83	0.65	0.72	1.00

Variables (proportion of the vote in 26 regions of Ukraine)

Yushchenko 2004	Vote for Yushchenko in the repeat second round of the 2004 presidential elections.
Our Ukraine 2002	Vote for the "Our Ukraine" bloc in the 2002 parliamentary elections.
Kuchma 1999	Vote for Kuchma in the second round of the 1999 presidential elections.
Nationalist 1998	Vote for nationalist parties in the 1998 parliamentary elections.
Kravchuk 1994	Vote for Kravchuk in the second round of the 1994 presidential elections.
Nationalist 1994	Vote for candidates from nationalist parties in the 1994 parliamentary elections.
Nationalist 1991	Vote for nationalist candidates in the 1991 presidential elections.
Referendum Dec. 1991	Vote for the independence of Ukraine in the December 1991 referendum.
Referendum March 1991	Vote for preservation of the Soviet Union in the March 1991 referendum.
Yanukovych 2004	Vote for Yanukovych in the repeat second round of the 2004 presidential elections.
Symonenko 1999	Vote for Symonenko in the second round of the 1999 presidential elections.
Communist 2002	Vote for Communist parties and *ZUBR* in the 2002 parliamentary elections.
Communist 1998	Vote for Communist parties and the Union Party in the 1998 parliamentary elections.
Communist 1994	Vote for candidates from Communist parties in the 1994 parliamentary elections.
Kuchma 1994	Vote for Kuchma in the second round of the 1994 presidential elections.
Kravchuk 1991	Vote for Kravchuk in the 1991 presidential elections.

Table A.3 Factor analysis of the vote for Communist/pro-Russian parties and candidates in the presidential and parliamentary elections and preservation of the Soviet Union in referendums in regions of Ukraine

Factor	Eigenvalue	Proportion	Cumulative
1	6.44	0.80	0.80
2	0.77	0.10	0.90
3	0.39	0.05	0.95
4	0.22	0.03	0.98
5	0.09	0.01	0.99
6	0.04	0.01	0.99
7	0.02	0.00	1.00
8	0.02	0.00	1.00

Table A.3 Cont. Factor Loadings

Variable	Factor 1
Referendum March 1991	0.95
Yanukovych 2004	0.72
Communist 2002	0.97
Symonenko 1999	0.94
Communist 1998	0.93
Communist 1994	0.93
Kuchma 1994	0.83
Kravchuk 1991	0.88

Scale Reliability Coefficient (Alpha): 0.96

Table A.4 Factor analysis of the vote for Nationalist/pro-Western parties and candidates in the presidential and parliamentary elections and support for independence in referendums in regions of Ukraine

Factor	Eigenvalue	Proportion	Cumulative
1	6.27	0.78	0.78
2	0.97	0.12	0.90
3	0.30	0.04	0.94
4	0.23	0.03	0.97
5	0.11	0.01	0.98
6	0.07	0.01	0.99
7	0.04	0.01	1.00
8	0.02	0.00	1.00

Table A.4 Cont. Factor Loadings

Variable	Factor 1
Yushchenko 2004	0.82
Our Ukraine 2002	0.97
Kuchma 1999	0.86
Nationalist 1998	0.95
Kravchuk 1994	0.96
Nationalist 1994	0.90
Nationalist 1991	0.94
Referendum Dec. 1991	0.62

Scale Reliability Coefficient (Alpha): 0.96

Index of pro-Soviet /pro-Russian attitudes in Moldova

Variables in the index of pro-Soviet /pro-Russian attitudes (1998 Laitin/Hough survey):

Russia Unification   What future state structure would you prefer to see in Moldova?

USSR citizen   To what degree do you consider yourself a citizen of the former U.S.S.R.?

Soviet Union   How do you assess the passing of the Soviet Union?

Table A.5 Factor analysis of pro-Soviet /pro-Russian attitudes in Moldova

Factor	Eigenvalue	Proportion	Cumulative
1	1.67	0.56	0.56
2	0.75	0.25	0.81
3	0.58	0.19	1.00

Table A.5 Cont. Factor Loadings

Variable	Factor 1
Russia Unification	0.72
USSR citizen	0.80
Soviet Union	0.72

Scale Reliability Coefficient (Alpha): 0.60

Bibliography

Aarebrot, Frank. 1982. "Norway: Centre and Periphery in a Peripheral State." In *The Politics of Territorial Identity: Studies in European Regionalism*, eds. Stein Rokkan and Derek Urwin. London: Sage.

Aarrevaara, Timo. 1998. *Councillors and Civil Servants in the Ukrainian Self-Government*. Kyiv: Naukova Dumka.

Aberg, Martin. 2000. "Putnam's Social Capital Theory Goes East: A Case Study of Western Ukraine and Lviv." *Europe-Asia Studies* 52 (2): 295–318.

Alapuro, Risto. 1982. "Finland: An Interface Periphery." In *The Politics of Territorial Identity: Studies in European Regionalism*, eds. Stein Rokkan and Derek Urwin. London: Sage.

Allardt, Erik, and Pesonen, Pertti. 1967. "Cleavages in Finnish Politics." In *Party Systems and Voter Alignments: Cross-national Perspectives*, eds. Seymour Martin Lipset and Stein Rokkan. New York: Free Press.

Almond, Gabriel. 1983. "Communism and Political Culture Theory," *Comparative Politics* 15 (2): 127-138.

Almond, Gabriel. 1990. *A Discipline Divided: Schools and Sects in Political Science*. Newbury Park: Sage.

Almond, Gabriel, and Sidney Verba. 1965. *The Civic Culture: Political Attitudes and Democracy in Five Nations*. Boston: Little, Brown and Company.

Aly, Götz and Susanne Heim. 2002. *Architects of Annihilation: Auschwitz and the Logic of Destruction*. Translated by A. G. Blunden. Princeton: Princeton University Press.

Armstrong, John Alexander. 1990. *Ukrainian Nationalism*, 3rd ed. Englewood, Colo.: Ukrainian Academic Press.

Arel, Dominique. 1995. "Ukraine: The Temptation of the Nationalizing State." In *Political Culture and Civil Society in Russia and the New States of Eurasia*, ed. Vladimir Tismaneanu. Armonk: M.E. Sharpe.

Arel, Dominique. 1996. "A Lurking Cascade of Assimilation in Kyiv?" *Post-Soviet Affairs* 12 (1): 73-90.

Arel, Dominique and Andrew Wilson. 1994. "The Ukrainian Parliamentary Elections." *RFE/RL Research Report* 3 (26): 6-17.

Aslund, Anders. 1999. "Problems with Economic Transformation in Ukraine." Paper Presented at the Fifth Dubrovnik Conference on Transition Economies, June 23-25.

Aslund, Anders. 2005. "The Economic Policy of Ukraine after the Orange Revolution." *Eurasian Geography and Economics* 46 (5): 327-353.

Babilunga, N., and B. Bomeshko. 1998. *Pridnestrovskii konflict: Istoricheskie, demograficheskie, politicheskie aspekty.* Tiraspol: Transdniestrian State University.

Babilunga, N. V., S. I. Beril, B. G. Bomeshko, I. N. Galinsky, V. R. Okushko, and P. M. Shornikov. 2000. *Fenomen Pridnestrov'ia.* Tiraspol: RIO PGU.

Barber, Benjamin. 1995. *Jihad vs. McWorld.* New York: Times Books.

Barraclough, Geoffrey, ed. 1998. *HarperCollins Atlas of World History.* Ann Arbor: Borders Press.

Barrington, Lowell. 1997. "The Geographic Component of Mass Attitudes in Ukraine." *Post-Soviet Geography* 38 (10): 601-614.

Barrington, Lowell. 2001. "Stereotypes of Russians and Ukrainians in Ukraine: Views of the Ethnic 'Other,' and Their Implications." Paper Presented at the 6th World Convention of the Association for the Study of Nationalities (ASN), New York, April 5-7.

Barrington, Lowell, and Erick Herron. 2004. "One Ukraine or Many?: Regionalism in Ukraine and its Political Consequences." *Nationalities Papers* 32 (1): 53-86.

Bekirova, Gulnara. 2004. *Krymskotatarskaia problema v SSSR (1944-1991.)* Simferopol: Odzhak.

Belarus and Moldova: Country Studies. 1995. Washington, D.C.: Federal Research Division, Library of Congress.

Berrington, Hugh. 1985. "Centre-Periphery Conflict and British Politics." In *Centre-Periphery Relations in Western Europe,* eds. Yves Meny and Vincent Wright. London: George Allan & Unwin.

"Better Later than Never, Maybe." 1995. *Economist,* July 22.

Bilinsky, Yaroslav. 1975. "The Incorporation of Western Ukraine and its Impact on Politics and Society in Soviet Ukraine." In *The Influence of*

East Europe and the Soviet West on the USSR, ed. Roman Szporluk. New York: Praeger.

Bilocerkowycz, Jaroslaw. 1988. *Soviet Ukrainian Dissent: A Study of Political Alienation.* Boulder: Westview Press.

Birch, Sarah. 1995. "Electoral Behaviour in Western Ukraine in National Elections and Referendums, 1989-91." *Europe-Asia Studies* 47 (7): 1145-1176.

Birch, Sarah. 2000a. *Elections and Democratization in Ukraine.* New York: St. Martin Press.

Birch, Sarah. 2000b. "Interpreting the Regional Effect in Ukrainian Politics." *Europe-Asia Studies* 52 (6): 1017-1042.

Boettke, Peter. 1990. *The Political Economy of Soviet Socialism: The Formative Years, 1918-1928.* Boston: Kluwer Academic.

Bojcun, Marko. 1995. "The Ukrainian Parliamentary Elections in March-April 1994." *Europe-Asia Studies* 47 (2): 229-249.

Bookman, Milica. 1991. *The Political Economy of Discontinuous Development: Regional Disparities and Inter-regional Conflict.* New York: Praeger.

Bookman, Milica. 1993. *The Economics of Secession.* New York: St. Martin Press.

Bookman, Milica. 1994. "War and Peace: The Divergent Break-ups of Yugoslavia and Czechoslovakia." *Journal of Peace Research* 31 (2): 175-187.

Borys, Jurij. 1977. "Political Parties in the Ukraine." In *The Ukraine, 1917-1921: A Study in Revolution*, ed. Taras Hunczak. Cambridge: Harvard Ukrainian Research Institute.

Bosacki, Marcin, Marcin Wojciechowski, and Damian Kramski. 2005. "Zakulisova historia revolutsii." *Gazeta wyborcza*, April 2.

Botev, Nikolai. 1994. "Where East Meets West: Ethnic Intermarriage in the Former Yugoslavia, 1962 to 1989." *American Sociological Review* 59 (3): 461-480.

Boudon, Raymond. 1996. "The 'Rational Choice Model': A Particular Case of the Cognitive Model." *Rationality and Society* 8 (2): 123-150.

Boudon, Raymond. 1998. "Limitations of Rational Choice Theory." *American Journal of Sociology* 104 (3): 817-828.

Bremmer, Ian, and Ray Taras, eds. 1997. *New States, New Politics: Building the Post-Soviet Nations*. Cambridge: Cambridge University Press.

Bremmer, Ian. 2005. "Investors Must Stay Cautious about Ukraine." *Financial Times*, January 24.

Brown, Kathryn Lake. 2000. *A Biography of No Place: The Ukrainian Borderlands and the Making of Nation-space*. Ph.D. Dissertation. Seattle: University of Washington.

Brown, Kathryn Lake. 2004. *A Biography of No Place: From Ethnic Borderland to Soviet Heartland*. Cambridge: Harvard University Press.

Brown, Michael. 1996. "The Causes and Regional Dimensions of Internal Conflict." In *The International Dimensions of Internal Conflict,* ed. Michael Brown. Cambridge: MIT Press.

Browne, Michael. 1971. *Ferment in the Ukraine*. New York: Praeger Publishers.

Buckley, Stephen. 2000. "Upheaval in Ecuador Shows Clout of Indians; Protests Ended in President's Ouster." *Washington Post*, January 27.

Bullock, Charles, and Mark Rozell. 1998. "Southern Politics at Century's End." In *The New Politics of the Old South: An Introduction to Southern Politics,* eds. Charles Bullock III and Mark Rozell. Lanham, Md.: Rowman & Littlefield.

Burds, Jeffrey 1997. "Agentura: Soviet Informants' Networks and the Ukrainian Underground in Galicia, 1944-48." *East European Politics and Societies* 11 (1): 89-130.

Burnham, Walter Dean. 1974. "The United States: The Politics of Heterogeneity." In *Electoral Behavior: A Comparative Handbook*, ed. Richard Rose. New York: Free Press.

Chang, David, and Richard Chuang. 1998. *Politics of Hong Kong's Reversion to China*. New York: St. Martin's Press.

Charakteristika Social Economica a Oraselor si Raioanelor Republicii Moldova. 1993. Chisinau: Departamentul de Stat Pentru Statistic al Republicii Moldova.

Chinn, Jeff, and Steven Roper. 1998. "Territorial Autonomy in Gagauzia." *Nationalities Papers* 26 (1): 87-101.

Chivers, C. J. 2005. "How Top Spies in Ukraine Changed the Nation's Path." *New York Times*, January 17.

Clem, Ralph S., and Peter R. Craumer. 2005. "Shades of Orange: The Electoral Geography of Ukraine's 2004 Presidential Elections." *Eurasian Geography and Economics* 46 (5): 364-385.

Coleman, James. 1988. "Social Capital in the Creation of Human Capital." *American Journal of Sociology* 94 (Supplement): 95-120.

Conaghan, Catherine. 1995. "Politicians Against Parties: Discord and Disconnection in Ecuador's Party System." In *Building Democratic Institutions: Party Systems in Latin America,* eds. Scott Mainwaring and Timothy Scully. Stanford: Stanford University Press.

Conquest, Robert. 1986. *Harvest of Sorrow: Soviet Collectivization and the Terror –Famine.* New York: Oxford University Press.

Conquest, Robert. 1990. *The Great Terror: A Reassessment.* New York: Oxford University Press.

Cotler, Julio. 1995. "Political Parties and the Problem of Democratic Consolidation in Peru." In *Building Democratic Institutions: Party Systems in Latin America,* eds. Scott Mainwaring and Timothy Scully. Stanford: Stanford University Press.

Coulon, Christian. 1995. "Senegal: The Development and Fragility of Semidemocracy." In *Politics in Developing Countries: Comparing Experience with Democracy*, eds. Larry Diamond, Juan Linz, and Seymour Martin Lipset. Boulder: Lynne Rienner.

Crampton, R. J. 1997. *A Concise History of Bulgaria.* Cambridge: Cambridge University Press.

Craumer, Peter, and James Clem. 1999. "Ukraine's Emerging Electoral Geography: A Regional Analysis of the 1998 Parliamentary Elections." *Post-Soviet Geography and Economics* 40 (1): 1-26.

Crowther, William. 1997a. "The Politics of Democratization in Post-Communist Moldova." In *Democratic Changes and Authoritarian Reactions in Russia, Ukraine, Belarus, and Moldova,* eds. Karen Dawisha and Bruce Parrott. Cambridge: Cambridge University Press.

Crowther, William. 1997b. "Moldova: Caught between Nation and Empire." In *New States, New Politics: Building the Post-Soviet Nations*, eds. Ian Bremmer and Ray Taras. Cambridge: Cambridge University Press.

CVK. 2000. Central Electoral Commission of Ukraine: *http://www.cvk. ukrpack.net/.*

CVK. 2002. Central Electoral Commission of Ukraine: *http://www.cvk.gov.ua.*

CVK. 2004. Central Electoral Commission of Ukraine: *http://www.cvk.gov.ua.*

D'Anieri, Paul, Robert Kravchuk, and Taras Kuzio. 1999. *Politics and Society in Ukraine.* Boulder, Colo.: Westview Press.

Dalton, Russell. 1996. "Political Cleavages, Issues, and Electoral Change." In *Comparing Democracies: Elections and Voting in Global Perspective,* eds. Lawrence LeDuc, Richard Niemi, and Pippa Norris. Thousand Oak: Sage.

Das Gupta, Jyotirinda. 1995. "India: Democratic Becoming and Developmental Transition." In *Politics in Developing Countries: Comparing Experience with Democracy,* eds. Larry Diamond, Juan Linz, and Seymour Martin Lipset. Boulder: Lynne Rienner.

Davies, Norman. 1996. *Europe: A History.* New York: Oxford University Press.

Department of State. 2000. *Ukraine and the World: Focus Groups in 5 Cities.* Prepared by Thomas Klobucar with Steven A. Grant. Research Report R-3-00. Washington: Office of Research, United States Department of State.

Derzhavnyi komitet statystyky Ukrainy. 2002. "Pro kilkist' ta sklad nasellenia Ukrainy za pidsumkamy vseukrains'koho perepysu naselennia 2001 roku." *http://www.ukrstat.gov.ua/Perepis/PidsPer.html.*

Diamond, Larry. 1993. "Causes and Effects." In *Political Culture and Democracy in Developing Countries,* ed., Larry Diamond. Boulder, Colo.: Lynne Rienner.

Diamond, Larry. 1995. "Nigeria: The Uncivic Society and the Descent into Praetorianism." In *Politics in Developing Countries: Comparing Experience with Democracy,* eds. Larry Diamond, Juan Linz, and Seymour Martin Lipset. Boulder: Lynne Rienner.

Diamond, Larry, Juan Linz, and Seymour Martin Lipset, eds. 1988. *Democracy in Developing Countries: Africa,* vol. II. Boulder: Lynne Rienner.

Diamond, Larry, Juan Linz, and Seymour Martin Lipset, eds. 1989a. *Democracy in Developing Countries: Asia,* vol. III. Boulder: Lynne Rienner.

Diamond, Larry, Juan Linz, and Seymour Martin Lipset, eds. 1989b. *Democracy in Developing Countries: Latin America*, vol. IV. Boulder: Lynne Rienner.

Diamond, Larry, Juan Linz, and Seymour Martin Lipset, eds. 1995. *Politics in Developing Countries: Comparing Experience with Democracy.* Boulder: Lynne Rienner.

Díez Medrano, Juan. 1995. *Divided Nations: Class, Politics, and Nationalism in the Basque Country and Catalonia.* Ithaca: Cornell University Press.

Dima, Nicholas. 1999. "The Moldavian-Dnestr Republic: A Geopolitical Game." *Journal of Social, Political and Economic Studies* 24 (1): 37-63.

Dnipropetrovs'ka Simia. 1996. Kyiv: Fond Demokratii.

Dogan, Mattei. 1967. "Political Cleavage and Social Stratification in France and Italy." In *Party Systems and Voter Alignments: Cross-National Perspectives*, eds. Seymour Martin Lipset and Stein Rokkan. New York: Free Press.

Drohobycky, Maria, ed. 1995. *Crimea: Dynamics, Challenges, and Prospects.* Lanham, Md.: Rowman and Littlefield.

Dunlop, John. 1997. "Aleksandr Lebed and Russian Foreign Policy." *SAIS Review* 17 (1): 47-72.

Dyrud, Keith. 1992. *The Quest for the Rusyn Soul: The Politics of Religion and Culture in Eastern Europe and in America, 1890- World War I.* Philadelphia: Balch Institute Press.

EBRD. 1997. *Transition Report: Enterprise Performance and Growth.* London: European Bank for Reconstruction and Development.

Elazar, Daniel. 1966. *American Federalism: A View from the States.* New York: Crowell.

Electorala '98. Documente si cifre. 1998. Chisinau: Tish.

Emmons, Terence. 1983. *The Formation of Political Parties and the First National Elections in Russia.* Cambridge: Harvard University Press.

Encyclopedia of Ukraine, eds. Volodymyr Kubijovyc and Danylo Struk. 1984-1993. Toronto: University of Toronto Press.

Erikson, Robert, McIver, John, and Gerald C. Wright, Jr. 1987. "State Political Culture and Public Opinion." *American Political Science Review* 81 (3): 797-813.

European Centre for Minority Issues. 1997. "From Ethnopolitical Conflict to Inter-Ethnic Accord in Moldova." A Report on a Seminar held in Flensburg, Germany, and Bjerremark, Denmark, 12-17, September 1997.

Evangelista, Matthew. 1996. "Historical Legacies and the Politics of Intervention in the Former Soviet Union." In *The International Dimensions of Internal Conflict*, ed. Michael Brown. Cambridge: MIT Press.

"Failed States Index." 2005. *Foreign Policy*, 149 (July/August): 56-65.

Faiola, Anthony. 2000. "Peruvian Candidate Reflects New Indian Pride." *Washington Post,* March 31.

Fearon, James, and David Laitin. 2003. "Ethnicity, Insurgency, and Civil War." *American Political Science Review* 97 (1): 75-90.

Finn, Peter. 2004. "Old Divisions Resurface in Ukraine." *Washington Post*, November 29.

Fireman, Ken. 2004. "Ukrainians Cleaved by Their Tortured Past." *Newsday*, December 5.

Fish, Steven. 1998. "The Determinants of Economic Reform in the Post-Communist World." *East European Politics and Societies* 12 (1): 31–78.

Fond "Demokratychni initsiatyvy." 2002. "Dumka hromadian shchodo vstupu Ukrainy do NATO." *http://www.dif.org.ua/*.

Forsberg, Tuomas. 1995. *Contested Territory: Border Disputes at the Edge of the Former Soviet Empire.* Aldershot: Edward Elgar.

Frank, Allen, and Ronald Wixman. 1997. "The Middle Volga: Exploring the Limits of Sovereignty." In *New States, New Politics: Building the Post-Soviet Nations,* eds. Ian Bremmer and Ray Taras. Cambridge: Cambridge University Press.

Friedman, Steven. 1995. "South Africa: Divided in a Special way." In *Politics in Developing Countries: Comparing Experience with Democracy*, eds. Larry Diamond, Juan Linz, and Seymour Martin Lipset. Boulder: Lynne Rienner.

Fukuyama, Francis. 1992. *The End of History and the Last Man.* New York: Free Press.

Fukuyama, Francis. 1995a. "The Primacy of Culture." *Journal of Democracy* 6 (1): 7-14.

Fukuyama, Francis. 1995b. *Trust.* New York: Free Press.

Gagnon, V. P. Jr. 1994. "Ethnic Nationalism and International Conflict: The Case of Serbia." *International Security* 19 (3): 130-166.

Gellner, Ernest. 1983. *Nations and Nationalism.* Ithaca: Cornell University Press.

Gellner, Ernest. 1997. *Nationalism.* New York: New York University Press.

Gitelman, Zvi. 1999. "The Jews of Ukraine and Moldova." In *Jewish Roots in Ukraine and Moldova: Pages from the Past and Archival Inventories,* ed. Miriam Weiner. Secaucus, N.J.: Miriam Weiner Routes to Roots Foundation.

Glaser, James. 1996. *Race, Campaign Politics, and the Realignment in the South.* New Haven: Yale University Press.

Gonzalez, Luis. 1995. "Continuity and Change in the Uruguayan Party System." In *Building Democratic Institutions: Party Systems in Latin America,* eds. Scott Mainwaring and Timothy Scully. Stanford: Stanford University Press.

Gorzelak, Grzegorz. 1998. *Regional and Local Potential for Transformation in Poland.* Warsaw: Euroreg.

Greenfeld, Liah. 1992. *Nationalism: Five Roads to Modernity.* Cambridge: Harvard University Press.

Gryb, Arsen. 2003. "Halychany hotovi do samostiinosti." *Postup*, January 11.

Guboglo, M., and A. Yakubovski. 1997. *Mnogonatsional'nyi Odesskii krai: Obraz i real'nost.* Vol. 3. Moskva: Staryi Sad.

Gurr, Ted Robert. 1993. *Minorities at Risk: A Global View of Ethnopolitical Conflicts.* Washington: United States Institute of Peace Press.

Gurr, Ted Robert, and Will Moore. 1997. "Ethnopolitical Rebellion: A Cross-sectional Analysis of the 1980s with Risk Assessments for the 1990s." *American Journal of Political Science* 41 (4): 1079-1103.

Gurr, Ted Robert, Monty Marshall, and Anne Pitsch. 1999. "The Minorities at Risk Project: Lessons, Limits, New Directions." Paper Presented at the 1999 APSA Annual Meeting in Atlanta.

Hagen, Mark von. 1995. "Does Ukraine Have a History?" *Slavic Review* 54 (3): 658-673.

Hale, Henry. 1998. "Secession From Ethnofederal Systems: A Statistical Study of Russia, India, and Ethiopia." Paper Presented at the 1998 APSA Annual Meeting in Boston.

Hardin, Russell. 1995. *One for All: The Logic of Group Conflict.* Princeton: Princeton University Press.

Hechter, Michael. 1999. *Internal Colonialism: The Celtic Fringe in British National Development.* New Brunswick: Transaction Publishers.

Heiberg, Marianne. 1982. "Urban Politics and Rural Culture: Basque Nationalism." In *The Politics of Territorial Identity: Studies in European Regionalism,* eds. Stein Rokkan and Derek Urwin. London: Sage.

Hellie, Richard. 1982. *Slavery in Russia, 1450-1725.* Chicago: University of Chicago Press.

Herrera, Yoshiko. 2005. *Imagined Economies: The Sources of Russian Regionalism.* New York: Cambridge University Press.

Hesli, Vicki. 1995. "Public Support for the Devolution of Power in Ukraine: Regional Patterns." *Europe-Asia Studies* 47 (1): 91-121.

Hesli, Vicki, William Reisinger, and Arthur Miller. 1998. "Political Party Development in Divided Societies: The Case of Ukraine." *Electoral Studies* 17 (2): 235-256.

Himka, John-Paul. 1999. *Religion and Nationality in Western Ukraine: The Greek Catholic Church and Ruthenian National Movement in Galicia, 1867-1900.* Montreal: McGill-Queen's University Press.

Hobsbawm, Eric. 1990. *Nations and Nationalism since 1780: Programme, Myth, Reality.* Cambridge: Cambridge University Press.

Holovakha, Evhen. 2000. "Popular Social and Political Attitudes in Ukraine." In *Ukraine: The Search for a National Identity,* eds. Sharon Wolchik and Volodymyr Zviglyanich. Lanham, Md.: Rowman and Littlefield.

Horowitz, Donald. 1985. *Ethnic Groups in Conflict.* Berkeley: University of California Press.

Huntington, Samuel. 1993. "The Clash of Civilizations?" *Foreign Affairs* 72 (3): 22-49.

Huntington, Samuel. 1997. *The Clash of Civilizations and the Remaking of World Order.* New York: Touchstone.

Hunter, Shireen. 1997. "Azerbaijan: Searching for New Neighbors." In *New States, New Politics: Building the Post-Soviet Nations*, eds. Ian Bremmer and Ray Taras. Cambridge: Cambridge University Press.

IFES (International Foundation for Election Systems.) 1994. *Republic of Moldova: Parliamentary Elections, February 27, 1994.* Chisinau: Tish.

IFES. (International Foundation for Election Systems.) 1995. *Republic of Moldova: Local Elections, April 16, 1995.* Chisinau: Tish.

IFES. (International Foundation for Election Systems.) 1996. *Republic of Moldova: Presidential Elections, November 17 & December 1, 1996.* Chisinau: Tish.

IFES. (International Foundation for Election Systems.) 1998. *Republic of Moldova: Parliamentary Elections, March 22, 1998.* Chisinau: Tish.

IFES. (International Foundation for Election Systems.) 1999. *Republic of Moldova: Local Elections, May 23, 1999.* Chisinau: Tish.

IFES. 2001a. 2001 Parliamentary Elections. *http://www.ifes.md.*

IFES. 2001b. *http://www.ifes-ukraine.org/english/Elections1998.*

Ignatieff, Michael. 1993. *Blood and Belonging: Journeys into the New Nationalism.* Toronto: Viking.

Inalcik, H. 1979. "Servile Labor in the Ottoman Empire." In *The Mutual Effects of the Islamic and Judeo-Christian Worlds: The East European Pattern*, eds. Abraham Ascher, Tibor Halasi-Kun, Bela K. Kiraly. New York: Brooklyn College Press.

Inglehart, Ronald, et al. 2000. 1995-1997 World Values Surveys [Computer file], ICPSR version. Ann Arbor: Institute for Social Research.

Isaievych, Iaroslav. 1994. "Galicia and Problems of National Identity," In *The Habsburg Legacy: National Identity in Historical Perspective*, eds. Ritchie Robertson and Edward Timms. Edinburgh: Edinburgh University Press.

Istoriia Ukrainy: Nove bachennia. 1995. Kyiv: Ukraina.

Iurash, Andrii. 2000. "Karta relihiinoi aktyvnosti v Ukraini." *Polityka i kul'tura* 36 (1.)

Iurov, Iurii. 1995. "Kryms'ka karta v donbas'komu pas'iansi." *Geneza* 1: 188-193.

Jalali, Rita, and Seymour Martin Lipset. 1992-93. "Racial and Ethnic Conflicts: A Global Perspective." *Political Science Quarterly* 107 (4): 585-606.

Johnson, Richard, Andre Blais, Henry Brady, and Jean Crete. 1992. *Letting the People Decide: Dynamics of a Canadian Election.* Stanford: Stanford University Press.

Judah, Tim. 1997. *The Serbs: History, Myth, and the Destruction of Yugoslavia.* New Haven: Yale University Press.

Kaiser, Robert. 1994. *The Geography of Nationalism in Russia and the USSR.* Princeton: Princeton University Press.

Katchanovski, Ivan. 1995. "Perspektivy liberal'noi demokratii v Rossii." *Obshchestvennye nauki i sovremennost'* 2: 52-56.

Katchanovski, Ivan. 2000. "Divergence in Growth in Post-Communist Countries." *Journal of Public Policy* 20 (1): 55-81.

Katchanovski, Ivan. 2001. *Regional Political and Policy Divisions in Ukraine and Moldova.* Ph.D. Dissertation. Fairfax: George Mason University.

Katchanovski, Ivan. 2005. "Small Nations but Great Differences: Political Orientations and Cultures of the Crimean Tatars and the Gagauz." *Europe-Asia Studies* 57 (6): 877-894.

Katchanovski, Ivan, and Todd La Porte. 2005. "Cyberdemocracy or Potemkin E-Villages: E-Government in OECD and Post-Communist Countries." *International Journal of Public Administration* 28 (7 & 8): 665-681.

Katchanovski, Ivan. 2006. "The Orange Evolution? The Political Realignment and Regional Divisions in Ukraine." Paper presented at the 11th World Convention of the ASN in New York, March 23-25.

Kaufman, Stuart. 1996. "Spiraling to Ethnic War: Elites, Masses, and Moscow in Moldova's Civil War." *International Security* 21 (2): 108-138.

Khmelko, Valeri, and Andrew Wilson. 1998. "Regionalism and Ethnic and Linguistic Cleavages in Ukraine." In *Contemporary Ukraine: Dynamics of Post-Soviet Transformation*, ed. Taras Kuzio. Armonk: M.E. Sharpe.

Khodarkovsky, Michael. 2002. *Russia's Steppe Frontier: The Making of a Colonial Empire, 1500-1800.* Bloomington: Indiana University Press.

Khrushchev, Nikita. 1970. *Khrushchev Remembers*, ed. and tr. Strobe Talbott. Boston: Little, Brown.

KIIS. 2000. Kyiv International Institute of Sociology: *http://kiis.com.ua/projects/po_poll_apr00.html.*

KIIS. 2002. "Hromads'ka dumka v Ukraini: Hruden' 2001." *http://www.kiis.com.ua/release-last2.htm.*

King, Charles. 1994a. "Moldova." In *Political Parties of Eastern Europe, Russia and the Successor States*, ed. Bogdan Szajkowski. London: Stockton.

King, Charles. 1994b. "Eurasia Letter: Moldova with a Russian Face." *Foreign Policy* 97 (Winter): 106-120.

King, Charles. 1997. "Minorities Policy in the Post-Soviet Republics: The Case of the Gagauzi." *Ethnic and Racial Studies* 20 (4): 738-756.

King, Charles. 2000. *The Moldovans: Romania, Russia, and the Politics of Culture.* Stanford: Hoover Institution Press.

King, Gary. 1997. *A Solution to the Ecological Inference Problem: Reconstructing Individual Behavior from Aggregate Data.* Princeton: Princeton University Press.

Kirschbaum, Stanislav. 1995. *A History of Slovakia: The Struggle for Survival.* New York: St. Martin's Press.

Kistiakowsky, George. 1976. *A Scientist at the White House: The Private Diary of President Eisenhower's Special Assistant for Science and Technology.* Cambridge: Harvard University Press.

Kohn, Hans. 1944. *The Idea of Nationalism: A Study in its Origins and Background.* New York: Macmillan.

Kohn, Hans. 1955. *Nationalism: Its Meaning and History.* Princeton: D. Van Nostrand Company.

Kohut, Zenon.1988. *Russian Centralism and Ukrainian Autonomy: Imperial Absorption of the Hetmanate, 1760s-1830s.* Cambridge: Harvard Ukrainian Research Institute.

Kolossov, Vladimir, and John O'Loughlin. 1999. "Pseudo-states as Harbingers of a New Geopolitics: The Example of the Trans-Dniester Moldovan Republic (TMR.)" *Geopolitics* 3 (1): 151-176.

Kolsto, Pal, Andrei Edemsky, with Natalya Kalashnikova. 1993. "The Dniester Conflict: Between Irredentism and Separatism." *Europe-Asia Studies* 45 (6): 973-1000.

Kolsto, Pal, and Andrei Malgin. 1998. "The Transdniestrian Republic: A Case of Politicized Regionalism." *Nationality Papers* 26 (1): 103-128.

Kolsto, Pal, ed. 2002. *National Integration and Violent Conflict in Post-Soviet Societies: The Cases of Estonia and Moldova.* Lanham, Md: Rowman & Littlefield.

Kopstein, Jeffrey, and David Reilly. 2000. "Geographic Diffusion and the Transformation of the PostCommunist World." *World Politics* 53 (1): 1-37.

Koropeckyj, I. S. 1990. *Development in the Shadow: Studies in Ukrainian Economics.* Edmonton: Canadian Institute of Ukrainian Studies Press.

Kosyk, Volodymyr. 1993. *Ukraina i Nimmechyna u Druhii svitovii viini.* Paryzh: Naukove Tovarystvo Imeni T. Shevchenka u L'vovi.

Krawchenko, Bohdan. 1985. *Social Change and National Consciousness in Twentieth-century Ukraine.* New York: St. Martin's Press.

Kremin, V., D. Bezluda, V. Bondarenko, O. Valevskii, M. Golovatyi, M. Mishchenko, S. Riabov, P. Sytnyk, and O. Yaremenko. 1997. *Sotsial'no-politychna sytuatsia v Ukraini: Postup piaty rokiv.* Kyiv: National Institute for Strategic Studies.

"Krym na politychnii karti Ukrainy." 2001. *Natsional'na bezpeka i oborona* 16 (4): 2-39.

Kryms'kyi, Ahatanhel. 1924/1996. *Istoriia Turechchyny.* Kyiv: Olir.

Kubicek, Paul. 2000. "Regional Polarisation in Ukraine: Public Opinion, Voting and Legislative Behaviour." *Europe-Asia Studies* 52 (2): 272-293.

Kucera, Milan, and Pavlik, Zdenek. 1995. "Czech and Slovak Demography." In *The End of Czechoslovakia*, ed. Jiri Musil. Budapest: Central European University Press.

Kulchytskyi, Stanislav, ed. 1995. *Holodomor 1932-1933 rr. v Ukraini – Prychyny i naslidky.* Kyiv: Institute of History of Ukraine.

Kuzio, Taras, and Andrew Wilson. 1994. *Ukraine: Perestroika to Independence.* New York: St. Martin's Press.

Laitin, David. 1995. "National Revivals and Violence." *Archives Europûennes de Sociologie* 36 (1): 3-43.

Laitin, David. 1998. *Identity in Formation: The Russian-Speaking Populations in the Near Abroad.* Ithaca: Cornell University Press.

Laitin, David. 2001. "Secessionist Rebellion in the Former Soviet Union." *Comparative Political Studies* 34 (8): 839-861.

Lake, David, and Donald Rothchild. 1998. "Spreading Fear: The Genesis of Transnational Ethnic Conflict." In *The International Spread of Ethnic Conflict: Fear, Diffusion, and Escalation.* Princeton: Princeton University Press.

Lamis, Alexander. 1999. "The Two Party South: From the 1960s to the 1990s." In *Southern Politics in the 1990s*, ed. Alexander Lamis. Baton Rouge: Louisiana State University Press.

Lawson, Chappell. 1998. "Development and Democratization in Mexico: A State Level Analysis of Political Change." *Policy Studies Review* 15 (2/3): 18-34.

Leff, Carol Skalnik. 1999. "Democratization and Disintegration in Multinational States: The Break-up of the Communist Federations." *World Politics* 51 (2): 205-235.

Leonov, Ivan. 2005. "Nedilia iaka ne stala kryvavoiu." *Ukraina moloda*, November 29.

Lerman, Zvi, Csaba Csaki, and Victor Moroz. 1998. "Land Reform and Farm Restructuring in Moldova." *World Bank Discussion Paper*, No. 398.

Lieberson, Stanley, and Mary Waters. 1988. *From Many Strands: Ethnic and Racial Groups in Contemporary America*. New York: Russell Sage Foundation.

Lieven, Anatol. 1998. *Chechnya: Tombstone of Russian Power*. New Haven: Yale University Press.

Lieven, Anatol. 1999. *Ukraine & Russia: A Fraternal Rivalry*. Washington: United States Institute of Peace Press.

Lieven, D. C. B. 2001. *Empire: The Russian Empire and its Rivals*. New Haven: Yale University Press.

Linz, Juan. 1967. "Cleavage and Consensus in West German Politics: The Early Fifties. In *Party Systems and Voter Alignments: Cross-National Perspectives*, eds. Seymour Martin Lipset and Stein Rokkan. New York: Free Press.

Lipset, Seymour Martin. 1968/1950. *Agrarian Socialism: The Cooperative Commonwealth Federation in Saskatchewan*. Berkeley: University of California Press.

Lipset, Seymour Martin. 1981/1959. *Political Man: Social Bases of Politics*. Baltimore: John Hopkins University Press.

Lipset, Seymour Martin. 1990. *Continental Divide: The Values and Institutions of the United States and Canada*. New York: Routledge.

Lipset, Seymour Martin. 1996. *American Exceptionalism*. New York: W. W. Norton.

Lipset, Seymour Martin, Noah Meltz, Rafael Gomez, and Ivan Katchanovski. 2004. *The Paradox of American and Canadian Unionism: Why Americans Like Unions More than Canadians Do, but Join Much Less.* Ithaca: Cornell University Press.

Lipset, Seymour Martin, and Stein Rokkan. 1967. "Cleavage Structures, Party Systems, and Voter Alignments." In *Party Systems and Voter Alignments: Cross-national Perspectives*, eds. Seymour Martin Lipset and Stein Rokkan. New York: Free Press.

Loughlin, John. 1985. "Regionalism and Ethnic Nationalism in France." In *Centre-Periphery Relations in Western Europe*, eds. Yves Meny and Vincent Wright. London: George Allan & Unwin.

Lykhovii, Dmytro. 2005. "Tanky Pomaranchevoi revoliutsii." *Ukraina moloda*, November 22.

Madajczyk, Ceslav. 1962. "Generalplan Ost." *Polish Western Affairs* 3 (2.)

Magocsi, Paul Robert, ed. 1993a. *Historical Atlas of East Central Europe.* Seattle: University of Washington Press.

Magocsi, Paul Robert. 1993b. *Galicia: A Historical Survey and Bibliographic Guide.* Toronto: University of Toronto Press.

Magocsi, Paul Robert.1994. *Our People: Carpatho-Rusyns and Their Descendants in North America.* Toronto: Multicultural History Society of Ontario.

Magocsi, Paul Robert. 1996. *History of Ukraine.* Seattle: University of Washington Press.

Magocsi, Paul Robert. 2002. *The Roots of Ukrainian Nationalism: Galicia as Ukraine's Piedmont. Toronto*: University of Toronto Press.

Mainwaring, Scott. 1995. "Brazil: Weak Parties, Feckless Democracy." In *Building Democratic Institutions: Party Systems in Latin America*, eds. Scott Mainwaring and Timothy Scully. Stanford: Stanford University Press.

Maksymiuk, Jan. 2000. "Doubts Remain over Ukraine's 16 April Referendum." *RFE/RL Newsline*, April 12.

Malanchuk, Oksana. 2005. "Social Identification Versus Regionalism in Contemporary Ukraine." *Nationalities Papers* 33 (3): 345-368.

Mares, David. 1997. "Latin American Perspectives on the Causes, Prevention and Resolution of Deadly Intra- and Interstate Conflicts, 1982-1996."

Carnegie   Commission   on   Preventing   Deadly   Conflict, *http://www.Ccpdc.org/pubs/mares/mrfr.htm.*

Marples, David. 1992. *Stalinism in Ukraine in the 1940*s. New York: St. Martin's Press.

Martyniuk, Jaroslaw. 1994. "The State of the Orthodox Church in Ukraine." *RFE/RL Research Report* 3 (7.)

McGuire, James. 1995. "Political Parties and Democracy in Argentina." In *Building Democratic Institutions: Party Systems in Latin America*, eds. Scott Mainwaring and Timothy Scully. Stanford: Stanford University Press.

McLaughlin, Daniel. 2005. "Walesa Says He Averted Ukraine Clashes." *Observer,* May 1.

Melnychenko Tapes Project. 2001. *http://www.wcfia.harvard.edu/ melnychenko/.*

Merton, Robert. 1941/1976. "Intermarriage and the Social Structure." *Sociological Ambivalence and Other Essays*, ed. Robert Merton. New York: Free Press.

Meurs, Wim van. 1994. *The Bessarabian Question in Communist Historiography: Nationalist and Communist Politics and History-Writing.* New York: East European Monographs.

Mihalisko, Kathleen. 1997. "Belarus: Retreat to Authoritarianism." In. *Democratic Changes and Authoritarian Reactions in Russia, Ukraine, Belarus, and Moldova*, eds. Karen Dawisha and Bruce Parrott. Cambridge: Cambridge University Press.

Miles, William F. S. 1994. *Hausaland Divided. Colonialism and Independence in Nigeria and Niger.* Ithaca: Cornell University Press.

Miller, Arthur, Thomas Klobucar, and William Reisinger. 2000. "Establishing Representation: Mass and Elite Political Attitudes in Ukraine." In *Ukraine: The Search for a National Identity,* eds. Sharon Wolchik and Volodymyr Zviglyanich. Lanham, Md.: Rowman and Littlefield.

Miller, Warren, and Merrill Shanks. 1996. *The New American Voter.* Cambridge: Harvard University Press.

Miller, William, Stephen White, and Paul Heywood. 1998. *Values and Political Change in Post-Communist Europe.* New York: St. Martin's Press.

Minahan, James. 1996. *Nations Without States: A Historical Dictionary of Contemporary National Movements.* Westport: Greenwood Press.

Minorities at Risk Project. 2000. *http://www.bsos.umd.edu/cidcm/mar/.*

Mises, von Ludwig. 1983/1919. *Nation, State, and Economy: Contributions to the Politics and History of Our Time.* New York: New York University Press.

"Moldavia's Minorities Vote to Quit." 1991. *Independent,* December 3.

"Moldova Contemplates a European Future." 2005. *Economist,* January 29.

Moreland, Laurence, Tod Baker, and Robert Steed, eds. 1982. *Contemporary Southern Political Attitudes and Behavior: Studies and Essays.* New York: Praeger.

Mostova, Iulia, and Serhii Rakhmanin. 2005. "Rik pislia Maidanu: Povtorennia neproidenoho." *Dzerkalo tyzhnia,* November 19.

Motyl, Alexander. 1993. *Dilemmas of Independence: Ukraine after Totalitarianism.* New York: Council on Foreign Relations Press.

Motyl, Alexander, and Bohdan Krawchenko. 1997. "Ukraine: From Empire to Statehood." In *New States, New Politics: Building the Post-Soviet Nations,* eds Ian Bremmer and Ray Taras. Cambridge: Cambridge University Press.

Mukovskyi, Ivan, and Oleksandr Lysenko. 1997. *Zvytiaha i zhertovnist': Ukraintsi na frontakh druhoi svitovoi viiny.* Kyiv: Knyha pamiati Ukrainy.

Musil, Jiri, ed. 1995. *The End of Czechoslovakia,* Budapest: Central European University Press.

Nadolishnii, P. 1998. *Etnonatsional'nyi faktor administratyvnoi reformy v Ukraini.* Kyiv: UADU.

Naselennia Ukrainy: Demohrafichnyi shchorichnyk. 1993. Kyiv: Tekhnika.

Nevitte, Neil, Andre Blais, Elisabeth Gidengil, and Richard Nadeau. 2000. *Unsteady State: The 1997 Canadian Federal Election.* Oxford: Oxford University Press.

Newman, Saul. 1996. *Ethnoregional Conflict in Democracies.* Westport: Greenwood Press.

O'Loughlin, John, Michael Shin, and Paul Talbot. 1996. "Political Geographies and Cleavages in the Russian Parliamentary Elections." *Post-Soviet Geography and Economics* 37 (6): 355-385.

O'Loughlin, John, V. Kolossov, and A. Tchepalyga. 1998. "National Construction, Territorial Separatism, and Post-Soviet Geopolitics in the Transdniester Moldovan Republic." *Post-Soviet Geography and Economics* 39 (6): 332-358.

O'Loughlin, John, and James Bell. 1999. "The Political Geography of Civic Engagement in Ukraine." *Post-Soviet Geography and Economics* 40 (4): 233-266.

Obshchestvennoe mnenie: Aktual'nye problemy sotsialnoi zhyzni SSR Moldova. 1990. Chishinau: Department of Sociology of the Academy of Sciences of Moldova.

Olcott, Martha Brill. 1997. "Kazakhstan: Pushing for Eurasia." In *New States, New Politics: Building the Post-Soviet Nations,* eds. Ian Bremmer and Ray Taras. Cambridge: Cambridge University Press.

"Oleksandr Turchynov: The Order to Crush the Revolution Came with Kuchma's Consent. The Land Forces Though, Were Ready to Switch to the Side of the People." 2005. *Ukraiinska pravda,* April 17.

Omrod, Jane. 1997. "The North Caucasus: Confederation in Conflict." In *New States, New Politics: Building the Post-Soviet Nations,* eds. Ian Bremmer and Ray Taras. Cambridge: Cambridge University Press.

Ozhiganov, Edward. 1997. "The Republic of Moldova: Transdniester and the 14th Army." In *Managing Conflict in the Former Soviet Union: Russian and American Perspectives*, eds. Alexei Arbatov, Abram Chayes, Antonia Chayes, and Lara Olson. Cambridge: MIT Press.

Paniotto, Volodymyr. 1999. "The Level of Anti-Semitism in Ukraine." *International Journal of Sociology* 29 (3): 66-75.

Panina, N. 2005. *Ukrainske suspil'stvo 1994-2005: Sotsiolohichnyi monitorynh.* Kyiv: Sophia.

Parliament of the Republic of Moldova. 2001. *http://www.parlament.md/en/structure/fractions/.*

Parliament of Ukraine. 2000. *http://guru.rada.kiev.ua:2000/web/ owa/fr_list.*

Piotrowski, Tadeusz. 1998. *Poland's Holocaust: Ethnic Strife, Col-laboration with Occupying Forces and Genocide in the Second Republic, 1918-1947.* Jefferson, N.C.: McFarland.

Pipes, Richard. 1974/1954. *The Formation of the Soviet Union: Communism and Nationalism, 1917-1923.* New York: Atheneum.

Pirie, Paul. 1996. "National Identity and Politics in Southern and Eastern Ukraine." *Europe-Asia Studies* 48 (7): 1079-1104.

Plokhy, Serhii. 1995. "The History of a "Non-Historical" Nation: Notes on the Nature and Current Problems of Ukrainian Historiography." *Slavic Review* 54 (3): 709-716.

Pohl, J. Otto. *Ethnic Cleansing in the USSR, 1937-1949.* 1999. Westport: Greenwood Press.

Polanyi, Michael. 1997. *Society, Economics & Philosophy: Selected Papers,* ed. R.T. Allen. New Brunswick: Transaction Publishers.

Politychna kul'tura: Teoria, problemy, perspektyvy. 2004. Kyiv: Parapan.

Polonsky, Antony. 1972. *Politics in Independent Poland 1921-1939: The Crisis of Constitutional Government.* Oxford: Clarendon Press.

Potichnyj, Peter. 1992. "The March 1990 Elections in Ukraine." In *Ukrainian Past, Ukrainian Present,* ed. Bohdan Krawchenko. New York: St. Martin's Press.

"Preliminary Results of the Parliamentary Elections in the Republic of Moldova." 2005. http://*www.alegeri2005.md.*

Prizel, Ilya. 1997. "Ukraine between Proto-democracy and "Soft" Authoritarianism." In *Democratic Changes and Authoritarian Reactions in Russia, Ukraine, Belarus, and Moldova,* eds. Karen Dawisha and Bruce Parrott. Cambridge: Cambridge University Press.

Prizel, Ilya. 1998. *National Identity and Foreign Policy: Nationalism and Leadership in Poland, Russia and Ukraine.* Cambridge: Cambridge University Press.

Pro khid ekonomichnoi reformy v Ukraini za 1998 rik. 1999. Kyiv: Derzhavnyi komitet statystyky Ukrainy.

Protsyk. Oleh. 2005. "Federalism and Democracy in Moldova." *Post-Soviet Affairs* 21 (1): 72-90.

Pulse of Europe: A Survey of Political and Social Values and Attitudes. 1991. Washington: Times Mirror Center for the People & the Press.

Putnam, Robert. 1993. *Making Democracy Work: Civic Traditions in Modern Italy.* Princeton: Princeton University Press.

Quataert, Donald. 2000. *The Ottoman Empire, 1700-1922.* New York: Cambridge University Press.

Quinlan, Paul D. 2004. "Back to the Future: An Overview of Moldova under Voronin." *Demokratizatsiya* 12 (4): 485-504.

Radkey, Oliver. 1989. *Russia Goes to the Polls: The Election to the All-Russian Constituent Assembly, 1917.* Ithaca: Cornell University Press.

Rapawy, Stephen. 1998. "Ethnic Reidentification in Ukraine." *http://www.census.gov/ipc/www/ebspr98a.html.*

Reed, John Shelton. 1972/1986. *The Enduring South: Subcultural Persistence in Mass Society.* Chapel Hill: University of North Carolina Press.

Reent, Oleksandr, and Oleksandr Lysenko. 1995. "Taemnytsi shcho buly za simoma zamkamy. Vtraty ukrains'koho narodu u Druhii svitovii viini." *Ridna shkola* 6.

Report on the Moldovan Parliamentary Elections: Southern Moldova, the "Security Zone and Gagauzia. 1998. Washington: The Commission on Security and Cooperation in Europe.

Republic of Moldova: Economic Review of the Transnistria Region. 1998. Washington: World Bank.

Riabchuk, Mykola. 2001. "Dvi Ukrainy." *Krytyka*, 4.

Riabchuk, Mykola. 2003. *Dvi Ukrainy: Realni mezhi, virtual'ni viiny.* Kyiv: Krytyka.

Richard, Madeline. 1991. *Ethnic Groups and Marital Choices: Ethnic History and Marital Assimilation in Canada, 1871 and 1971.* Vancouver: UBC Press.

Rokkan, Stein. 1967. "Geography, Religion, and Social Class: Crosscutting Cleavages in Norwegian Politics." In *Party Systems and Voter Alignments: Cross-national Perspectives,* eds. Seymour Martin Lipset and Stein Rokkan. New York: Free Press.

Rohrschneider, Robert. 1996. "Cultural Transmission versus Perceptions of the Economy." *Comparative Politics* 29 (1): 78-104.

Romaniuk, Anatolii, and Natalia Chernysh. 1995. "Shid - Zahid: Kompromis chy konfrontatsia." *Filosofs'ka i sotsiolohichna dumka* 3-4: 104-116.

Roper, Steven D., and Florin Fesnic. 2003. "Historical Legacies and Their Impact on Post-Communist Voting Behaviour." *Europe-Asia Studies* 55 (1): 119-131.

Rose, Richard. 1974a. "Britain: Simple Abstractions and Complex Realities." In *Electoral Behavior: A Comparative Handbook*, ed. Richard Rose. New York: Free Press.

Rose, Richard, ed. 1974b. *Electoral Behavior: A Comparative Handbook.* New York: Free Press.

Rummel, R. J. 1992. *Democide: Nazi Genocide and Mass Murder.* New Brunswick: Transaction Publishers.

Rummel, R. J. 1994. *Death by Government.* New Brunswick: Transactions Publishers.

Rusinow, Dennison. 1996. "Yugoslavia's Disintegration and the Ottoman Past." In *Imperial Legacy: the Ottoman Imprint on the Balkans and the Middle East*, ed. Carl L. Brown. New York: Columbia University Press.

Sadovyi, Andrii. 2002. "Naselennia L'vova v dzerkali opytuvannia hromads'koi dumky (Hruden' 2000 roku.)" *I* 23.

Saideman, Stephen. 1998. "Is Pandora's Box Half Empty or Half Full? The Limited Virulence of Secessionism and the Domestic Sources of Disintegration. In *The International Spread of Ethnic Conflict: Fear, Diffusion, and Escalation.* Princeton: Princeton University Press.

Sallnow, John, and Anna John. 1982. *An Electoral Atlas of Europe: 1968-1981.* London: Butterworth Scientific.

Saunders, David. 1993. "Mikhail Katkov and Mykola Kostomarov: A Note on Petr A. Valuev's Anti-Ukrainian Edict of 1863," *Harvard Ukrainian Studies* 17 (3/4), 364-377.

"Schemes and Scandals in Ukraine." 2001. *Economist*, January 18.

Schutz, Alfred. 1971. *Collected Papers.* Hague: M. Nijhoff.

Schwartz, Mildred. 1995. "Regions and Regionalism in Canada." In *Politics, Society and Democracy,* eds. H. E. Chebabi and Alfred Stepan. Boulder: Westview Press.

Selivanova, I. F. 1996. "Trans-Dniestria." In *U.S. and Russian Policymaking with Respect to the Use of Force*, eds. Jeremy Azrael and Emil Payin. Santa Monica: RAND.

Sestanovich, Stephen. 2004. "Ukraine's Democratic Strengths." *Washington Post*, November 19.

Shepot'ko, L., I. Prokopa, O. Maksymiuk, et al. 1997. *Selo: Suchasna polityka i stratehiia rozvytku.* Kyiv: Instytut ekonomiky NAN Ukrainy.

Shulman, Stephen.1999a. "Asymmetrical International Integration and Ukrainian National Disunity." *Political Geography* 18 (8): 913-939.

Shulman, Stephen.1999b. "The Cultural Foundations of Ukrainian National Identity." *Ethnic and Racial Studies* 22 (6): 1011-1036.

Siegfried, Andre. 1930. *France: A Study in Nationality*. New Haven: Yale University Press.

Siegfried, Andre. 1949. *Geographie Electorale de l'Ardeche sous la IIIe Republique*. Paris: A. Colin.

Sikorsky, Igor. 1958. *The Story of the Winged-S; Late Developments and Recent Photographs of the Helicopter. An Autobiography*. New York: Dodd, Mead.

Silske hospodarstvo Ukrainy: Statystychnyi zbirnyk. 1995. Kyiv: Ministerstvo statystyky Ukrainy.

Slezkine, Yuri. 2004. *The Jewish Century*. Princeton: Princeton University Press.

Smith, Anthony. 1998. *Nationalism and Modernism: A Critical Survey of Recent Theories of Nations and Nationalism*. London: Routledge.

Snyder, Timothy. 1999. "'To Resolve the Ukrainian Problem Once and for All': The Ethnic Cleansing of Ukrainians in Poland, 1943-1947." *Journal of Cold War Studies* 1 (2): 86-120.

Solchanyk, Roman. 1991. "The Referendum in Ukraine: Preliminary Results." *Report on the USSR*, March 29: 5-7.

Solchanyk, Roman. 1995. "Crimea: Between Ukraine and Russia," In *Crimea: Dynamics, Challenges, and Prospects*, ed. Maria Drohobycky. Lanham, Md: Rowman and Littlefield.

Solchanyk, Roman. 1998. "Prospects for Stability." In *Contemporary Ukraine: Dynamics of Post-Soviet Transformation,* ed. Taras Kuzio. Armonk: M.E. Sharpe.

Solohubenko, Olexiy. 2005. "How Ukraine 'Verged on Civil War.'" *BBC News*, November 22, *http://news.bbc.co.uk/2/hi/europe/4459876.stm*.

Speel, Robert. 1998. *Changing Patterns of Voting in the United States: Electoral Realignment: 1952-1996*. University Park, Pa.: Pennsylvania State University.

Statystychnyi shchorichnyk Ukrainy za 1996 rik. 1997. Kyiv: Ukrains'ka ent-syklopedia.

Steed, Robert, Laurence Moreland, and Tod Baker. 1990. *Disappearing South? Studies in Regional Change and Continuity.* Tuscaloosa: University of Alabama Press.

Stephen, Chris. 2004. "East-West Split Feared in Ukraine." *Observer,* December 1.

Subtelny, Orest. 1981. "Cossack Ukraine and the Turco-Islamic World." In *Rethinking Ukrainian History,* ed. Ivan L. Rudnytsky. Edmonton: Canadian Institute of Ukrainian Studies.

Subtelny, Orest. 1988. *Ukraine: A History.* Toronto: University of Toronto Press.

Subtelny, Orest. 1995. "Russocentrism, Regionalism, and the Political Culture of Ukraine." In *Political Culture and Civil Society in Russia and the New States of Eurasia,* ed. Vladimir Tismaneanu, Armonk: M. E. Sharpe.

Symonenko, Petro. 1996. *Holos Ukrainy,* March 21.

Szporluk, Roman. 1979. "West Ukraine and West Belorussia." *Soviet Studies* 31 (1): 76-98.

Timoshenko, Stephen. 1968. *As I Remember.* Princeton: Van Nostrand.

Ther, Philipp, and Ana Siljak. 2001. *Redrawing Nations: Ethnic Cleansing in East-Central Europe, 1944-1948.* Lanham: Rowman and Littlefield.

Todorova, Maria. 1996. "The Ottoman Legacy in the Balkans." In *Imperial Legacy: The Ottoman Imprint on the Balkans and the Middle East,* ed. Carl L. Brown. New York: Columbia University Press.

Treisman, Daniel. 1997. "Russia's "Ethnic Revival": The Separatist Activism of Regional Leaders in a PostCommunist Order." *World Politics* 49 (2): 212-249.

Trials of War Criminals Before the Nuremberg Military Tribunals under Control Council Law no. 10. 1946-1949. Washington: U. S. Government Printing Office.

Tsentr "Suspil'stvo." 2000. "Hromads'ka ekspertyza: Svoboda slova." *http://www.suspilstvo.com.ua/rozpodil.htm.*

Tyler, Patrick. 2001. "From under a Couch, an Effort to Stop Corruption in Ukraine," *New York Times,* February 26.

Ukrains'ke suspil'stvo 1994-2001: Rezul'taty opytuvannia hromads'koi dumky. 2002. Instytut sotsiolohii NAN Ukrainy. *http://www.dif.org.ua/.*

Ulc, Otto. 1996. "Czechoslovakia's Velvet Divorce." *East European Quarterly* 30 (3): 331-350.

UNDP. 1996. *National Human Development Report: Ukraine, 1995.* United Nations Development Program.

UNDP. 1999. *National Human Development Report: Republic of Moldova, 1998.* United Nations Development Program.

UNDP-Moldova and Administration of the Territorial Autonomous Unit Gagauzia (Gagauz-Yeri.) 2001. *Regional Development Programme "Gagauz-Yeri."* Chisinau-Comrat.

Urwin, Derek. 1982a. "Territorial Structures and Political Developments in the United Kingdom." In *The Politics of Territorial Identity: Studies in European Regionalism,* eds. Stein Rokkan and Derek Urwin. London: Sage.

Urwin, Derek. 1982b. "Germany: From Geographical Expression to Regional Accommodation." In *The Politics of Territorial Identity: Studies in European Regionalism,* eds. Stein Rokkan and Derek Urwin. London: Sage.

Urwin, Derek. 1983. "Harbinger, Fossil or Fleabite? "Regionalism" and the Western European Party Mosaic." In *Western European Party Systems: Continuity and Change,* eds. Hans Daalder and Peter Mair. Beverly Hills: Sage.

USIA. 1996. *Crimean Views Differ Sharply from Ukrainian Opinion on Key Issues.* March, 15.

USIA Opinion Analysis. 1998. "Russians and Ukrainians Regret Demise of the USSR, Lose Confidence in NATO," February 24.

Valen, Henry, and Stein Rokkan. 1974. "Norway: Conflict Structure and Mass Politics in a European Periphery." In *Electoral Behavior: A Comparative Handbook,* ed. Richard Rose. New York: Free Press.

Van den Berghe, Pierre. 1981. *The Ethnic Phenomenon.* New York: Praeger.

Van den Berghe, Pierre. 1986. "Ethnicity and Sociobiology Debate." In *Theories of Race and Ethnic Relations,* eds. John Rex and David Mason. Cambridge: Cambridge University Press.

Varnalii, Zakharii. (Editor). 2005. *Rehiony Ukrainy: Problemy ta priorytety sotsial'no-ekonomichnoho rozvytku.* Kyiv: Natsional'nyi instytut stratehichnykh doslidzhen.

Vengroff, Richard, and F. L. Morton. 2000. "Regional Perspectives on Canada's Charter of Rights and Freedoms: A Reexamination of Democratic Elitism." *Canadian Journal of Political Science* 33 (2): 359-382.

Wagstyl, Stefan, Chrystia Freeland, and Tom Warner 2004. "Ukrainian President Spurned Pressure Over Protesters." *Financial Times*, December 13.

Wandycz, Piotr. 1974/1994. *The Lands of Partitioned Poland, 1975-1918.* Seattle: University of Washington Press.

Way, Lucan. 2005. "Authoritarian State Building and the Sources of Regime Competitiveness in the Fourth Wave: The Cases of Belarus, Moldova, Russia, and Ukraine." *World Politics* 57 (2): 231-261.

Weakliem, David and Robert Biggert. 1999. "Region and Political Opinion in the Contemporary United States." *Social Forces* 77 (3): 863–886.

Weber, Eugen Joseph. 1976. *Peasants into Frenchmen: The Modernization of Rural France, 1870-1914.* Stanford: Stanford University Press.

Weber, Max. 1904-1905/1958. *Protestant Ethic and Spirit of Capitalism.* New York: Charles Scribner's Sons.

Weber, Max. 1922/1978. *Economy and Society: An Outline of Interpretive Sociology*, eds. Guenther Roth and Claus Wittich. Berkeley: University of California Press.

Weber, Max. 1946. "The Protestant Sects and the Spirit of Capitalism." In *From Max Weber: Essays in Sociology*, eds. H. Gerth and Wright Mills. New York: Oxford University Press.

Weber, Max. 1949. *The Methodology of the Social Sciences.* Eds. Edward A. Shils and Henry A. Finch. Glencoe: Free Press.

Weiner, Miriam, ed. 1999. *Jewish Roots in Ukraine and Moldova: Pages from the Past and Archival Inventories,* Secaucus, N.J.: Miriam Weiner Routes to Roots Foundation.

Welch, Steven R. 1999. "The Annihilation of Superfluous Eaters": Nazi Plans for and Uses of Famine in Eastern Europe." Genocide Studies Program, Yale University. *http://www.yale.edu/gsp/index.html.*

Who's Who in the Ukrainian Political Elite. 1997. Kyiv: KIS.

Williams, Brian Glyn. 2001. *The Crimean Tatars. The Diaspora Experience and the Forging of a Nation.* Leiden: Brill.

Wilson, Andrew, and Artur Bilous. 1993. "Political Parties in Ukraine." *Europe-Asia Studies* 45 (4): 693-703.

Wilson, Andrew. 1994. "Ukraine." In *Political Parties of Eastern Europe, Russia and the Successor States*, ed. Bogdan Szajkowski. London: Stockton.

Wilson, Andrew. 1995. "Presidential and Parliamentary Elections in Ukraine: The Issue of Crimea," In *Crimea: Dynamics, Challenges, and Prospects*, ed. Maria Drohobycky. Lanham, Md.: Rowman and Littlefield.

Wilson, Andrew. 1997a. "The Ukrainian Left: In Transition to Social Democracy or Still in Thrall to the USSR?" *Europe-Asia Studies* 49 (7): 1293-1316.

Wilson, Andrew. 1997b. *Ukrainian Nationalism in the 1990s: A Minority Faith.* Cambridge: Cambridge University Press.

Wilson, Andrew and Sarah Birch. 1999. "Voting Stability, Political Gridlock: Ukraine's 1998 Parliamentary Elections." *Europe-Asia Studies* 51 (6): 1039-1068.

Wilson, Andrew. 2000. *The Ukrainians: Unexpected Nation.* New Haven: Yale University Press.

Wilson, Andrew. 2005. *Ukraine's Orange Revolution.* New Haven: Yale University Press.

Woods, Dwayne. 1995. "The Crisis of Center-Periphery Integration in Italy and the Rise of Regional Populism: the Lombard League." *Comparative Politics* 27 (2): 187-203.

Yevtoukh, Volodymyr. 1995. "The Dynamics of Interethnic Relations in Crimea," In *Crimea: Dynamics, Challenges, and Prospects*, ed. Maria Drohobycky. Lanham, Md.: Rowman and Littlefield.

"Zaiava Kurultaiu kryms'kotatars'koho narodu "Pro vybory prezydenta Ukrainy."" 2005. Tsentr informatsii ta dokumentatsii kryms'kych tatar, *http://www.cidct.org.ua.*

Zaprudnik, Jan, and Michael Urban. 1997. "Belarus: From Statehood to Empire?" In *New States, New Politics: Building the Post-Soviet Nations*, eds. Ian Bremmer and Ray Taras. Cambridge: Cambridge University Press.

Zarycki, Tomasz, and Andrzej Nowak. 2000. "Hidden Dimensions: The Stability and Structure of Regional Political Cleavages in Poland," *Communist and Post-Communist Studies* 33 (3): 331-354.

Zickel, Raymond E., and Walter R. Iwaskiw, eds. 1994. *Albania: A Country Study.* Washington: Headquarters, Department of the Army.

Zinchenko, Iurii. 1998. *Kryms'ki tatary: Istorychnyi narys.* Kyiv: Holovna spetsializovana redaktsiia literatury movamy natsional'nych menshyn Ukrainy.

Index

Dr. Andreas Umland (Ed.)

SOVIET AND POST-SOVIET POLITICS AND SOCIETY

ISSN 1614-3515

This book series makes available, to the academic community and general public, affordable English-, German- and Russian-language scholarly studies of various *empirical* aspects of the recent history and current affairs of the former Soviet bloc. The series features narrowly focused research on a variety of phenomena in Central and Eastern Europe as well as Central Asia and the Caucasus. It highlights, in particular, so far understudied aspects of late Tsarist, Soviet, and post-Soviet political, social, economic and cultural history from 1905 until today. Topics covered within this focus are, among others, political extremism, the history of ideas, religious affairs, higher education, and human rights protection. In addition, the series covers selected aspects of post-Soviet transitions such as economic crisis, civil society formation, and constitutional reform.

SOVIET AND POST-SOVIET POLITICS AND SOCIETY

Edited by Dr. Andreas Umland

ISSN 1614-3515

Михаил Лукянов
Российский консерватизм и реформа, 1905-1917
ISBN 3-89821-503-2

Robert Pyrah
Cultural Memory and Identity
Literature, Criticism and the Theatre in Lviv - Lwow - Lemberg, 1918-1939 and in post-Soviet Ukraine
ISBN 3-89821-505-9

Dmitrij Chmelnizki
Die Architektur Stalins
Ideologie und Stil 1929-1960
ISBN 3-89821-515-6

Andrei Rogatchevski
The National-Bolshevik Party
ISBN 3-89821-532-6

Zenon Victor Wasyliw
Soviet Culture in the Ukrainian Village
The Transformation of Everyday Life and Values, 1921-1928
ISBN 3-89821-536-9

Nele Sass
Das gegenkulturelle Milieu im postsowjetischen Russland
ISBN 3-89821-543-1

Josette Baer
Preparing Modernity in Central Europe
Political Thought and the Independent Nation State
ISBN 3-89821-546-6

Julie Elkner
Maternalism versus Militarism
The Russian Soldiers' Mothers Committee
ISBN 3-89821-575-X

Maryna Romanets
Displaced Subjects, Anamorphosic Texts, Reconfigured Visions
Improvised Traditions in Contemporary Ukrainian and Irish Literature
ISBN 3-89821-576-8

Alexandra Kamarowsky
Russia's Post-crisis Growth
ISBN 3-89821-580-6

Martin Friessnegg
Das Problem der Medienfreiheit in Russland seit dem Ende der Sowjetunion
ISBN 3-89821-588-1

Florian Mühlfried
Postsowjetische Feiern
Das Georgische Bankett im Wandel
ISBN 3-89821-601-2

Nikolaj Nikiforowitsch Borobow
Führende Persönlichkeiten in Russland vom 12. bis 20 Jhd.: Ein Lexikon
Aus dem Russischen übersetzt und herausgegeben von Eberhard Schneider
ISBN 3-89821-638-1

Anton Burkov
The Impact of the European Convention for the Protection of Human Rights and Fundamental
Freedoms on Russian Law
ISBN 3-89821-639-X

Katsiaryna Yafimava
The Role of Gas Transit Routes in Belarus' Relations with Russia and the EU
ISBN 3-89821-655-1

Christopher Ford
Borotbism: A Chapter in the History of Ukrainian Communism
ISBN 3-89821-697-7

Series Subscription

Please enter my subscription to the series *Soviet and Post-Soviet Politics and Society*, ISSN 1614-3515, as follows:

❏ complete series   OR   ❏ English-language titles
                                                    ❏ German-language titles
                                                    ❏ Russian-language titles

starting with
❏ volume # 1
❏ volume # ___
      ❏ please also include the following volumes: #___, ___, ___, ___, ___, ___, ___
❏ the next volume being published
      ❏ please also include the following volumes: #___, ___, ___, ___, ___, ___, ___

❏ 1 copy per volume   OR   ❏ ___ copies per volume

Subscription within Germany:

You will receive every volume at 1st publication at the regular bookseller's price – incl. s & h and VAT.
Payment:
❏ Please bill me for every volume.
❏ Lastschriftverfahren: Ich/wir ermächtige(n) Sie hiermit widerruflich, den Rechnungsbetrag je Band von meinem/unserem folgendem Konto einzuziehen.

Kontoinhaber: _____Kreditinstitut: _____

Kontonummer: _____Bankleitzahl:_____

International Subscription:

Payment (incl. s & h and VAT) in advance for
❏ 10 volumes/copies (€ 319.80)   ❏ 20 volumes/copies (€ 599.80)
❏ 40 volumes/copies (€ 1,099.80)
Please send my books to:

NAME_____DEPARTMENT_____
ADDRESS _____
POST/ZIP CODE_____COUNTRY _____
TELEPHONE _____EMAIL_____

date/signature_____

A hint for librarians in the former Soviet Union: Your academic library might be eligible to receive free-of-cost scholarly literature from Germany via the German Research Foundation. For Russian-language information on this program, see
       http://www.dfg.de/forschungsfoerderung/formulare/download/12_54.pdf.

Please fax to: **0511 / 262 2201 (+49 511 262 2201)**
or mail to: *ibidem*-Verlag, Julius-Leber-Weg 11, D-30457 Hannover,Germany
or send an e-mail: ibidem@ibidem-verlag.de

ibidem-Verlag

Melchiorstr. 15

D-70439 Stuttgart

info@ibidem-verlag.de

www.ibidem-verlag.de
www.edition-noema.de
www.autorenbetreuung.de